On Samuel R. Delany's *Dhalgren*

Etching by Gregory W. Frux, Fruxart.com

On Samuel R. Delany's *Dhalgren*

edited by Bill Wood

Fantastic Books
1380 East 17 Street, Suite 2233
Brooklyn, New York 11230
www.FantasticBooks.biz

Simultaneous hardcover and trade paperback publication.

Hardcover ISBN: 978-1-5154-4772-6
Trade Paperback ISBN: 978-1-5154-2419-2

First Edition

Table of Contents

Contemporary Reviews, 1975–76

Born in New York City's black ghetto Harlem in 1942, Samuel R. Delany was the first African-American to come up through the professional channels open to commercial American science fiction writers. After 1968 (a year before Stonewall), he was the first openly gay science fiction writer—although others, later to come out, included Frank Robinson, Arthur C. Clarke, Thomas M. Disch, Joanna Russ, and Murray Leinster ("outed" posthumously), who followed Delany's late-sixties' lead.

Today Samuel Delany's novel *Dhalgren* is published in trade paperback by Vintage Books, a division of Random House, the publishers and publishers' imprint that produce the general edition of Joyce's *Ulysses*—an eminently respectable publishing venue. In January 1975, however, *Dhalgren* first appeared as an 879-page paperback original science fiction novel from Bantam Books. (It carried the banner, "A Frederik Pohl selection": a long-time science fiction writer, Pohl then edited for Bantam Books and had acquired the novel the year before, while Delany was living in London.) Although Bantam Books was one of the most successful American paperback reprint houses, paperback original novels of any genre, which appeared without a previous hardcover edition, were considered the lowest rung in the publication hierarchy.

Copies of *Dhalgren* were available in book stores, on newsstands, and in airport bookracks by the second week in December 1974. Thanks to enthusiastic early sales and solicitation orders, the book went through three printings by its official publication date, January 1st, 1975, a week after Delany, his wife, and infant daughter returned to the States to spend the Christmas season with his family.

Three months later, in April, *Dhalgren* had gone through two more printings.

Dhalgren was not a bestseller in the usual sense. Nevertheless—and unexpectedly—it was something of a publishing phenomenon. (See

Delany's discussion of what constitutes a "bestseller" in the excerpt from his interview "The Semiology of Silence" with McCaffrey and Gregory, in **Delany on *Dhalgren*.**) In its first year, with no advertising budget at all, *Dhalgren* sold approximately half-a-million copies. The book was clearly a literary experiment. It had begun life as a paperback original without any previous hardcover appearance. Thus Bantam was leery of sinking any advertising money into it, for fear the commercial crest would have passed by the time the advertising appeared. In its second year, however, *Dhalgren* sold another 250-thousand copies. Over the next ten years, it sold just over that amount again, bringing its total sales, after a dozen years, to slightly over a million copies. In November 1987, after 19 paperback printings, Bantam Books put *Dhalgren* out of print.

Though *Dhalgren* was published as a science fiction novel (and it was as a science fiction writer than Delany had amassed a notable reputation by his twenty-sixth year, before he began the five years' work on the novel that appeared three months before his thirty-third birthday), within weeks it became clear that its considerable audience was largely among college-age readers, most without any particular interest in science fiction *per se*.

The full-page review by southern student Steven Paley for his college newspaper *The Daily Cardinal* (Monday, April 14, 1975) is both indicative and exemplary of the initial intelligent reader enthusiasm for the book.

Following Paley's review is Gerald Jonas's cautious *New York Times Book Review* appraisal of February 16. (Actually Jonas's review appeared two months before Paley's.) A year later, for *Penthouse Magazine* (May 1976), Jonas reviewed *Dhalgren* again, now that it was clear the book was a commercial success. It's interesting to compare the tone of the two pieces and the different nature of both the praise and reservations. In its first six weeks, *Dhalgren* received a mention on a brief-lived NBC News segment, where Pia Lindstrom (daughter of Ingrid Bergman, half-sister of Isabella Rossellini) gave spot one-to-three sentence responses to new SF and mystery novels and pronounced the book: "Some pretty weird stuff." But that exhausts the "advertising" the book received during the whole of its 12 years with Bantam.

Within the science fiction community, *Dhalgren* was easily the most controversial novel of its decade. An example of that controversy is the Harlan Ellison and Theodore Sturgeon reviews from, respectively, the *Los*

Angeles Times (February 1975) and *Galaxy Magazine* (March 1975). Only a few years previously, for several months, Ellison and Sturgeon had been housemates. The October 1975 issue of the fanzine *Outworld*, edited by William Bowers, ran a section entitled "Stand on *Dhalgren*," featuring pro and con articles by Douglas Barbour of Vancouver, British Columbia, and Darrell Schweitzer of Philadelphia, Pennsylvania. Barbour would go on to publish the first book-length study of Delany's work, *Worlds Out of Words: The S-F Novels of Samuel R. Delany*. Based on his dissertation of some years before at the University of British Columbia at Vancouver, Barbour's book appeared in Great Britain from Bran's Head Books in 1979.

Y8554 ★ $1.95 ★ BANTAM SCIENCE FICTION

A FREDERIK POHL SELECTION

STRANGER IN A STRANGE LAND,
THEN **DUNE** AND NOW,
THE MAJOR NOVEL OF LOVE
AND TERROR AT THE END OF TIME

DHALGREN

BY SAMUEL R. DELANY

FOUR-TIME NEBULA AWARD-WINNER

BELLONA TIMES

Roger Calkins
—Editor—

TUESDAY
JUNE 7, 1837

Today's weather—Autumn
Moonrise—7:22 p.m. Georgerise—8:57 p.m.

Only One Hundred Years Till Death of Harlow!

WE FIND OURSELVES in the uncomfortable position of being stared at. Bellona has been put under a microscope, and we are squirming. The microscope is a book called *Dhalgren* which was recently published in the outside world. We find it encouraging that the outside world has again taken notice of us (we are easily flattered) but regret that many of our urgent problems (the water shortage, for example) are given very little attention. But *Dhalgren* is a novel, and water shortages are not the traditional theme of novels.

We are uncomfortable under the view of the author. We recognize ourselves, so we do not know how to write this review. Shall we point out the differences between our view of the city, and how the author, Samuel R. Delany, sees Bellona? This would be to confuse the factual with the subjective, the event with the experience, or, as Delany quotes in the beginning of his saga: "You have confused the true and the real." What is true about our city is not necessarily real. The same may be said of the novel.

BELLONA, AS WE VIEW and live it, is a city sorely beset by the destruction that has caused us to lose over 95% of our population. The fires still burn, the city is colored grey, and we have not seen a recognizable sky for too long a time. Our remaining citizens survive as scavengers looting and re-looting the artifacts of the past. Whether it's the Scorpions or the commune in the park, we have not made any significant progress in rebuilding our city. We plan, but we have been incapable of channeling our plans into action. Perhaps the saddest comment we can make is that the Scorpions have done the most in the way of action, while their actions have accomplished nothing.

We are, as is everyone in Bellona, familiar with the Scorpions. As you know from our previous editorials (and with luck, this review might escape that fate) we take a rather sour view of these street gangs. They have too much opportunity to terrorize what's left of our city at will. They are clans of lost and dangerous youth. They gather themselves into nests and pour into our unprotected streets. We look at them and are reminded of a quote that started a different book. A quote attributed to one Dr. Johnson: "He who makes a beast of himself rids himself of the pain of being a man."

But Delany does not seem to take this view. He has humanized these creatures of the night. He has given them names (Dragon Lady, Nightmare, Glass, The Lady of Spain . . .) and given them qualities of which we were unaware. The Scorpions rise above their pack mentality and reveal themselves to be men and women with their own dreams and plans, people who desire more than simple survival, and who have an almost preternatural ability and willingness to dissect our city, to cut through the tedium even at the cost of some spilled blood. Delany uses the city as a massive backdrop for their wanderings. The billows of smoke that shroud Bellona into a uniform darkness become a cloud from which the Scorpions and others appear and stand, independent of the structures behind them. So the Scorpions, with their lamps that cast animal images about them, become a sort of atmospheric disturbance. Which is real, which is true?

WE DO NOT INTEND to deceive you. *Dhalgren* is not about Scorpions. The central character, the hero if you will, is none other than the Kid (or Kidd), the author of our locally published book of poems, Brass Orchids. Kidd, as we knew him, was like most of us in Bellona. He was a drifter, quieter than most until he met up with the Scorpions, unwilling or unable to describe his own history, anxious to find one for the city, willing to share a part of himself in his poems.

Yet this is not the man we meet in *Dhalgren*. Kidd becomes an intense searcher, so intense that he often loses the geography of his search. He is a man like the city, out of place in both time and space. Like the city, he suffers from some break in his past. He cannot remember his name, or what caused him to forget it. He is plagued by the knowledge of his own mortality, and sees this mirrored in the appearance of the second moon, the rising of the unnamed sun, the approach of the final storm and riot.

The Kid comes into our city covered with the prisms, mirrors, and lenses that lie between the links of a strangely acquired chain. He is given an Orchid (the familiar wrist knife with talons that enclose the fist) to protect himself. These are the tools to unlock Bellona. The chain to alter perception, to see beyond sight, to go past simple amazement at Bellona's survival, and the Orchid to cut away the unnecessary whether it be time or flesh. But thus armed, he becomes a man not so concerned with the essence of Bellona as with the experience of life. Again, Bellona becomes a cloud, its people are allowed to stand out and be real. (Or true?)

WHO ARE THE PEOPLE of Bellona? Fighters, drinkers, talkers, dancers, actors, winners, losers, survivors—and lovers, with an incredible kind of love. Incredible because we live in a disaster area, a spasm of city where any love is unexpected. That the Kid makes physical love with Tak, Lanya, Denny, and a few others would be interesting enough for its honest novelty. But there is passion along with the motions, passion that is sometimes as ashen as one would anticipate, but is also a blinding, consuming passion, honest in its own right.

But we are forgetting the purpose of this article. This is a review and not a critique. We have, perhaps, taken too much liberty with the paper we print on.

Dhalgren is a book, a complex novel that, in our opinion, rivals anything we have read in terms of quality, truth, honesty, reality. Delany has created a city that is very similar to our own, and we squirm in discomfort as we try to escape his vision. We would like to show our better sides; we would like to discuss our plans and projects. But we must seek our totality. We must admit that Bellona is—

- a place where a rapist is an object of worship, a quasi-religious figure, a black christ who has sinned for us all.
- a violence of Scorpion runs, gangs chasing wildly into nights filled with blood.
- a newspaper that switches days and dates at whim, that headlines the past while writing of the future.
- no longer listed on the maps of the outside world, either forgotten or suppressed.
- a preacher preaching, "Where is this city? Struck out of time! Where is it builded? On the brink of truths and lies. Not truth and falsity—Oh, no. No. Nothing so grand. Here we are sunk in an abyss of discrete fibs, innocent misobservations, brilliant speculations that turn out wrong and kill."
- a killing.
- a killer.
- a blood red contact lens.
- a dead boy crushed at the bottom of an elevator shaft.
- a Brass Orchid, as in orchis, the Greek word for testicle.
- an astronaut saying "It's another world, and when you're there, you have no way of knowing what anything means."
- a book

Called *Dhalgren*, written by Samuel Delany, it is a description of our city. We are troubled by it, but we enjoyed it. If you find a stray copy of it, open it up. Your time will not be wasted.

STEVEN PALEY

[For the full text of this review, see the following pages.]

WE FIND OURSELVES in the uncomfortable position of being stared at. Bellona has been put under a microscope, and we are squirming. The microscope is a book called *Dhalgren* which was recently published in the outside world. We find it encouraging that the outside world has again taken notice of us (we are easily flattered) but regret that many of our urgent problems (the water shortage, for example) are given very little attention. But *Dhalgren* is a novel, and water shortages are not the traditional theme of novels.

We are uncomfortable under the view of the author. We recognize ourselves, so we do not know how to write this review. Shall we point out the differences between our view of the city, and how the author, Samuel R. Delany, sees Bellona? This would be to confuse the factual with the subjective, the event with the experience, or, as Delany quotes in the beginning of his saga: "You have confused the true and the real." What is true about our city is not necessarily real. The same may be said of the novel.

BELLONA, AS WE VIEW and live it, is a city sorely beset by the destruction that has caused us to lose over 95% of our population. The fires still burn, the city is colored grey, and we have not seen a recognizable sky for too long a time. Our remaining citizens survive as scavengers looting and re-looting the artifacts of the past. Whether it's the Scorpions or the commune in the park, we have not made any significant progress in rebuilding our city. We plan, but we have been incapable of channeling our plans into action. Perhaps the saddest comment we can make is that the Scorpions have done the most in the way of action, while their actions have accomplished nothing.

We are, as is everyone in Bellona, familiar with the Scorpions. As you know from our previous editorials (and with luck, this review might escape that fate) we take a rather sour view of these street gangs. They have too much opportunity to terrorize what's left of our city at will. They are clans of lost and dangerous youth. They gather themselves into nests and pour into our unprotected streets. We look at them and are reminded of a quote that started a different book. A quote attributed to one Dr. Johnson: "He who makes a beast of himself rids himself of the pain of being a man."

But Delany does not seem to take this view. He has humanized these creatures of the night. He has given them names (Dragon Lady,

Nightmare, Glass, The Lady of Spain…) and given them qualities of which we were unaware. The Scorpions rise above their pack mentality and reveal themselves to be men and women with their own dreams and plans, people who desire more than simple survival, and who have an almost preternatural ability and willingness to dissect our city, to cut through the tedium even at the cost of some spilled blood. Delany uses the city as a massive backdrop for their wanderings. The billows of smoke that shroud Bellona into a uniform darkness become a cloud from which the Scorpions and others appear and stand, independent of the structures behind them. So the Scorpions, with their lamps that cast animal images about them, become a sort of atmospheric disturbance. Which is real, which is true?

WE DO NOT INTEND to deceive you. *Dhalgren* is not about Scorpions. The central character, the hero if you will, is none other than the Kid (or Kidd), the author of our locally published book of poems, *Brass Orchids*. Kidd, as we knew him, was like most of us in Bellona. He was a drifter, quieter than most until he met up with the Scorpions, unwilling or unable to describe his own history, anxious to find one for the city, willing to share a part of himself in his poems.

Yet this is not the man we meet in *Dhalgren*. Kidd becomes an intense searcher, so intense that he often loses the geography of his search. He is a man like the city, out of place in both time and space. Like the city, he suffers from some break in his past. He cannot remember his name, or what caused him to forget it. He is plagued by the knowledge of his own mortality, and sees this mirrored in the appearance of the second moon, the rising of the unnamed sun, the approach of the final storm and riot.

The Kid comes into our city covered with the prisms, mirrors, and lenses that lie between the links of a strangely acquired chain. He is given an Orchid (the familiar wrist knife with talons that enclose the fist) to protect himself. These are the tools to unlock Bellona. The chain to alter perception, to see beyond sight, to go past simple amazement at Bellona's survival, and the Orchid to cut away the unnecessary whether it be time or flesh. But thus armed, he becomes a man not so concerned with the essence of Bellona as with the experience of life. Again, Bellona becomes a cloud; its people are allowed to stand out and be real. (Or true?)

WHO ARE THE PEOPLE of Bellona? Fighters, drinkers, talkers, dancers, actors, winners, losers, survivors—and lovers, with an incredible kind of love. Incredible because we live in a disaster area, a spasm of city where any love is unexpected. That the Kid makes physical love with Tak, Lanya, Denny, and a few others would be interesting enough for its honest novelty. But there is passion along with the motions, passion that is sometimes as ashen as one would anticipate, but is also a blinding, consuming passion, honest in its own right.

But we are forgetting the purpose of this article. This is a review and not a critique. We have, perhaps, taken too much liberty with the paper we print on.

Dhalgren is a book, a complex novel that, in our opinion, rivals anything we have read in terms of quality, truth, honesty, reality. Delany has created a city that is very similar to our own, and we squirm in discomfort as we try to escape his vision. We would like to show our better sides; we would like to discuss our plans and projects. But we must seek our totality. We must admit that Bellona is—

• a place where a rapist is an object of worship, a quasi-religious figure, a black christ who has sinned for us all.
• a violence of Scorpion runs, gangs chasing wildly into nights filled with blood.
• a newspaper that switches days and dates at whim, that headlines the past while writing of the future.
• no longer listed on the maps of the outside world, either forgotten or suppressed.
• a preacher preaching: "Where is this city? Struck out of time! Where is it builded? On the brink of truths and lies. Not truth and falsity—Oh, no. No. Nothing so grand. Here we are sunk in an abyss of discrete fibs, innocent misobservations, brilliant speculations that turn out wrong and kill."
• a killing.
• a killer.
• a blood red contact lens.
• a dead boy crushed at the bottom of an elevator shaft.
• a Brass Orchid, as in orchis, the Greek word for testicle.
• an astronaut saying "It's another world, and when you're there, you have no way of knowing what anything means."
• a book

called *Dhalgren*, written by Samuel Delany; it is a description of our city. We are troubled by it, but we enjoyed it. If you find a stray copy of it, open it up. Your time will not be wasted.

STEVEN PALEY

S. F.

by Gerald Jonas

[Sunday, February 16, 1975, *New York Times Book Review*]

Dhalgren, by Samuel R. Delany (Bantam, paper, $1.95) is the long-awaited major novel by a writer who won four Nebula Awards in the 1960s and who was undoubtedly the most interesting member of that group of S.F. mavericks known collectively as the New Wave. His last novel appeared in 1968. Since then, by all accounts, he has been hard at work on a truly big book, his magnum opus. In some S.F. circles, Delany's project has been treated as the equivalent of Normal Mailer's self-touted major novel—the book that Mailer insists will prove to the world that he belongs in the same room with Mr. Tolstoy and Mr. Dostoevsky.

It takes a writer of unusual gifts to make a work-in-progress seem more interesting than most published novels. The world is still waiting for Mailer's big one. Delany, at the age of 32, has now delivered. The cover copy of *Dhalgren* includes the tag: "Bantam Science Fiction." But from the first page, Delany lets the reader know that his ambitions extend even beyond challenging Mr. Wells and Mr. Verne.

Dhalgren is 879 pages long. Its form is unmistakably circular. The first words in the book—"to wound the autumnal city."—seem to be the end of a sentence, and the last words of the book—"I have come to"—seem to be the beginning of the same sentence. This obvious echo of *Finnegan's Wake* is both daring and defensible. It is Delany's way of flagging his intent, of proclaiming the standards by which he wishes to be judged. Among science fiction fans, his book is bound to set off a new round of that interminable debate over what is S.F. and what isn't S.F. Delany himself is on record as preferring the label "speculative fiction."

One thing is certain: *Dhalgren* is not a conventional novel, whether considered in terms of S.F. or the mainstream. But since a great deal of science fiction falls into the subcategory of "space opera"—callow adventure stories that use outer space and the far future as convenient backdrops—perhaps *Dhalgren* can best be classified as a "space-time opera." If the book can be said to be *about* anything, it is about nothing less than the nature of reality.

The "autumnal city" is a metropolis, somewhere in America, called Bellona. An unexplained disaster has destroyed Bellona's normal social fabric, and done something irreparable to the space-time continuum itself. Most of the inhabitants have fled; the few who remain and those who arrive by choice have coalesced into a new kind of community, an unstable mixture of civility and anarchy. The hero who comes to "wound" this already stricken city has forgotten his name; he is known variously as Kidd, kid, and the Kid, and he may or may not be a madman named William Dhalgren. More or less by accident, he becomes the poet laureate of Bellona; he also assumes the leadership of a youth gang loosely modeled on the Hell's Angels; he falls in love with (and repeatedly makes love to) a young girl and a young boy; he has numerous encounters with a large cast of characters who all too obviously represent a cross section (seen through a distorting prism) of modern civilization; and as he moves through the city, he records many of his reactions in a battered notebook, which may or may not be the original manuscript of the vast creation entitled "Dhalgren."

Any further synopsis would be misleading. As in Joyce's *Ulysses*, mythological allusions abound. However, the most important fact about Delany's novel—in terms of contemporary science fiction, at least—is that nothing in it is clear. Nothing is *meant* to be clear. An event may be described two or three times, and each recounting is slightly, disconcertingly different from the one before. What appear to be close parallels dissolve on closer inspection into ambiguity. The nameless narrator experiences time discontinuously; whole days seem to be excised from his memory. Strange portents appear briefly in the sky—a second moon, an impossibly large sun—but none of the characters shows much curiosity about what is happening. As for the rest of the world, Delany implies that the events in Bellona are being ignored outside the city limits. In a very real sense, every adventure in Bellona is subjective, because the city provides no objective landmarks, either physical or social; there is no common reference. "We live, Kid though; and die in different cities."

If what I have said makes *Dhalgren* sound like another entry in the parade of "head" novels—another self-indulgent trip through someone's drug-induced fantasies—let me correct this impression. The dissolving landscape, the ambiguous characters, the freakish events are all presented as having a reality (of some kind) outside the author's mind. Bellona may be a nightmare, but it is, to paraphrase Joyce, a nightmare of history.

Most so-called modern science fiction is rooted in the world-view of 19th-century physics. Every effect is presumed to have an ascertainable cause, and there is nothing that you cannot know, in principle, if you have the time to make the necessary observations and work out the mathematics. But physics today makes no such assumptions. It is not merely that advances like Heisenberg's Uncertainty Principle and Goedel's Theorem have set theoretical limits to our possible knowledge. On a more practical level, scientists who peer down into the atom and out into interstellar space have encountered a bewildering array of wonders—from quarks to quasars—that suggest there is more to the universe than has been dreamed of by Einstein or Heisenberg or anyone else.

Delany once wrote a brilliant short novel called *The Einstein Intersection* (which won the Nebula Award for Best S.F. Novel of 1967), about a future universe where all the laws of physics had been subtly altered by a cosmic catastrophe. Despite some stylistic sleight of hand, *The Einstein Intersection* (Ace, paper, 95 cents) could still be read as a "conventional" S.F. novel that merely played with its dazzling theme. *Dhalgren* expounds what the earlier book only hinted at. It is as if Delany were saying, "This is what science fiction might be, if the science in it were really up-to-date." In *Dhalgren*, the premonitions of subatomic physics and cosmology are given flesh. The universe, as experienced by an ordinary person from day to day, no longer follows the old rules. Presumably, there are some rules, but they are not understood yet, and there is no assurance that men can ever know them.

To thrust the reader into this universe (instead of merely telling him about it, as in *The Einstein Intersection*), Delany has found a style to match his theme: the texture of *Dhalgren* is dense and intricate, totally unlike anything else in recent science fiction. Most S.F. is written as if the characters and events were being viewed through a telescope: everything is described from the outside, only large gestures count and things happen in a hurry. The characters and events in *Dhalgren* are observed through a microscope: conversations go on and on; the smallest actions are analyzed and re-analyzed: "Actions are interesting to watch. [Kid thinks.] I learn about the actors. Their movements are emblems of the tensions in this internal landscape, which their actions resolve. About-to-act is an interesting state to experience, because I am conscious of just those tensions. Acting itself feels fairly dull: it not only resolves, it obliterates those tensions from my consciousness." And so on.

The quotation reveals the flaw in Delany's strategy. I am afraid that *Dhalgren* is precisely the kind of book that most people turn to S.F. to get away from. Its virtues are apparent, but it is a chore to read. In fact, a book like *Dhalgren*—genuine S.F. conceived and executed on this level of sophistication—would have been unimaginable 10 years ago. Only in the last decade has the Academic Critical Apparatus taken serious note of science fiction. *Dhalgren* may be the first S.F. novel written with at least one eye on this new S.F. audience—the students and professors of literature who are always seeking grist for their mills of exegesis.

One clue to what Delany is doing can be found in the title. S.F. titles are often marvelously evocative—as might be expected in a genre that is not far removed from its pulp origins, when a good story with a dull title never made it off the newsstand rack. Delany himself, while still in his teens, wrote a novel called *The Jewels of Aptor* (Ace, paper, 75 cents), followed by a trilogy: *Captives of the Flame*, *The Towers of Toron*, and *City of a Thousand Suns* available in a single volume under the title of *The Fall of the Towers* (Ace, paper, $1.25). He went on to write much better books with even more evocative titles, like *The Einstein Intersection*, *Babel-17* (Ace, paper, 95 cents), and *Nova* (which Bantam will reissue later this year). And now: *Dhalgren*. His latest title is nothing if not discreet. It evokes no pictures, sets no echoes resonating. Cool, flat, and unyielding as a formica tabletop, it does not even invite speculation. In short, there is not a trace of pulp in it.

Gerald Jonas is the author of *Visceral Learning: Toward a Science of Self-Control*.

Breakdown of a Breakthrough Novel

by Harlan Ellison

Dhalgren by Samuel R. Delany (Bantam Books: $1.95)

[Sunday, February 23, 1975, *Los Angeles Times*, Page 64]

The millennium is at hand and, to quote Gulley Jimson in *The Horse's Mouth*, "It's not the vision I had." Speculative fiction has been banging down the barriers of the ghetto for 20 years and apologists of the idiom have been saying, "Just wait till the important novels of human conflict are written utilizing the tools of science fiction. Just wait! Then you'll see some dynamite literature." Well, I was one of the prime shouters, and some of those novels have been published in the last few months, and frankly I feel as if my mouth ought to be washed out with a copy of *The Charterhouse of Parma*.

Probably the most anxiously awaited of these promised "big" novels intended to merge SF with the mainstream, written not by academic dabblers or best-seller-list poseurs but by Our Crowd, was *Dhalgren* by Delany. Of all the post-New Wave writers, young Delany had the most stuff going for him: consummate storyteller, poet, four-time Nebula award winner, au courant, flashy stylist; hell, he'd even been published in *New American Review*.

Rumors of its length, the depth of its perception, the range of its subject matter have circulated in the world of the fantasy writers for a fistful of years: it's huge, more than 300,000 words; it synthesizes everything Chip Delany was going for in *The Einstein Intersection* and *Nova*[1]; it's sexually explicit in a way the genre's never been. Then came delays, and the book was always coming, coming, coming. The rumors grew more interesting. Chip refuses to sell it to any publisher who won't

---

1. SRD: The only connection between *Nova* and *Dhalgren* was the borrowing of one rhetorical figure: the use of a broken sentence at the end of *Nova* and then at the beginning and end of *Dhalgren*. Other than that, the novels had nothing to do with one another in my mind.

guarantee it'll be released uncut[2]; Chip won't let anyone edit a word of it; Chip had to change the title from "Brodecky" to "Dhalgren"[3]; Chip's book has been turned down by all the hardcover houses.[4]

Now *Dhalgren* is with us, all 879 pages of it, and the questions are answered. Who could have known that all the answers would be unsatisfying?

For *Dhalgren* is a tragic failure. An unrelenting bore of a literary exercise afflicted with elephantiasis, anemia of ideas and malnutrition of plot and character development. It is a master talent run amuck, suiciding endlessly for chapter after chapter of turgid, impenetrable prose.

---

2. SRD: No one ever asked me to cut it. The original company, who had contracted for five novels from me, decided it was too long to publish in a single volume and simply let me buy back the contract.

3. The story of the change from "Brodecky" to "Dhalgren" had nothing to do with publishers but, rather, with a friend of mine named Bill Brodecky, who, as a joke, had said I could use his name for the title. At a certain point, he had an argument with his father and decided he wanted to change his own name to William Alvin Moore and did not want his father's name to appear anywhere. Moore wasn't the name I wanted; I wanted a name that was more than one syllable, and so I chose "Dhalgren" largely because of its phonic similarity—when the syllables are rearranged—to Grendel. As well, I was looking for a name that was not in the Manhattan telephone directory, and the best I came up with was "Dhalgren" with that spelling.

4. SRD: To my knowledge, the only hardcover house that turned it down was Doubleday. I don't believe it was ever shown to anyone else—besides Doubleday and Bantam. Bantam was both hardcover and softcover, and the editor there was Fred Pohl: The decision there was to make it a paperback original.

At Doubleday, Mark Haefele received the novel on a Friday and, by the following Tuesday, was told it was simply too long to publish. My suspicion is that was the only hardcover house it could have been published at because of the timing.

Meanwhile, Fred Pohl dropped in to see Marilyn and me in London one evening after dinner; as I recall, he saw the manuscript sitting on the floor and asked what it was, and I told him it was a new long novel I was coming to the end of. He said I should keep him in mind. At this point, it was being retyped by Jo Batterham. She and her partner were the two people who had rediscovered Jean Rhys in Cornwall, where she had been hiding out, which led to her writing her most famous novel, *Wide Sargasso Sea*.

I must be honest: I gave up after 361 pages.[5] I could not permit myself to be gulled or bored any further. Realizing from the git-go that the opening lines of the novel would tie into the closing lines, forming one of those Laocoonian Moebius gimmicks considered too hoary for use 30 years ago, the travels of the nameless hero with one sandal did not seem sufficiently enriching to permit my engaging in the reading of the book as a career. Others who leaped on the first available copies of the novel, as I did, who began reading it avidly, as I did, who began breathing raggedly and faltered in the sprint, as I did, have assured me the book goes nowhere, does nothing, says nothing, and is sunk to its binding in mythological symbolism that is both flagrant and embarrassing. Three hundred and sixty-one pages had delivered me of the same conclusions.

It is possible the trendy and the impressionable who conceived of "great" books as being those that are sententious and muddled may take to *Dhalgren* in cult as did the poor saps who think *Stranger in a Strange Land* is a hot item.

But for those of us who have read Delany's previous work, who have admired it and who have rooted for him, hoping *Dhalgren* would be the breakthrough novel that won for him and for science fiction all the legitimacy for which both have been crying… this sorry compendium of pointless ramblings is a dry hole over which we will weep and wail for years to come.

---

5. SRD: Only when I was rereading this screed did it occur to me to look at the original and see what had been going on on page 361. What apparently had caused Harlan to stop reading was the discussion of a gay sexual encounter, which, I have a feeling, Ellison simply thought had no place in science fiction. Years later, I mentioned this to him, and he said he had no memory of it. It never stopped him being friends with me, however.

Galaxy Bookshelf

by Theodore Sturgeon

[March 1975, *Galaxy Magazine*]

And now, *now*, I can get into what I have been wanting to do for weeks, what I have been getting other things out of the way for, what I have, at the same time, ignored duties and rituals, my wife, my child, my rabbits and my dog. And now I hardly know where to begin.

How about this: I have just read the very best ever to come out of the science fiction field.

How about that.

Or I could start like this: *Dhalgren*, by Samuel R. Delany (New York, Bantam, 896 pp., $1.95) is the all-time Best Buy.

There are so many things to be said about this astonishing achievement that it would take many more than 879 pages to cover them all, and I make the flat prediction that criticism and commentary on *Dhalgren* will exceed that page-count very many times over. Further (and I think one must read the book before thoroughly appreciating this point) the urge to comment evokes an instant fury of frustration because of the necessity of putting down words in a linear fashion while the pressure is to say it all at once on every one of the many levels in which the book itself communicates. Seat the greatest performer in the world on the bench of the world's most elaborate organ, facing the orchestral score of the most celebrated symphony ever composed, and then amputate nine of his fingers, and he will tell you about this kind of frustration. Nothing one can lucidly state about this book can emerge like anything but one-finger music. Delany calls for response in chords because he writes in chords.

Looking back over the immense experience of having read *Dhalgren*, one recalls certain crests and peaks: a strophe on rape, great crystalline stretches of poetry and about poetry, sex sequences so exquisitely delineated that dirt cannot adhere to their polish, and above all, the injection of atmosphere—all kinds of atmosphere, meteorological, ecological, aural, emotional, and spiritual. And character! The Scorpions, ragged and deadly kid gangs armed with holographic projectors which surround them with huge, brilliant, terrifying shapes; Mr. Newboy, whose profound literary criticism would not be amiss in William Carlos Williams or T.S. Eliot; frightened blonde June, the obsessive rapee, fifteen-year-old Denny, a depraved innocent who knew, perhaps, some things about love which could benefit us all, and Lanya, whom I love, whom I shall always love. There are dozens more, and perhaps the most memorable character of all is the city itself, Bellona. It is somewhere in the U.S., and has experienced an unnamed disaster; but it is more than that. Metaphorically it is "here"—any man's "here"—and unless you are very different from the rest of us, you will allow that from time to time "here" shifts and changes in remarkable ways while "why" remains a mystery. In addition, the protagonist is never sure of his own name; that is to say, he spends a lot of this gigantic novel in not knowing who he is.

Do you know who you are?

Have you noticed how often recently, in sf shorts and novels, this theme of transient or alternate reality occurs, and how it increases? For some rather fascinating reason which I must seek out some day, this looks like the trickle which will be a torrent in most literature in the near future. Who am I? What am I? Where am I, and what, really, is "here"? The natural pressure of growth and change, decay and rebirth, has always been in direct conflict with our hunger for stasis, solidity, permanence, security. It is in these areas in which Delany and other truly great, finished writers live and work; it is in these areas where live the wonders and astonishments, the surprises, the new learnings, the discoveries of things and processes hitherto unknown or (a very different thing) unrecognized.

The ultimate test of great and lasting literature is its usefulness. I have said it and said it: the big ones, from Homer through Shakespeare to Nabokov and Delany, are fables, metaphors, parallels to your thought and actions and passions and mine. The usefulness of *Dhalgren* to you and to me is beyond question. Having experienced it, you will stand taller, understand more, and press your horizons back a little further away than you ever knew they could go.

I have space to say only one more thing about *Dhalgren*. It is a paperback original, and as such is going to be by-passed by serious critics everywhere. Some of us have been fighting this especially pernicious snobbery for a long time, with a certain but regrettably small amount of success. Rumor has it that a whole series of hardback houses turned this one down, until paperback release was the only course. I'll try to get the facts on this and will share them with you if I can, but in the meantime proclaim with me our gratitude to Bantam Books. The ultimate recognition of *Dhalgren* as the literary landmark it truly is, as expressed in strong sales and wide acceptance, will do more to eliminate this snobbery than any amount of fulmination from this chair.

This is the first of a pair of articles by Douglas Barbour and Darrell Schweitzer published side-by-side in *Outworld* #27, edited by Bill Bowers, 1975, in a section of the 'zine called "Stand on *Dhalgren*"

The Autumnal City

by Douglas Barbour

Some Notes Towards a Putative Review of Samuel R. Delany's Dhalgren

1. Let's get this out of the way at once: I liked this book. That I also found so much to provoke thought, various kinds of aesthetic & emotional responses, critical theorizing, & delight follows, though not necessarily (I rather liked—to take a fairly far-flung example—Phyllis Einstein's Alaric stories, but they did not *demand* the spectrum of complex responses *Dhalgren* does). I suspect it is necessary to like something this big if you are even going to finish it (I liked *Gravity's Rainbow*, too). I further suspect that a lot of sf readers are not going to like *Dhalgren* sufficiently to keep going through all 880 pages of it. Fine, but that doesn't give them the right to dismiss it as a poor job. And I, for one, believe it is a very strong, major work of contemporary fiction.

2. Is it science (or even speculative) fiction? Even Fred Pohl, who showed great editorial courage in purchasing it for Bantam (he may be doing less, but I think he's worth a lot more than Roger Elwood—partly because he does know the field, & does have high standards, but no special social/political/spiritual drums to beat as editor), has admitted in conversation (fall, 1973, Penn State) that he is not sure if it really is sf. Well, by my very broad definition of 'speculative,' it certainly fits that category: &, if we accept the idea of science fiction that Delany & Joanna Russ have suggested—that it deals with events that have not happened (but—implied—possibly could, or could have)—then it is definitely science fiction, too: at least it's sf. Of course, it's so much more than *mere* sf, that perhaps such categorization is an insult to it. Perhaps, but I'm not

sure. Delany has remarked somewhere that science fiction provides marvelous metaphors for a writer to play with. Indeed, as he implies, sf *is* a marvelous metaphor. How many sf titles can you think of with a phrase something like 'other worlds' in it? In *Dhalgren*, Delany does not use the usual sf trappings, yet Bellona (named for the Roman goddess of war, if for anything) *is* an 'other world,' to which we—along with the kid—travel by means of a bridge (the bridge of art?). This wounded, autumnal city is, like most sf landscapes, both terribly familiar & terribly alien, & strangers (aliens) live strange lives within its wall. Delany is just not that interested in telling us ('scientifically') how Bellona came to be such a strange place, but he does exercise his very subtle art in rendering its presence—as an alien, yet not totally unrecognizable, landscape against which humans can act out their various roles—with great verisimilitude. This is good sf writing: create the 'other world' as fully as possible, & put some believable characters in it, whose actions will intrigue, interest, & perhaps overwhelm us.

3. What a lot of people will *not* like: the frank enjoyment (or sometimes simply acceptance) of human detritus. Most of the people we meet at any length in *Dhalgren*, especially those who hang out, or about, the scorpions' nests, aren't too clean. There is quite a bit of description of human smells, etc., very little of washing (though the one bath the kid has, to clean off a lot of blood, is described with Delany's usual precision). Delany may be attacking the western bourgeois' concern with hygiene here. Anyway, those who were turned off by Delany's description—very light, & doing double duty as part of a scientific explanation of the changes in health by the year 3,000—of Mouse's dirty foot in *Nova*, will definitely be turned off by the kid, & unable to understand, or even appreciate (perhaps—though it's always possible Delany's articulation of these things will win said reader over), Lanya's desire for him, *that way*.

Why go into this? Well, those people have every right to say they don't want to read this book. They have none to say that Delany's exquisitely detailed rendering of human funkiness represents some kind of falling off in his artistry. He is doing something *beyond* what he has done before. In 880 pages he can attempt—at some length—scenes that have never before been a focal part of his work. I think of the dinner at the Richards' apartment, where his representation of 'polite conversation' is so devastatingly accurate it creates its own satiric context. The whole shifting scene of the party at Roger Calkins' carries some of the social conflicts suggested in Prince Red's Paris party in *Nova* to new heights of subtle confrontation; it's an exquisitely realized piece of writing.

4. "But what is this huge wallop of a novel about?" I hear some poor readers crying in the wilderness of Lit 100. After all, any book this huge has got to be about something. But then, there are others who accuse it of being 'relevant,' & therefore out of date already. Well: precisely. It is *about* what it *surrounds*, & that is as relevant as you—or any single reader—wants to make it, taking it as a whole as you can, & responding to it—this other world where things happen which you can or cannot relate to—as fully as possible (or you wish to). It is—precisely because it is so big—about too many things for me to even attempt to list them. (Can they be listed? No. It *is* a fictional construct, an artifact, an other world; in it many wonderous events happen. As is true of any experience, the experience of reading this novel can be a learning experience. So can getting up in the morning, if you want it to be.) The point I'm laboring to make here is that Delany is not interested in messages, but in creating a fiction so multiplex & profound (i.e., something we can dive deeper, deeper into every time we enter it) it will stand for itself alone. Has he succeeded? It will be a long time before anyone can pronounce authoritatively on that.

5. "Nothing we look at is ever seen without some shift and flicker—that constant flaking of vision which we take as imperfections of the eye, or simply the instability of attention itself; and we ignore this illusory screen for the solid reality behind it. But the solid reality is the illusion: the shift and the flicker is all there is. (Where do sf writers get their crazy ideas? From watching all there is *very* carefully."[6] Delany, I believe, is interested in perception (yes, yes, I am going to tell you one of the many things I think *Dhalgren* is about; like poets or lovers, critics reserve the right to contradict themselves in a good cause).

---

6. S.R. Delany in "Appendix: Shadows," §3 p. 254, *Longer Views: Extended Essays*, by Samuel R. Delany, Middletown: Wesleyan UP, 1996

Delany has been accused, & has accused himself in *The Tides of Lust*, of being pretentious. The word is applicable if we can remove the sense of derogation from it. I think the sheer clottedness of his recent style, the increasingly ragged difficulty of it, is due to his interest in reconstructing what happens, from *here* to *here*, the *perceived* particles of event (by particles, here, I mean something akin to what happens at the subatomic level in physics—to measure that, record what is going on—Delany wants to record what is perceived as happening—which does *not* include *all* that is going on—in a language that will represent the *perceived* event. Perceived, because any event is too full & complex to be caught whole in words, but some uses of language, such as a highly compacted style used phenomenologically, may get at perceptual knowledge, what one individual could perceive as happening *now*). I think Delany's desire—articulated in his essay in *Those Who Can*—to write down exactly what is happening is one reason for the high pretentiousness of his style in his latest work: he is attempting to capture physical & psychological events in as full a manner as possible.

And he does this much of the time, right from the strange—possibly dream—fuck in the first few pages, through many different actions, including a number of other sexual encounters. But he does something else as well. There is one triple sex scene that is described—from the kid's perceiving point of view—in exquisite detail. Shortly afterwards there is another similar scene, only this time the kid loves *both* other partners, Lanya & Denny: he can't remember the details because he wasn't concentrating on perceiving the act, but the shared emotion of the act. This is *done*; it is not simply *talked about*.

6. Things I don't like that much? Yes, quite a few, but then such failures to continually achieve perfection must be expected in a novel that dares as much, over such a great distance, as this one. Sometimes it is a pretentious use of language that does not come off. A small example: "swive-juice," in which the word "swive" in its archaic presence calls too much attention to itself, thus loosening the bonds the story has on my imagination at that point. Possibly Delany overdoes his explanations of brass orchids, so they aren't allowed to achieve their own resonance the way Lobey's hollow blade and Mouse's syrinx do. On the other hand, when *Brass Orchids* becomes the title of a book of poems, the art/weapon

paradox Delany has long been obsessed with is neatly made literary rather than musical. There are some places, especially in *The Anathemata: a plague journal*, where the style becomes too clotted for me, though I'm not sure the passages won't clear up with rereadings.

7. Things I do like. Lots. Much of the characterization. The sex scenes: they are erotically stimulating & yet demand intellectual response as well, & they're written with grace & sensitivity. The handling of interpersonal tensions and the way such tensions can lead to quickly erupting violence. The descriptions of the landscape of Bellona & of the sky. The marvelous scene where another young poet, Frank, tells kid—& he's the only one to do so—that he doesn't like the poems of *Brass Orchids*. The tensions of that confrontation is perfectly rendered: I know that scene, & Delany has caught it perfectly. Too much else to go into. But there is more than enough to allow me to cry, riches galore.

8. Delany's literary obsessions. They're all here. The sexual/loving triple relationship. The conjunction of artist & criminal—an old Romantic notion (see my article in *Khatru 2*). The continual discussion—in fictional terms—of the place, effect & value of art & the artist in society (one of Delany's finer minor characters in *Dhalgren* is the Audenesque Mr. Newboy, who holds forth on these matters most wittily & at some length). The analytical interest in violence. Linguistic theory & philosophy (what, after all, is real, & how can we name it?) ("These things I'm writing, they're not *descriptions* of anything. They're complex names," *Dhalgren*, p. 177).

9. Look, when I say I *enjoyed* reading this book, I mean it. If other people don't or can't, that's their worry finally, not mine. But I did not enjoy it in the same way I enjoyed earlier Delany works. I couldn't put them down—with the books & stories following *Empire Star*, I couldn't put them down even on 3rd or 4th reading. Well, of course, with an 880-page book you *can't* read it straight through, but my point is I could put *Dhalgren* aside, even in the middle of a paragraph, & not feel any pressing need to finish at least this chapter. Unlike most of Delany's earlier books, there is no urgent plot movement urging me on (as in Bester's *Tiger, Tiger*, as well). There is a very diluted quest pattern here, but it too isn't as central in the drive of the narrative.

Indeed, Delany is not, apparently, interested in narrative thrust in this book the way he was in earlier novels. One of the possible reasons it is his longest novel is that he is filling in the perceived moments of a life slowly passed in an autumnal space rather than rushing us through larger happenings with precision, wit & a delicate complexity of understanding —& only a few, important scenes taken close-up. So *Dhalgren* is different, as is my response. I savored scenes, & lines, argued with some, thought a lot about what was happening between readings, & eventually, happily, reached the end of the book. It's a difficult book, not always a nice book, a demanding book. Don't read it because I say it's good. It's good, all right, & I like it, but I know it's for certain tastes only. Still, I hope there are enough people out there (both steady readers of sf and others) who will be intrigued by this book, & will eventually find enough in it to stimulate them, that it makes enough money to satisfy Bantam's accountants that Fred Pohl is a worthy editor (after all, he also bought Joanna Russ's *The Female Man*, yes!). *Dhalgren* is but one step on the way; Delany is still a maturing author. I want to read the book that will follow. I think it's entirely possible that it will be shorter & apparently lighter of touch. Possibly it will appeal to a wider audience. If so it won't be because *Dhalgren* doesn't mark a necessary & artistically important stage in Delany's development as a major writer of contemporary sf.

—Douglas Barbour

Dully Grinning Delany Descends to Disaster

by Darrell Schweitzer

Refuting Douglas Barbour

An Essay with Numbered Sections

1. In 1970 James Blish wrote an article on what was then called "The New Wave," and you can find it in his collection of critical essays, *More Issues at Hand* (Advent, 1970). One of the more interesting points made, from the viewpoint of 1975, is a rather cautious statement about Samuel R. Delany:

> That Delany has drive, insight, and a certain music I cannot doubt, but neither his clotted style nor his zigzag way of organizing a story strike me as being much better than self-indulgent and misdirected. If I am right about this—and my experience with Ellison suggests that I am more likely to be wrong—Delany's early popularity, laid on well before he was either in control or was convinced of the necessity of being in control of his manner or his matter, may well turn out to be destructive. He would not be the first writer whom early praise (though every writer longs for it) put out of business, at least for a damagingly long period… (p. 135)

Back in 1970 I was reading Delany and I considered him to be one of the greatest living science fiction writers in English. He had the drive, the insight, and the music Blish spoke of to an enormous degree. He was interesting, occasionally profound, brilliant once in a while, and ceaselessly inventive. I found him to be better organized than Blish did occasionally. Only *The Einstein Intersection* teetered on the brink of chaos, and even that pulled itself back by the end to become a meaningful whole.

But now with the publication of *Dhalgren* (Bantam, 1975) I'm afraid I have to admit Blish was right. Chalk up one astoundingly perceptive prediction for him, but still it hurts to do so. Writers of the first water are worth more than all the critics there will ever be.

Dhalgren isn't just a poor book; it is a shockingly bad one. This sudden disintegration of all Delany's artistic strengths is numbing. If it can happen to Delany it can happen to the best of us. It *has*.

In retrospect, there were a few telltale signs, but I dismissed them at the time. There was a story called *Night and the Loves of Joe Dicostanzo*, published in an anthology called *Alchemy and Academe* (Doubleday 1969, edited by Anne McCaffrey), which was the first time Delany ever did slip off the handle and go spiraling out of control into non-meaning. I met a rabid Delany fan who read the story in the collection *Driftglass* and said of it, "Well, I assume that one was just filler." No way. Delany isn't the kind of writer who produces filler. Something was fundamentally wrong.

Also there's something called *The Tides of Lust* which I cannot evaluate because I have not read it. It apparently sold all of a half a dozen copies before going out of print, and is now extremely rare. It would be quite valuable if anybody wanted it. I saw a copy only once, in the hands of another Delany admirer. He told me the book was bilge, that it made sex dull, and the only point of interest was trying to figure out who was doing what to whom in some of the more complicated orgies. You needed a diagram, he said. I dismissed this, too. I thought maybe Delany was just goofing off. But I can't believe that now, in the light of *Dhalgren*.

2. One of the most curious things about *Dhalgren* is the fact that very few people manage to finish it. I'd like to see *Locus* take a poll asking "How far did *you* get?" The answers would be fascinating. *Dhalgren* has become a fannish endurance game, and few people make it to the end. I did because I was reviewing the book for a magazine called *Concert* and felt obligated. I've taken a little survey of my own, and discovered that among maybe thirty or so people asked, one (1) person finished *Dhalgren*. The most common breaking point is about page 200. About half the people gave up there, and of those who went further, the next most common point was page 500. That took care of all but the people who lasted [for] less than 50 pages (maybe 15%, including two well-known SF writers) and a few oddballs like the guy who went as far as page 800 before abandoning the thing.

This is amazing. There have been controversial books before in SF, and terrible books, but a score like that is without precedent I think. The obvious question is *why*? Style isn't it. The prose is inferior prose, which sometimes becomes so concerned with putting words into novel combinations that meaning is lost—sound becomes more important than sense, a classic symptom of self-indulgence—but for the most part the book is extremely readable. The descriptions are usually clear with a few exceptions, like what seemed to be an "attack" on a deserted department store by people without weapons facing guards with rifles, in a sequence I can't make heads or tails out of, and for the most part people talk like people; the prose flows along nicely. In the best parts the style is almost invisible.

How many books are unreadable because of turgid prose. Henry James had an absolutely tin ear for language, and few people have been able to finish his novels. James Fenimore Cooper suffered from the problem of being only partially literate, with no genuine powers of observation, and again no ear for language. On the opposite end of the spectrum there's Joyce's *Finnegans Wake*, which is unreadable to most people because it is too difficult. It has to be studied rather than merely read before any meaning comes out at all, and most novel readers are unwilling to exert that sort of effort. But *Dhalgren* isn't like the works of James, or Cooper, or the later Joyce. It is easy to read, so the problem must lie elsewhere.

3. The universal complaint of all those people who failed to finish the book is that it is dull. It did not interest them, and when I read it I saw why. The overwhelming impression it left was one of rambling emptiness. It is a dreary, *dead* book, about as devoid of content as any piece of writing can be and still have the words arranged in any coherent order. In the review I did for *Concert* I synopsized the whole thing in a single paragraph, and said that meant a lot, because I'd like to see you do the same with another novel of the same length, say, *War and Peace*. You can't. Tolstoy's book is too complicated. Delany's is very simple, and doesn't merit its length.

For the first time Delany is wasting words wholesale.

4. Fred Pohl insists that *Dhalgren* is great literature, even though its meaning may not be known to us at this time. He's said this several times at conventions, in conversation and on panels, and I respect him for his faith. It's a very dangerous thing for an editor to buy a book he doesn't

understand, because he could be making a mistake, and one mistake is all you get in publishing.

I'm not holding my breath for the Great Revelation, because I don't think it will come. *Dhalgren* has no meaning. By traditional rules it isn't even a novel, because a novel has to be a story, and a story is a series of significant events which lead to some sort of character change. If the character is the same at the end it is because the development has run a complete circle, and the sameness is the point of the story. *Dhalgren* makes a few weak noises about a circular structure, but the essential movements aren't there. You can excise any section you want, and there's no difference, because nothing is being dismembered. The book has no structure beyond the kid's entering and leaving the city. The great bulk of it is a formless lump.

It's a very literary lump, to be sure. It has lots of Symbols in it, most of them sexual, the most obvious ones being the huge red sun and the double moons. Delany is not subtle about this. He all but stands up and shouts, "Hey! This is symbolic!" But do the symbols do anything but hang there, like art Christmas tree ornaments? They do not. They do not illuminate, expand, parallel, or otherwise work on the thematic material, because there is no theme, just as there is no plot or character development.

Pohl seems to think *Dhalgren* is great literature, but I would have to disagree. Great literature is something which speaks to people of all ages and all times. It's something you read when you're young, maybe only enjoying it for the superficial story. Then when you're a little older you come back, and it means something new to you, something visible only now that you have entered a new phase of life. You keep coming back, and the work continues to speak to you. I've had that reaction with Shakespeare's *Macbeth*.

This isn't the case with *Dhalgren*. It is all vague touching and feeling, with no personality dominant, no intellectual content. It does not speak because it has no voice.

5. When you get down to it, *Dhalgren* is pornographic in the strictest sense of the word. I don't say this to condemn it, only to describe it. The book works on no other level but the erotic, and even that is only in passing intervals between large chunks of complete non-function. I've

been suggesting rather cynically for a while now that the thing should be subtitled "The Collected Fetishes of Samuel R. Delany," and that's how I explain much of what others call the book's kinkiness, the fascination with dirt, human odors, and chains. There have been traces of this sort of thing before, in *Time Considered As a Helix of Semi-Precious Stones*, in *Nova*, and in *Night and the Loves* [sic] *of Joe Dicostanzo*. Delany seems to be on a grime and bondage trip. To each his own.

The book has been enormously successful in America. It has sold something like a half a million copies since its initial publication, and has gone through at least five printings as of this writing. I suspect much of its appeal is that it isn't just anti-intellectual, but non-intellectual, and this fits the temper of the times. The middle Seventies seems to be a period of regression and exhaustion for this country, filled with a hazy mental apathy. Nothing matters anymore. Hence it's just the right time for a book which allows the reader to escape into a fantasy world where people can lounge around without cares, where the rigidities of modern society are gone, and all the people Samuel Delany doesn't like don't exist anymore. There's no mental stimulation at all, no challenge, as is to be expected in a daydream. Delany compromises the basics of human experience, overlooking such things as greed, lust of power, and brutality. Nobody in *Dhalgren* seems to worry much about territory, property, or taking over the whole scene and ruling others, as people really do in life. Even the hoodlums are basically nice people.

The thing about all this is that the self-conscious reader who imagines himself to be an intellectual can read this soothing mind-wash and pretend all the while that he's experiencing great art. And the sexual angle shouldn't be overlooked. Most people are ashamed to be seen reading hardcore smut. *Dhalgren* is packaged respectably. No one will ever know.

6. *Dhalgren* is, I think, the most disappointing thing to happen to science fiction since Robert Heinlein made a complete fool out of himself with *I Will Fear No Evil*. Heinlein proved with that book and the subsequent *Time Enough for Love* that he was artistically exhausted, written out, and had lost his touch. But then Heinlein is an old man, and has a large body of respectable work behind him. For this to happen to Delany at the age of 32, after he had shown such tremendous promise and begun to fulfill it, is nothing short of tragic. Of course it has happened before: Stephen

Crane burned himself out at an early age, as many flaming geniuses have, but the catastrophe of it is undiminished. Blish is right: the damage has been done, and Delany has been put out of business artistically. *Dhalgren* might have made a mildly interesting 10,000 word novelet [sic], but beyond that it's all padding.

Science Fiction's Great Hope of the late 1960s has just fizzled out

—Darrell Schweitzer

A Response to Myself

by Darrell Schweitzer

Wow. I was 23 when I wrote that. As an essay, not bad in its form, but clearly the argument of this piece has not withstood the test of time. I am 68 now and I have to admit that *Dhalgren* seems well on its way to fulfilling the definition of "great literature" I give here, i.e., that it means something different to readers at different points in their lives, and they keep coming back to it. That the book has remained in print all this time indicates that they do. It has, in sales jargon, "legs." It goes on and on. *Dhalgren* is now being read and enjoyed by people who were not even born when it was first published, and there is every indication this will continue well into the future.

I have come to the conclusion over the years that a critic is at a disadvantage trying to tell people why they should not have enjoyed something they already did. Mark Twain almost did that in his famous essay "Fenimore Cooper's Literary Offenses," but I do not think he was actually addressing Cooper's *fans*. It is too late to explain *Dhalgren* away. The task for the critic now is to determine why the book appeals and what its influence has been. Obviously I have not done that here.

—Philadelphia, PA

Sept 4, 2020

Words: And Now Tomorrow

by Gerald Jonas

[*Penthouse*, May 1976 (pp. 48–50)]

Just because a science fiction story takes place in the year 2001—or 1984—doesn't necessarily mean that the author is trying to predict what the future will be like. Politicians, economists, weathermen, and astrologers claim the power of prediction; some may even believe their claims. Science fiction writers are more modest; they treat the future as an enormous grab bag filled with so many surprises and uncertainties that one guess about what will happen is just as good as any other guess. This attitude toward the future gives the SF writer the freedom to invent situations and characters without worrying too much about how everything fits together. A writer who wipes out the human race with a nuclear holocaust in one novel will cheerfully describe man's triumphant conquest of the galaxy in his next book. But too much freedom can become a burden too, and the more serious SF writers usually restrict their flights of imagination to stories describing what might happen if *this* trend or *that* trend is allowed to continue. Not surprisingly, most of these futuristic fictions read like cautionary tales, warning us of the doom that awaits if we don't mend our ways. There are also a few Utopian fables which try to influence the shape of things to come by holding up the author's vision of the "ideal society" for our edification. But the most intriguing SF stories are those that fall in between these extremes, stories depicting a future that simultaneously attracts and repels the reader, while throwing an oddly revealing light on the present. There was a rich crop of such books within the last few months.

Samuel R. Delany, one of the best young writers in the field, produced a huge enigmatic volume called *Dhalgren* (Bantam, paper, $1.95). Its 879 pages were devoted to the portrait of a city called Bellona which has suffered a disaster so cataclysmic that the very fabric of the space-time continuum has been distorted. We never learn exactly what the disaster was; Delany perversely concentrates on its aftermath. Buildings burn endlessly but are not consumed. Radio and television broadcasts cannot enter or leave the city. The sky is sealed with thick haze. When it clears briefly, strange portents are seen: two moons, a grotesquely swollen sun. The people who live in the city—survivors and a few adventurers who have come by choice—are even stranger. The hero is an amnesiac whose search for identity is the only consistent plot-element in the book. At various times, he becomes a poet, a leader of a youth gang, a bisexual lover, the author's alter ego. More than anything else, he likes to talk; so do most of the other characters. They seem determined to talk their way out of their predicament and back into a recognizable universe. But nothing is resolved; in fact the book literally ends where it began, with the last sentence hooking into the first like a snake trying to swallow its tail. It could have been monumentally dull, but Delany's kaleidoscopic prose—and his powerful vision of a society trying to come to terms with chaos—make the whole journey worthwhile.

Reviews of the 1996 Wesleyan University Press reprint

Despite its density and difficulty, many of *Dhalgren*'s initial readers read the book three, four, or more times. One woman—Mrs. Ann Dawson, of San Mateo, CA—read *Dhalgren* once a year for more than twenty years. Though Delany never met her during that time, eventually they exchanged letters.[7] Along with a number of other multiple-time readers of *Dhalgren*, Mrs. Dawson helped locate many typographical errors in various printings. Eventually Delany dedicated one of his essay collections, *The Straits of Messina* (Serconia Press: Seattle, 1989), to her.

After *Dhalgren* had gone through 19 printings over almost 12 years, Bantam Books put the book out of print at the end of 1986.

Eight years later, Wesleyan University Press, under the editorial directorship of Terry Cochran, reissued *Dhalgren* as a university press trade paperback. Most reviews of the reprint concentrate—as did the book's new foreword by William Gibson—on the emotional effect the book had on its first generation of readers.

The following reviews of the Wesleyan reprint are from *The Telluride Times-Journal* (August/September 1996) and the summer 1996 issue of *Rain Taxi*.

---

7. In 2003, when Delany was on a Spring book tour of the West Coast for the Vintage Books edition of his collected early science-fiction and fantasy short stories, *Aye, and Gomorrah and other stories* (Vintage Books: New York, 2003), he and Mrs. Dawson finally met—and, with a number of mutual friends, had dinner together—on the May evening of his reading at the Modern Times Bookstore in San Francisco. There was a small earthquake during dinner.

SAMUEL R. DELANY

Dhalgren

With a new foreword by William Gibson

Now Read This

by John Nizalowski

[*Telluride Times-Journal*, Aug 29–Sept 4, 1996, §2B:]

Classic countercultural novel returns to haunt you

In my life I have encountered a handful of novels that created a personal metamorphosis central to my identity.

Samuel R. Delany's *Dhalgren* is one of those crucial novels, and I am extremely grateful to Wesleyan University Press for making *Dhalgren* available again after nearly a decade of being out of print.

Dhalgren affected me so profoundly that I vividly remember reading it for the first time.

It was the summer of 1975, just months after the novel first appeared.

That summer, I worked at painting my parents' two-century-old home in upstate New York and refinishing the attic of my grandfather's rental property.

Two settings dominated my outer experience: high ladders, thick layers of white latex paint, and summer sunlight diffused by maple and locust leaves; and hot, empty rooms, the smell of sawdust and clean maple planking, and daylight filtered through streaked, dusty attic windows.

Meanwhile, *Dhalgren* consumed my interior universe with stylistically captivating passages: "Charcoal, like the bodies of beetles, heaped below the glittering wall on the far corner. The sharpness of incinerated upholstery cut the street's gritty stink. Through a cellar window, broken, a gray eel of smoke slithered the sidewalk to vaporize in the gutter. Through another, intact, flickerings.... The singular burning among the dozens of whole buildings was the most uncanny thing he'd seen."

That summer I became obsessed with *Dhalgren*'s fictional mid-western city of Bellona—adrift in time and space, severed from the outside world, an anarchist paradise of drugs, deviant sex, gangs and a complex urban landscape that shifted with the rising and setting of its occasional double moons and monstrous red sun.

I have gone on to re-read *Dhalgren* six times, and the settings for these re-readings are also vivid—including an old farmhouse in Virginia, where I huddled under an art deco floor lamp set beside a crackling wood stove, reading well toward dawn while the winter wind tore at the walls. Another reading was in a Santa Fe Laundromat, where the spinning machines rumbled and the fluorescent lights flickered. Outside, the dangerous south side barrio night was witness to heroin deals, robbed drunks and the occasional knifing, a sinister echo of Bellona's violent labyrinth of perpetual dusk streets.

The locales of re-reading *Dhalgren* remain sharp and clear because *Dhalgren*'s power has never diminished.

Every time I read *Dhalgren*, I feel like a jeweler turning a precious stone under a magnifying lens. New facets keep appearing—new imagery, new thematic motifs, new archetypes, and always fresh mysteries appear in this surreal novel about the shifting edges between the real and the magical.

To borrow a phrase from Ursula K. Le Guin, I believe that Samuel R. Delany is our home-grown Gabriel Garcia Marquez, and *Dhalgren* is one of the ten best American novels written since 1950.

Born in Harlem in 1942, Delany was a key voice of the '60's counterculture.

In the early '60s, he was a member of New York City's emerging gay scene and also an important folk music performer. At one time he was billed above Bob Dylan.

Later, Delany helped start a commune, Heavenly Breakfast, named after his rock band.

By 1968, Delany had also published numerous award-winning and critically acclaimed science-fiction works, including the richly textured novels *Babel-17*, *The Einstein Intersection*, and *Nova*.

Then, after a seven-year wait, *Dhalgren* appeared, signaling a new direction in Delany's work.

While his previous novels and stories explored stock science-fiction motifs (star travel, alternate dimensions, interstellar empire), *Dhalgren* traveled a path closer to Latin American magic realism.

Set in the 1970s, *Dhalgren* takes place in Bellona, a fictional American city.

In Bellona, time runs in loops. Even physical constraints, like where the sun rises, can transform in the night.

Most people have fled Bellona, but about a thousand remain, and others have drifted in since the disaster.

Bellona has no police, no government, no authority. Instead, there are drifters living out their fantasies, former suburban and ghetto residents clinging to a neurotic echo of their pre-disaster lifestyle, and gangs who conceal their bodies behind holographic projections of archetypal beast images—griffins, dragons, spiders and the like.

This anarchic condition reveals the essential nature of people by destroying masks and self-deceptions, a notion stated best by Bellona's Tak Loufer, former industrial engineer, leather freak and homosexual.

"You know here… you're free. No laws: to break, or to follow. Do anything you want. Which does funny things to you. Very quickly, surprisingly quickly, you become… exactly who you are.… If you're ready for that, this is where it's at."

Dhalgren's main character is Kid, a young drifter who has forgotten his identity and has a history of far more disturbing psychiatric problems.

While in Bellona, Kid writes a book of poetry, leads a gang of scorpions, and enters into a three-member sexual partnership with a man and a woman.

However, just before he enters Bellona, Kid meets a strange oriental woman in a forest. After they make love, she gives Kid loops and loops of chain ornamented with prisms and lenses. She then turns into a tree.

The encounter deeply disturbs Kid, and it also begins one of the novel's central narrative puzzles.

Many strange events will happen to Kid—gaps occurring in time; people appearing with entirely red eyes; buildings, streets, and bridges switching their location; double moons and giant red suns appearing in the sky.

The reader cannot tell much of the time whether these are objective events occurring for all residents of this strange city or are instead distortions created by the Kid's twisted mind.

Also, to complicate matters Delany makes use of meta-fictional techniques. For instance, Kid finds a notebook with an author's notes on *Dhalgren*, and later Kid looks into a mirror and sees Samuel R. Delany.

So, is Kid simply trapped in a narrative? But whose? Kid's? A character named Dhalgren (who appears only on a list of names in the mysterious notebook)? Delany's?

As in Joyce's *Finnegans Wake*, *Dhalgren*'s last line is a fragment which completes the novel's opening half sentence, creating a perpetual, closed narrative circle.

Is *Dhalgren* therefore a portrait of a character caught in a time loop, forever condemned to re-enter Bellona and re-enact his experiences? Or is the whole business Kid's (or Delany's) fictional exercise?

Dhalgren explores the nature of reality, the boundaries between the true and the imagined, and the relationship between art and life.

It also examines the nature of race, American social structure, the power of mythic patterns, the origins of violence, alternative sexual practices, and the connections between art and the criminal underground.

Altogether, *Dhalgren* is a unique and powerful literary masterpiece.

Dhalgren

by Rudi Dornemann

[Summer, 1996, *Rain Taxi,* Vol 1, #4: p. 30]

The first time I heard Samuel R. Delany speak, he was giving a talk on how changes in the publishing industry in the 1980s put an end to the extensive science fiction back catalogues that once kept science fiction's past accessible to readers just coming into the genre. Delany, a master of science fiction, has also written autobiography, comics, pornography, a series of semiotic sword-and-sorcery, and critical essays that are as insightful as they are learned. Thanks to Wesleyan University Press, readers inside (and outside) science fiction now have ready access to the works of one of the genre's most remarkable artists and critics. In the last three years, Wesleyan has reissued all four volumes of his Nevèrÿon fantasy series, as well as the nonfiction *Silent Interviews: On Languages, Sex, Science Fiction and Some Comics* and the non-science fiction *Atlantis: Three Tales*. This year, they have reissued two of his major science fiction novels, *Trouble on Triton* (with an introduction by Kathy Acker) and *Dhalgren* (with an introduction by William Gibson) and another book of essays, *Longer Views: Extended Essays*, will also appear shortly.

At a glance, the understated and elegant covers of the Wesleyan books say "literature" louder than "science fiction." Some of the writers who were, like Delany, identified with the "New Wave" movement in science fiction during the 1960s worked to distance themselves from the genre and define themselves as literary writers. Delany, however, has always maintained that the genre identification is integral to his writing—he uses the conventions and the traditions of one particular "paraliterature" and is best understood with reference to those conventions and traditions. *Dhalgren*, first published in the mid-1970s and perhaps Delany's most unusual work, is an interesting case in point.

In *Dhalgren*, Delany is interested in how we understand, how we misunderstand, how perception shifts from the one to the other. He zeroes in on moments of misreading, tracks the dynamics of rumor and reputation, and shows us a character continually grappling with a world either overdetermined or underdetermined by the information at hand.

Delany's main character, who can't remember his own name and winds up variously going by "kid," "Kid," "Kidd," or "the kid," arrives in a city called Bellona where space and time have been warped by some never quite specified disaster. Science fiction usually tours us through its fictional worlds by tracing the course of the logic, the underlying order, behind the strangeness. Not *Dhalgren*. We barely get hints as to why the city is in the midst of an ever-ongoing apocalypse; we move right into life with chaos. As one character observes:

> I go down a street: buildings are burning. I go down the same street the next day. They're still burning. Two weeks later, I go down the same street and nothing looks like it's been burned at all.

Radio and television signals cannot leave or enter the city. Street signs never seem to read the same way twice. The publisher of the local paper gets into the spirit of things by putting wildly different dates on the masthead from day to day. One night, Kid is just coming out of the city's only bar when—

> The smoke, so low and limitless before, had raddled into billows, torn and flung by some high wind that did not reach down to the street.
>
> Hints of a moon struck webs of silver on the raveling mist. . . .
>
> Through one rent, the lunar disk appeared; then, as the aperture moved with the wind, he saw a *second* moon!

Delany is not just being postmodern when Kid experiences a vertiginous sense of déjà vu when reading the novel's opening almost verbatim in a notebook that he finds. Such a metafictional move is also a science fictional sign of what's going on in the world Delany has created. Heisenberg's uncertainty principle has become a guiding aesthetic—hold any one element of the narrative fixed, and something else shifts, melts, morphs.

We see small groups cohering in the general anarchy, some struggling to hold onto normalcy, others exploring the possibilities opened up by the upheaval. We follow the course of Kid's friendships and acquaintances as he moves among these groups, we delve into the dynamics of the three-way relationship between kid and his lovers, we watch as he gains a measure of notoriety and responsibility in the city.

Amid all the chaos, Kid questions everything—having been in a mental hospital a few years back, he can never trust that the strangeness is entirely outside and not inside. The novel's title may or may not be that name that's on the tip of his tongue, the name he can't remember, the name that might be his own, or maybe just someone's he once knew.

Dhalgren is a book that, if you didn't find it in the science fiction section of your local bookstore or library, you might consider magic realism (c.f. the woman who turns into a tree on page five) or surrealism (look no further than the opening line: "to wound the autumnal city," or to the linguistic implosion in the book's last pages). You might be tempted to employ science fiction writer and critic Bruce Sterling's new genre category, and call it slipstream fiction. (Sterling's definition of slipstream fiction: "It is fantastic, surreal sometimes, speculative on occasion, but not rigorously so. It does not aim to provoke 'a sense of wonder' or to systematically extrapolate in the manner of classic science fiction. Instead, this is a kind of writing that simply makes you feel very strange; the way that living in the late twentieth century makes you feel, if you are a person of a certain sensibility.")

Part of the confusion might stem from *Dhalgren*'s being set in the present day—almost all the rest of Delany's science fiction is set in the far future or far past, clearly signaling "science fiction." The novel's language further complicates its categorization: *Dhalgren* isn't written in the "transparent prose" to which science fiction authors have so often aspired. Delany's prose follows Kid with intimate closeness, gets right into the flux of certainly and uncertainty with a specificity that charges the most mundane moment with fever-dream clarity. For a magic realist, specific attention to everyday details sets up the reader for a sudden turn, a twist into the fantastic. For a science fiction writer (as Delany has pointed out more than once in his essays), specificity has another function—in science fiction, the readers pays unusually vigorous attention to each word, knowing that words may move unexpectedly to describe what is everyday in the world of the story, but fantastic to us. Borrowing Delany's own illustrations, you can't just take "her world exploded" to mean she had a bad day, it might mean her planet is now a cloud of dust. When a sentence begins "The door," you can't assume that the verb following will be either "opened" or "closed" since it might just as well be "dilated," "flickered," or "effervesced"—and each would mean something entirely different.

In *Dhalgren*, Delany focuses this science fictionally acute attention on a fairly everyday world. (For all its strangeness, there are far more ordinary events in *Dhalgren* than extraordinary—any three paragraphs of Delany's *Trouble on Triton* offer more science fictional exoticisms than your average twenty pages of *Dhalgren*.) Into this heightened mundanity he introduces moments of the fantastic—each time ringing yet another resonance throughout the text, until he's built up a fugue of harmonic overtones and echoes. The book's structure is as much musical as it is narrative. Plot and character are just a couple of the modes in which Dealny works, and not necessarily the most privileged.

A considerable architecture of writerly structure lies just beneath *Dhalgren*'s surface. An early scene or exchange of dialogue mirrors and counterpoints another scene two hundred pages later. Some of these reflections are very close, at times almost line-for-line. The reader only glimpses others, but these hinted passages, in the context of Delany's writing, can loom as solidly as anything that actually is in the text. (Clues dropped throughout the novel point to an unwritten mirror book following the character of a woman whose heritage is Asian and European to Kid's African and Native American, who's a sculptor to his poet, whose odyssey in Bellona reflects and contrasts Kid's.) Hardly noticeable on the first reading, these parallels create a cumulative, almost subliminal effect, deepening the book's complexity and intensifying the dynamic reading experience created for the reader.

To read *Dhalgren* is to move in a field charged with semiotic potential at every point. It's a big book, more complex than its seemingly wandering plot might suggest. (The plot is not non-linear *per se*; it's perhaps better described as planar, exploring a space rather than simply moving the reader from point A to point B.) The reader, following Kid's example, is constantly making associations, realizing that the character you're meeting on page 241 is someone you've heard about or seen in a different role earlier, someone you'll see from yet another perspective later.

Dhalgren seems so strange (and is so hard to describe) in part because Delany is holding up a mirror to parts of reality that are not usually described in art. As William Gibson mentions in his evocative introduction to the Wesleyan University Press edition, *Dhalgren* conveys the feeling that someone else has seen this facet of human experience, it's not just me, I didn't just imagine it or lose my mind. In the anecdote Gibson relates, it's a look he glimpsed in a woman's eye as a demonstration was dispersed in Washington in the sixties. Whatever the catalyst, though, it's a very Kid-like emotion, this searching for collaboration, this reaching out for a witness. *Dhalgren* is as unique and valuable a work for evoking this need as it is for answering.

—Rudi Dornemann

Delany on *Dhalgren*

As its introductory note explains, Delany wrote "Of Sex, Objects, Signs, and Systems, Sales, SF, and Other Things" initially as an open letter to the fanzine *S-Forum*, published by the Science Fiction Club of the University of New Hampshire during the mid-1970s.

"Some Remarks Toward a Reading of *Dhalgren*," by K. Leslie Steiner, is a literary joke. In 18th century England, the poet Alexander Pope invented a critical alter-ego, "Barnivelt," who penned several essays about Pope's own poetry. Using Pope's "Barnivelt" as a model, Delany created "K. Leslie Steiner" (the K. stands for "Karen"), a black woman academic living in Ann Arbor, Michigan, where she presumably teaches at the U. Of M. "Steiner" has written several appraisals of Delany—and has even "interviewed" him (*q.v.* "The K. Leslie Steiner Interview," in *Silent Interviews*, Wesleyan UP, 1994, p. 296). Most of Steiner's pieces were collected in Delany's essay collection *The Straits of Messina* (Sarconia: Seattle, 1989), which includes all of Delany's writing between 1974 and 1988 about his own work, whether under his own name or as by Steiner.[8] The major uncollected Steiner material is a letter exchange between "Steiner" and the writer Richard Grant in *SF Eye* (1989), over a review by Grant's then-wife, Elizabeth Hand (another well-known science fiction writer), of Delany's Return to Nevèrÿon series, whose eleven stories and novels initially appeared between 1979 and 1987 and which was reissued by Wesleyan University Press in four volumes over 1993 and 1994.

The penultimate piece here is an excerpt from another interview ("The Semiology of Silence," also collected in *Silent Interviews*), conducted by Larry McCaffrey and his wife Sinda Gregory in New York City in 1982. McCaffrey, who would shortly be a major contributor to the *Columbia Literary History of the United States* (edited by Emory Elliot, Columbia

8. Within the SF Community, James Blish invented his own critical alter-ego, William Atheling, Jr.

University Press: New York, 1988), in his own personal list of the hundred most important American novels published in the 20th century ("The 20th Century's Hundred Greatest Hits"), includes two novels by Delany, both *Dhalgren* and Delany's novel *Hogg* (FC-2: Normal, 1995: "The most shocking novel published in the 20th century"), written at about the same time as *Dhalgren* but not published until almost 22 years afterward.

In Spring of 2001, the *Barnes & Noble Newsletter* commissioned from Delany the final meditation here, "Looking Back at the Autumnal City." The occasion was the Vintage Books edition of *Dhalgren*, which appeared that year. They asked Delany to address briefly what he felt made his novel retain its interest for readers 26 years after its initial 1975 appearance. "Looking Back at the Autumnal City" is his low-key response.

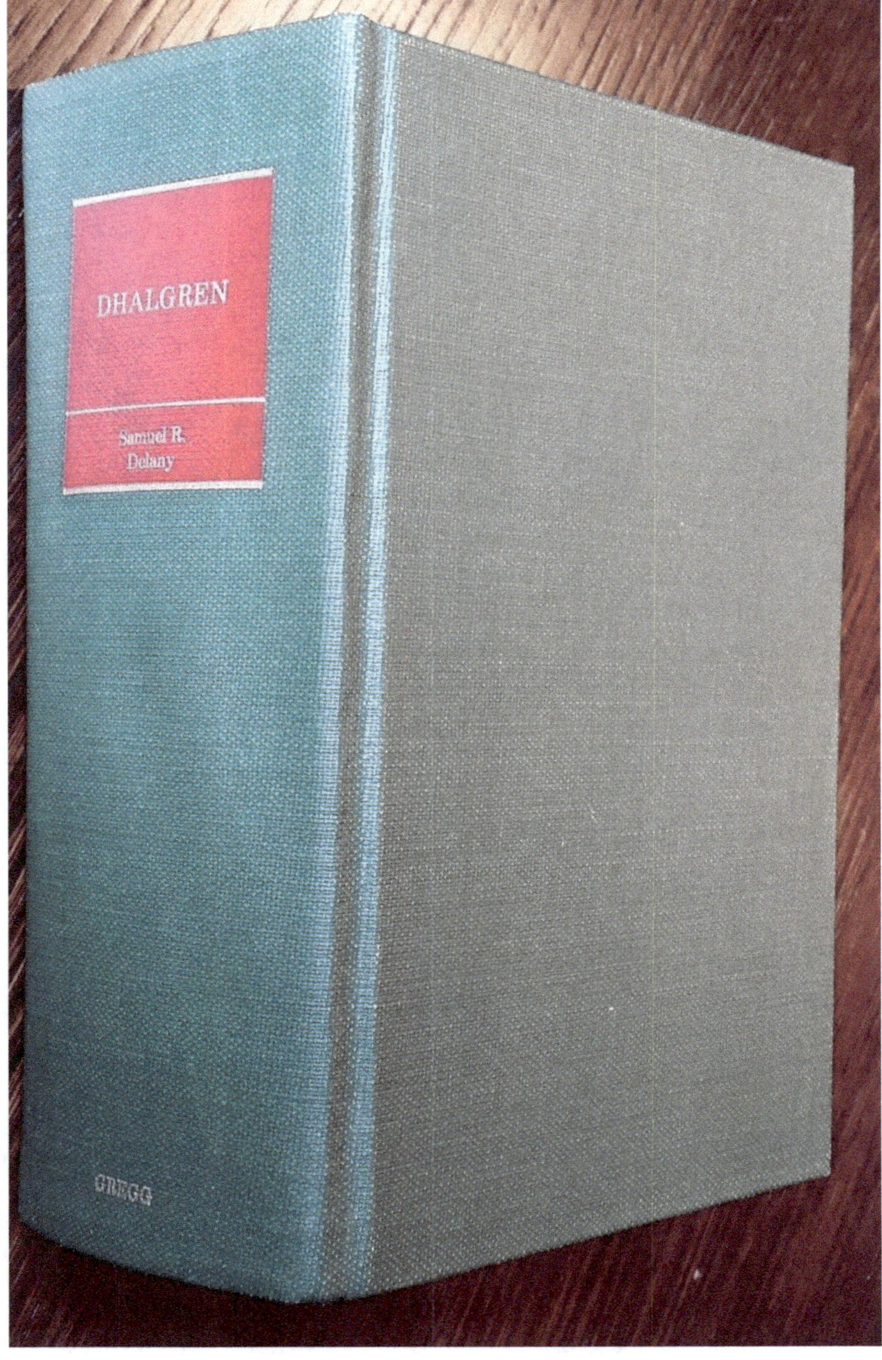
DHALGREN
Samuel R.
Delany
GREGG

Of Sex, Objects, Signs, Systems, Sales, Sf, And Other Things

Note: Tesseract was the name of the science fiction society of the University of New Hampshire. In August or September 1975, their then-president, Frank Brunner, extended an informal invitation to me through Bernard Kay to come and discuss my science fiction novel Dhalgren, *which had been published eight or nine months before in January 1975. I sent them the following open letter, which, I was later told, would appear in the Tesseract-sponsored 'zine,* S-Forum. *At the end of that year, however, Brunner graduated from the university, and* S-Forum *suspended publication before the piece could appear there. A dozen years later, it appeared in* Australian Science Fiction Review.

Samuel R. Delany
Albert Hotel
23 East 10th St.
New York, NY 10003

Dear Frank—

Thanks muchly for your letter. (Bernie Kay read it to me over the phone; so I haven't, as it were, been exposed to the actual text.) Thanks also for the invitation to sit in on Tesseract's *Dhalgren* meeting. I'm afraid, however, I have to decline. A couple of years back I would have replied to such an invitation, quite imperiously, "I never discuss my work in public," and let it go. But I've mellowed. I dislike discussing my own work for a host of reasons, some highly admirable I'm sure, others no doubt suspect, lowdown, and neurotic. Nevertheless, that's me.

The discourse of personal criticism is useful as it treats the writer as a fictional Other. For A to ask B what B thinks writer Y was trying to do (and for B to return an answer either the same as or different from A's) is a useful, even a rich enterprise. For A or B to turn to writer Y and ask such a question (and for Y to come back with an answer) defeats the whole enterprise of fiction. (As you can see, I love to theorize about language/writing and will do it at the drop of a postcard; the fact that I enjoy it so much is one of the [possibly neurotic] reasons I like to stay away from such discussions of my own work.) Such discussions, for me as a writer at any rate, are essentially fictions—as much as any story or novel. The relation between two fictions is a complex business to map out, especially when it must be done by the creation of a third. Julia Kristeva, Carol Jacobs, and Jacques Lacan (among others) have been exploring, from their respective positions, the complexities that lurk behind that most complex of fictions: commentary. Fictive discourse aims at producing a range of reactions, a field of multiple responses, responses not as in a scatter-pattern of buckshot, but as interrelated and ordered as lightwaves in a spectrum. Critical discourse between two readers, both by its disagreements and by its angles of agreement, no matter how linear, preserves that plurality in emblem and embryo. The same discourse between reader and writer rotates the lines of communication ninety degrees away from the currents that pass between equals so that now it lies directly across those currents, stalled in that ill-charged space auctority (authority) creates, that plurality abolished.

I work hard on my science fiction. Much of that work is theoretical (though the theorizing done when entangled in the text of fiction has a very different feel to it from the theorizing whose end is a theoretical, rather than a fictive, text); but the work is to read, and reread, reform, and respond to (making sure they proliferate properly) the resonances of whatever is being put down on paper. In a live question-and-answer situation, the spontaneity alone—on my part at any rate—would defeat all accuracy in linearly verbalizing what was (as is so much of writing) such a many-layered and finally non-verbal process.

I am perfectly happy to write about what's outside the text. You asked about sales, for example. Last time Bantam communicated with me anent the subject, there were 273,000 copies of *Dhalgren* in print, with more to come. Actual sales are hard to judge after only six months, but the general Bantam policy is not to order a new printing until at least 80% of the previous one has sold out; the sixth printing is currently on the book racks. The seventh is on order. Yes, it's a minor record for an SF novel in the first half of 1975, but in only a few weeks *The Mote in God's Eye* will raise its braying yawp in paperback and go galumphing off, I'm sure, with all the medals.[9]

Because I love the SF field, in some respects I'm downright gleeful to discuss what's outside the text! In a giant field like the Post-Modern Novel, with thousands upon thousands of examples high and low produced each year, it would be terribly presumptuous for any single author, even a postmodern Proust or Mann, to hope that a single work, or even a series of works, might restructure to whatever extent the concept of the form. In a field like SF, with not quite 325 original SF novels produced this year from substantially less than that number of writers—and most of these novels in a commercially fixed form the writers themselves would be the first to admit was dead from the outset—it is not so preposterous for a writer to hope that a single work, fermenting in the acknowledged live area of the field, might loosen and recontour the web of possibilities, charging that web at each repositioned intersection of possible word and possible word. I think, in exactly that slow and inevitable way that causes shrieks both of rage and delight, *Dhalgren* is doing that. And I like it. What I don't mean here is that I want to see more novels that resemble *Dhalgren* either in texture, form, or subject matter. (What writer would?) But I would like to see the range—the space of possibilities—that the textures and organization in *Dhalgren* imply explored by other SF writers.

Of course the line between what is inside the text and what is outside the text is frequently foggy—especially for the writer. And it is at least as permeable as Lacan's version of the Saussurian bar between signifier and signified.[10] Another reason I hesitate to attend a live discussion is because in live discussions that line may be too easily transgressed, by auctorial accident or enthusiasm—with disastrous results. I prefer the reflection afforded by ballpoint and notebook. As an SF writer I frequently see myself as trying to reach the boundary, the edge, the limit of fiction, a

9. A dozen years later (November 1987), *Dhalgren*'s sales have settled at about a million. It is still in print and sells a few more thousand each year. While more popular with the hardcore SF readership, *The Mote in God's Eye* never did catch up.

10. Lacan, Jacques, "The Insistence of the Letter in the Unconscious," included in *Structuralism*, edited by Jacques Ehrmann, (Doubleday Anchor), New York, 1970.

journey that can only be made on paper. Similarly, I am tempted to come as close to the line as possible from the critical side—one wants to live not just dangerously, but dangerously and intelligently.

Is this, for example, outside or in?

I've always wanted to write books that I wished to read but could not find on any library shelf or bookstore rack. A kind of book I've always liked is one that is witty, intelligent, formal, colorful, written with life and brio. But there's another that, from time to time, I hunt out as well:

Oddly enough, you will find it described in occasional contemporary introductions to various novels by Eliot and Stendhal. It is a long book, covering exhaustively the social workings of some heretofore unexplored sector of society, orienting it within the greater social context—but it does this almost off-handedly, as if in a passing nod to Arnold's observation that the life of fiction lies in the exactitude with which it can evoke the surfaces of life. But much more than that, it is a complex metaphysical construct: to understand it requires considered and deep response, measured and multiple readings. We note, at this point, the novels described in these introductions are novels-of-the-mind. They are seldom the novels of Eliot or Stendhal that follow. I do not mean that Eliot's and Stendhal's are not rich works, or that they do not benefit from close attention or careful rereading. But the entire critical stance these introductions assume is, in historical terms, a back-reading. A critical gaze that has no existence before the commentary garnered from the specific aesthetic undertakings of, first, Flaubert and, second, Joyce, can only meet with its true object as long as it gazes forward.

It has been known as long as narratives have been recognized for what they are that stories are made more coherent, vivid, exciting, and energetic by resonances leap-frogging from one section over another to relate to yet another; a multiplicity of such resonances binds the living and lively construct together. (What else is "plot" other than something at the end of the tale relating clearly and strongly to something at the beginning? And if "plot" is "dead," it is only because in most people's minds the only relations they will respond to have become far too limited, formalized, and restricted to a ridiculously narrow repertoire of revelatory actions.) But for a writer to expend such Flaubertian labors to make a complex web of responses the experience of the fiction is a specifically post-Joycean enterprise. And it is worth reminding ourselves that Joyce, to do this, had to shatter, more and more as *Ulysses* progressed, the novel's fictive foreground (though he allowed one to retrieve a foreground structure by means of the referent myth); in *Finnegans Wake*, he shattered not only the fictive foreground but all foreground mythical reference as well, so that all could be used, in fragmentia, to form the infrastructure to which the recomplicated resonantial textus was moored. Yes, Stendhal and Eliot used such resonances to bind their work together; but they did not use them in the same way as Joyce, to the same extent, or with the same intentional charge: this charge is fixed on so many other things in their work that it makes the kind of modern criticism that frequently introduces them court distortion of them each time it is evoked. Nor does such criticism fit, say, with Proust, Mann, or Kafka. These are all very nineteenth-century-oriented artists. If they add an obsessional concern with one sensibility or another, reflected in "excessive" (with Proust and Kafka, at any rate) labor over the text itself,[11] this still only winds up the decadent ends of the nineteenth century. We still have not approached the parameters of Stein, Charles Olson, and Frank O'Hara around which the vital art of the second half of this century organizes itself. (And if Olson and O'Hara respected Pound and Williams, it was as much for their negative as for their positive examples—the only truly rich examples one generation of artists can bequeath another.)

Fictive discourse contains within it (as one of its most powerful fictions) the possibility of exhaustiveness. Critical discourse, as Foucault showed in *The Order of Things*, is inexhaustive by virtue of the very épistémè in which it generated back with its birth in medieval commentary. (The basic reaction of most readers of Barthes' *S/Z* has to be, when all is said and done, how much more could have been said! The margins of my own copy crawl with commentary upon his.) Which brings me, abruptly, back to *Dhalgren*. Was it written for the critics, as various of them have megalomaniacally suggested? Well, it was definitely written to appease a certain richly critical response in myself—a response which, in myself, I associate with something mature and measured. I wanted to read a book—solid, sedate, sexual, and complex—full of mysteries that

11. Roland Barthes has quipped in *Writing Degree Zero* that Flaubert made writing acceptable to the bourgeoisie by welding the idea of "labor" to the creation of the text.

proliferate in orderly fashion by the very fact of their solution, a book I could sink my mental teeth into after they had been sharpened by what I'd found valid in the art and aesthetic discourse of the past century-and-a-quarter. But if it was written "for critics," it was not written for any fancied reward to be gleaned from any critical commentary.

The largest influences on the book that I am aware of, at any rate, were Michel Foucault (primarily *Madness and Civilization*, secondarily *The Order of Things*), John Ashbery's poems "The Instruction Manual" (and the Richard Howard essay on Ashbery in *Alone with America*) and "These Lacustrine Cities," G. Spencer Brown's *Laws of Form* (given me as a birthday present, months after its publication, by a young Harvard student when I lived in San Francisco[12]), Frank Kermode's *The Sense of an Ending* (bits and pieces of *Dhalgren* were worked on in Kermode's old office at Wesleyan University's Center for the Humanities, where I was a guest for a couple of weeks in 1971), and, of course, the works of Jack Spicer, whose memory and whose poems haunted San Francisco the years I lived there, where much of *Dhalgren*'s first draft was written, as Cavafy's hovered over Durrell's Alexandria. Anyone who thinks the elucidation of my science fiction novel worth the trouble might pursue these works with hope of at least a small reward over and above the great interest of the works themselves.[13] But certainly anyone who had read the Foucault thoroughly would know I could not expect much commentary: We can separate fiction into foreground and récit: récit is the written commentary that occurs within fictive discourse. Foreground is the referential presentation of "what was there" and "what happened to it."

---

12. Henry Kaiser, IIIrd, when I was living in a commune at Oak St., and he was staying at his family house in Oakland. As a return gift, I gave him my personal copy of Auden's *The Dyer's Hand*, with my various marginal notes.

Some years later in New York, John Mark Gawron (with me metaphorically reading over his shoulder) went over the Spencer Brown so that I began to get a comfortable grip on Brown's notion of "the arithmetic behind the Boolean algebras."

When I last saw Henry and his wife at a lecture I gave at Santa Cruz (March 10, 2016), he still had it.

13. Readers who detected the pastiche of "Caliban to the Audience" in Newboy's second monologue might wonder if Auden shouldn't be included. Let me say, Auden is a writer who concerns me and delights me—rather than who influences me.

Foucault demonstrates clearly that it is commentary which breeds commentary—and very little else. By a simple extension, only those novels proportionately rich in récit (James, Proust, Joyce, Stendhal, Kafka, or Faulkner, for examples) are likely to be much commented on at length. Novels proportionately rich in foreground (Chandler—whom no less than Gide called the finest stylist in America and of whose works no less than Auden said, "…they are darkly powerful works of art…"—R.L. Stevenson or D. Merezhkovsky, for examples) are experienced as more or less richly detailed slabs of experience itself; if this presentation is done with a rich web of language (to do it in a conscientiously impoverished language, e.g., Robbe-Grillet, to whom we shall return, reduces foreground to the status of récit; thus the commentary), the effect is of a double text of structured reality highlighted by a complex superstructure of attentional nodes. Mapping the relation between the two illusory texts (the "referent" [or even "meaning"] of the text and the nodal highlights of the text) is an infinite job because the separation between them—only the old warhorse "content vs. style" in another guise—is illusory and vanishes into an ungraduated unity wherever we fix our attention on it. Possibilities of commentary in such cases are so endless (they will generate wherever we decide to fix gradations) that the sane critic must eschew them. The only thing that, as a reasonable endeavor, we can comment on in such works is what they have to say about certain subjects. But heaven protect us once we get lost in the primary critical task of discovering and recovering what such works, phenomenologically, are. That is best left to the solitary dialogue between sovereign reader and playful page; those are the only participants in the dialogue that I, or the novel I wrote, are concerned with.

Dhalgren is (as is most SF) practically all foreground—at any rate, the proportion of foreground to récit is high enough to assure a paucity of serious (written) analysis. Here, standing on the line, it would be most presumptuous for me to suggest that the language within the text was rich, complex, or worked. It may well (and from my own, most unprivileged position, despite what anyone says, I shall never know) be simply flabby, opaque, and confusing. What I can hazard—not as my own response to any of the words on paper but merely as a projected observation that someone who visited me at any of the places I lived while I was writing it would have had to make—is that the language was worked on. (And what a Lacanian plenitude of readings that little preposition offers up to that most Calvinistic of verbs!) Where one goes with *Dhalgren* after that is entirely a matter of personal temperament. The reasons I wrote it are precisely those which prevent me from urging anyone else to read it. I can far more easily think of reasons to encourage people to avoid it.

My most vituperative critic (not Lester del Rey, but Harlan Ellison, in his review in the *Los Angeles Times*), abandoned the book at page 361, remarking that *Dhalgren* was not a novel but a "career." I wonder if it doesn't mean something when the most violent detractor hits the point precisely. Certainly the greatest single fiction among the many that weave together to make up the text are subsumed by the two dates which, nominally, enclose its creation—the last writing of mine one reads in the novel.

One person who has read *Dhalgren* a number of times writes me she found it easier to hear the voice of the writing if she actually paused, when reading to herself, between sentences. Many hundreds of sentences in the book were written down on index cards and/or separate notebook pages, worked over and revised as autonomous verbal objects to assure they did their particular micro-jobs as economically as possible before they were mortared back in edificial place. (Many of the sentences I am least satisfied with are ones I did not give this kind of attention to and which only underwent their various buffings on their half dozen trips through the typewriter.) Is there any relation between this reader's discovery of a way to respond to the text and my way of composition?

I don't know.

But her method and mine are ultimately outside the text and of merely anecdotal interest.

But let me see how closely I can approach the dangerous city-limit from a different direction.

A few months ago someone doing an article on "Sex in the Future" called me, along with a number of other SF writers, for a quote. I sent him:

> There's a prevalent theory that society, in some mysterious way, is and will always be a mirror of some mysteriously eternal sex act, i.e., standard missionary position. This theory, of course, is nonsense. Every sex

> act, from the most "normal" to the most "perverse," is an internalization of one or another set of social parameters. Once internalized, however, they are sexual and no longer social—save in their social effect as sexual behavior. Though an easy and uncritical passage from the social to the sexual is, therefore, always suspect, I would hazard that sex in the future will be no better or worse than society in the future. If future society is vigorous, open, and varied, then so will future sex. If future society is repressive, authoritarian and monotonous, you won't be able to hope for too much better in bed.

Somewhere in the text of the last chapter of *Dhalgren*, readers have noted some sentences that they feel express more or less the same thoughts as the first four sentences of the above. It would ill behoove me to argue.

Without commenting on what is in *Dhalgren*, I will say that the first four sentences of my quote (we can ignore the last three speculative ones) are about psycho/social facts-in-the-world. One might quibble with terms —perhaps it is not a "theory" so much as a largely unexamined model that explains much ill-considered action, many glib statements, and vast numbers of movies, novels, and plays; one could argue over how and in what way and when and exactly which social parameters are internalized to give specific forms to the varieties of human sexual responses. But that is arguing over whether the earth is a sphere, an oval, or a pear—not whether it is flat or round. *Dhalgren* certainly isn't about this psycho/social fact—nor the conflict between those who are aware of it and those who are its unknowing victims and/or exploiters—any more than Shakespeare's *Tempest* is about the fact that the Earth is round, a fact which the discovery of Bermuda had brought to the general attention of the British public only a few years before the play was written. Nevertheless, to know about the discovery of Bermuda and the new status of both magic and science that had resulted from it is certainly to make the *Tempest* more comprehensible. More to the point, contemporary playgoers who did not "believe" in the roundness of the earth, nor in the existence of outlying tropical islands, and had no feeling for the new distinctions between fantasy/magic/reality/science that were then being etched on the modern English-speaking consciousness, though they might recognize the form of the Masque, would, with all else in the play, be totally at sea. They simply would not be able to make the storm-tossed landing on that tropical island, nor read properly the emblems of what is real and what is not and the dialogue between them which are the structure, significance, and charm of the play. It is not that they would miss the surface plot: they would miss the subtext which gives the surface plot its reason for being what it is.

I think a good number of *Dhalgren*'s more incensed readers, the ones bewildered or angered by the book, simply cannot read the proper distinction between sex and society and the nature and direction of the causal arrows between them, a vision of which lies just below the novel's surface and which gives the book its logical coherence. Though these readers are perfectly willing to respond to a "sympathetic portrayal of the social problems of those who deviate sexually from the statistical norm," they are at first confused by and ultimately angered with a presentation that completely subverts the entire subtext that informs a discourse of "social problems/sympathetic/sexual deviate/normal" in the first place. They still see "real" society as a projection of an "idealized" sex act (which somehow involves vast amounts of male aggression inchoately coupled with total female passivity), and read all fictional accounts of sex-and/or-society as accurate, relevant, and charged with value as they constitute themselves under the shadow of this model. Such a mistake is understandable. Precisely this model charges with sense the fiction of writers as diverse as Lawrence, Mailer, Malzberg, Oates, Ellison, Barth, Roth, Bellow, and Thomas Berger (not to mention Le Guin). To read *Dhalgren* against this model, however—that is, to use this model as a template against which to discern the sense and weight of various scenes and sentences—is to render the book a non-sense far greater than any which might come under the rubric of "unorthodox plot," "sexual explicitness," or "reality vs. fantasy." It renders a very long book a mere mass of unordered, quotidian psycho/social detail.

I think this model—a platonically ideal sex act after which all social relations must be formed in order to partake of the good—is pure literary excrescence. (To call it "literary invention" implies that someone, sometime, somewhere invented it with malice aforethought: and I do not think this is the case.) I would like to see it dispelled. It distorts the true polarities of the human universe, mystifying the known and the knowable, subverting and diffusing human energies away from where they might help real women and real men: because it makes human problems accessible to analysis appear adamantine, monolithic.

Sex is sex, pleasure is pleasure, anger is anger, sadness is sadness, joy is joy, and fear is fear: all are intricately and intimately related, and the sudden paths from one to the other are endlessly surprising. All of them, and all the paths between, are affected by the material universe we live in. All affect our picture of that universe. Also, each of us experiences the complex of them differently, first because we are in different positions vis-a-vis the ordered external universe and moving through that order at different trajectories, and second because we are different individuals at our respective positions and the internal factors—capacities for pleasure, anger, joy, sex, etc.—are constituted vis-a-vis themselves differently in each of us.

Mapping all of this, either with the fictive device of "character" or "narrator," or employing such a map to move with words the "character" of the reader through such a territory, is one of the writer's possible tasks. Confusion in the map (or generalizing too quickly between one element and another) is an aesthetic flaw.

To use the sex-produces-society model as a mapping tool (rather than society-contours-sex) in any sort of narrative fictions (science or otherwise) foredooms us to losing our way, both practically and ethically, once we turn back to the world—and it does so without any implication that any particular set of morals need be reflected in the fictions themselves.

2.

This thing that hath a code and not a core...
—"An Object," Ezra Pound

Here follows a random galaxy of notes, most of them no doubt familiar to anyone who has read at all in the last decade-and-a-half's work in semiotics and structuralism, which, from their disorder, will hopefully force at least some coherence between what has gone before and what will come after them.

(1) Our actions influence the material world.

The material world (not just the modes of production!) influences (among many other things) our emotions and our general psychology. Frequently we are unaware of it—often we are only partially aware of it.

(2) Our landscape, entirely true for any urban environment (and, today, almost entirely true for any rural environment in Europe, the United States, and Canada), is made up totally of emblems of former human actions. From the sky (overcast because of the industrial effect or the greenhouse phenomenon), to each tree or grass blade in the city parks (the trees are there because someone put them there, or because someone left them there when clearing away others), the landscape is a dense, interlocked web of the detritus of haphazard human action and/or intentional human undertaking.

One way to look at it is as a vastly recomplicated code of human signs (or semes). As we walk down any street, we read (or sometimes misread), consciously or unconsciously, this code.

What it says affects us. It is the real world influencing (among many other things) our emotions and general psychology.

(3) I call it a code; but this code has many aspects of a true language. For one thing, syntax is all important:

A new building encountered in a section of the city where all the buildings around it are new has one meaning; a new building encountered in a section of the city where all the buildings around it are decrepit slums and tenements has another.

As well, these signs, semes, or codons affect one another in purely autonomous ways that change their meanings so that those meanings cannot be traced back to any intention on the part of the initial human actors:

Soot in the air (one seme) defaces a new building (another seme), creating a new seme—a grimy building—with a new meaning for the city itself. An unused sewer main beneath the street (one seme) collapses and causes a tenement (another seme) to drop a wall and collapse at one corner.

The abandoned, half-ruined building where people have been injured and have fled from it is a different seme (with a different meaning) from either an over-crowded tenement or an abandoned sewer main.

(4) Fiction as we know it today begins as a response to an industrial phenomenon, to which the social analysis of Marx was equally a response. To quote Sartre quoting Marx: "The means of production affect the political, spiritual, and economic life of the people." Responding to the same phenomenon that Marx's words were attempting to model, various nineteenth-century novelists (in France, they included Balzac, Stendhal, the Goncourts, and Zola; in England, they included Thackeray, Charlotte Brontë, George Eliot, and Dickens) realized, more or less articulately, that to describe the products of production, to evoke their textures and suggest their syntagmatic relation to one another in various settings, in the novel's foreground social space, not only fleshed out the representation of material life, but was also a way of implying—through their relation with the means of production—a commentary, in the novel's background social space, on the values, aspirations, and ethics (political, economic, and spiritual) of everyone involved in the described object's production, distribution, and purchase. Thus to describe an object was to generate a web of commentary, just beyond direct apprehension yet nevertheless strongly felt as one reads the texts at hand on the politics, economics, and religion of both the material and the fictive world, charging the whole work with significance and a sense of coherent worldly knowledge. This is what all those descriptions of furniture, fashion, fabrics, and carriages are doing in the novels of Balzac. More or less under control, this is (more or less) what they have been doing in the novels of all fictioneers since—and this includes science fictioneers.

(5) Consider: Our clothes are a sign system. So are our hairstyles; and whether or not we wear makeup, whether or not we shave; natural pigment in our skins is a direct sign (or an indirect reminder) of others' actions. The pigment acquired by exposure to sunlight is a sign of our own recent histories. Again, syntactic relation is all: deeply tanned skin on a well-dressed young man carrying an attaché case means one thing. Deeply tanned skin on a ragged old woman carrying a bulging, frayed shopping bag speaks something else entirely.

The entire visible surface of every urban landscape we walk or ride through, as well as ninety-nine percent of the visible surface of every human being in it, is constituted of signs of specifically human actions, human reactions, class and individual histories, ordered in informative, syntactic relations. (At a previous point in history, it might have been useful to distinguish between human signs and natural signs. Today the distinction is meaningless. The reading of "purely natural signs" generates the whole discourse we know as science; but with its humanly organized "controlled experiments" we have devised to verify our readings, the natural signs at this point have been absorbed by that discourse—at least for the West. Nature, or the study of nature, as soon as we turn to a book to help us pursue it, is absorbed in the implied discourse of human technology.) The autonomous inter-effects of these signs on one another and one another's meanings suggest the volatility of a living language—rather than the lexical extensionality of a simple code or cipher.

We may, for a moment, locate two areas in this language of human signs: the signs constituted under the rubrics of nature, architecture, furniture, cooking, craft and science form one area; and in general they are far more ambiguous, resonantial, and connotative than the signs in the other area we can locate, i.e., those signs constituted under the rubrics of bodies (gestures, deformations, and wounds), fashions, faces (expressions), texts, and voices, which, by comparison, are straightforward, clear, and denotative.

(6) Marx still provides the basic transformation by which the rare, simple declarative statement in the nonstop din of this language of human-made, human-charged, and human-structured signs may be translated into its political, economic and emotional/psychological/spiritual equivalent: "Who made it? How much were they paid? Who profited, and by how

much, from its sale? Who profits most from its having been put specifically *there*—in that specific syntagmatic order with the world around it?" Though they may use the answers differently, both the poet, the politician, and writer/reader of narratives will find these good questions to ask of the objects they encounter on their trek and trajectory.

(7) But "simple declarative utterances" in the total surround of the sign language we live in today are rare.

We tend to forget that Shakespeare's art was precisely an art of bodies, fashions, faces, texts, and voices—with a little music thrown in on the side: lavishly costumed, full of poetry, and from report brilliantly acted. But how many thousands of post-Elizabethan performances have obscured the fact that the plays were performed without scenery and with an astonishingly meager prop-box: letters, handkerchiefs, swords (which are really part of fashion), jewel boxes (ditto), cups, chairs, and a few musical instruments practically exhaust the lot. Precisely what there was of the sixteenth century language of objects, so connotative and resonantial, Shakespeare, on his bare boards, collapsed with the language of the actors. Another thing we tend to overlook is that, thanks to the fleshing out provided by the imagination of modern theatrical and film directors, for all the rich gallery of character types, covering such a goodly span of Elizabethan society, high and middle (if not low), it would be next to impossible, from the corpus of thirty-seven, to construct a rich vision of the material life of any of those types: details of architecture and shelter, food and food preparation, textile weaving and sartorial technology are just not terribly forthcoming from his texts. And these are the same details that the novels of the Goncourts and Zola—following from examples begun in Balzac—threaten to collapse under. The list of foods, clothing, and shelter mentioned in Shakespeare is thin and generalized: wine, roast meat, bread, fruit, "sweets" and "sweet meats," doublet, hose, cloak, hat, bonnet, gown, armor, sword, shield (encore ditto), castle, courtyard, dungeon. And an unbiased translator would confirm for us that there were not many more things on this list than could be found, say, mentioned in the *Iliad*, written twenty-five hundred years before (we except the descriptions of war articles—we are talking of the texture of material life).

The language of artifacted objects did not become the relative treasure of connotative riches it now represents for literature until it had been recomplicated by industrial development, as well as given a clear reading by that development's political consequences.

But the social developments that made the language of objects literarily decipherable did not halt; those developments that made this language both rich and clear (by providing an industrial, or sometimes an industrial vs. cottage, reading) continued to lay complexity atop complexity in that language so that its resonances, by the end of the First World War, if not well before, were too complex for the orthodox rhetoric of nineteenth-century fiction to represent clearly and precisely.

(8) Some months ago, I happened to encounter, by one of those chains of coincidences which are fiction, six Sony eight-inch portable color television sets:

The first was in the office of the chairman of the philosophy department at the University of Buffalo where I was teaching. The chairman was keeping it, on top of his filing cabinet, he explained, for a woman professor who was picking it up from him later that afternoon.

The same model set, a few days later, was brought around to the bachelor digs of one of my older students (who worked as a carpenter when not in class, and who had bought the house with three other young men some two years ago, though now its kitchen was filled with dirty dishes, its carpet worn through, its bathroom always in the midst of home repair, and its porch steps in need of new boards), by a rather scroungy, bearded seventeen-year-old, who wanted to sell it. My student didn't want to buy, and it was carried away across a wet, leaf-plastered Buffalo street.

Several weeks later, in New York City, I encountered the same set on the large, teakwood desk of a successful homosexual novelist in his largish, plant-filled, one-room studio apartment in Soho.

That same evening I found it on the cigarette-burned table top in the room of my next-door neighbor in the residence hotel where I'd been staying: he was a twenty-two-year-old black, a year out of North Carolina and ten months into a job as a security guard for an uptown building. He was sharing the room with (and I suspect supporting as well) a friend who was a not very effectual grass-dealer and their two girlfriends, who were always in to borrow my iron.

I'd already resolved to write down this chain encounter, so it was something of a humorous footnote to my proposed text when, almost two months later (and no writing actually done), I noticed the same model set under the elbow of a fortyish salesman in a green banlon shirt in a Fourteenth Street appliance store where I had gone to buy a digital clock radio.

What finally impelled pen to paper, however, was encountering a half-mad old woman who used to wander, mumbling, around Union Square and who later turned out to live on welfare in the basement of a building on Avenue D where a friend of mine lived on the third floor. In her basement room, where she beckoned us in to see, were piles and stacks of old TV chasses, broken sets and discarded pieces found all over the streets. I did not see the Sony. But there was a plastic Sony colophon in a large paper bag full of knobs and electronic parts, leaning against the leg of a rickety table—all of which, considering what had gone before, brought up quite clearly a Sony-of-the-mind.

Now the point of all this: the Sony eight-inch color portable speaks in far more muted tones than, say, the Aubusson tapestry on the wall of a Proustian drawing room—a simple cipher of money and taste, a simple symbol of time, if not history, passed in sight of an emblem of both.

The sociological syntagmatic accompaniments to solid state circuitry, both synchronically and diachronically, are too complex for us to read from these half dozen situations a simple, industrial message. We live in a world where the language of signs has grown too complicated for money, morals, aesthetics, philosophy, and technology to collapse all, as in the case of Proust's Aubusson, under a single sign.

This does not mean that the objects of modern technology—by virtue of their likelihood to appear in such varied social syntagms—have gone literarily mute. Rather, we simply must listen much more carefully if we are to hear what such a TV set truly has to say. Certainly it fulfills its task in generating a Marxist commentary, trailing the image of myriad Japanese women technicians (like a sexually inverted Hamlet's ghost viewed through the eye of a fly) as well as implications about wealth, supply, demand, production and production values, international tariffs, and the like. But in complex harmony with these, it signs a whole web of social values and social values denied, of communication—between classes, sexes, ages—and communication subverted. Even to say, "Several weeks later, in New York City, I encountered the same set..." generates a discourse almost totally congruent with one of those tedious aesthetic texts that begins, "Can we locate the single object under consideration in, say, six copies of *Ulysses*...?"—a problem that does not raise its head with the individually fashioned wall hanging. The Sony, if only through the greater multiplicity of its possible environments, sings a far more complicated, if quieter, song. One must constantly invoke the clanking music-box of nineteenth-century novelistic rhetoric just to make clear that these jigs and brass cadenzas are not what we are listening for: that we are attempting to hear a much subtler and more complicated interweave of melodies.

(9) The best-known attempt to present fictively the language of objects in all its modern complexity is, of course, the novels of Robbe-Grillet. By suppressing all traditional novelistic rhetoric, he hoped that the complex interrelation of object and object (or object perception and object perception), would speak forth loudly and state itself with its own, inchoate voice. The flaw in his strategy, a shy quarter of a century after the appearance of the first of the novels that made Robbe-Grillet a scandal and then an institution, is today too apparent:

Objects in the world speak the language of objects in the world: material life. Words on paper speak the language of words on paper: writing.

The other thing one must remember is that a good deal of that suppressed nineteenth-century novelistic rhetoric grew up precisely to represent in words the growing complexity in the language of objects that industrialism had rendered so aesthetically rich. Much of that rhetoric, frankly, was successful. (There is also the fact that the language of human signs in the seventies is substantially more complex than it was at the appearance of *Les Gommes* [*The Erasers*] in 1953.) The solution to the problem of the fictive representation of signs is more complicated than Robbe-Grillet's solution—indeed, it is not likely to be found in any specifically unilateral method. Like any other artist, the contemporary novelist must take from the past what seems to remain useful, discard what is irrelevant or what specifically distorts, and invent an artistic structure or set of structures adequate for what she or he feels has not been dealt with before. For the novelist, this means devising a set of fictive tropes, rhetorical devices, etc., complex enough to present/represent what one wants.

If Robbe-Grillet's novels are powerful works and remain viable, it is rather in the way Seurat's paintings remain forceful nodes of aesthetic tension/attention, i.e., not because of the method but because of the artists' faithfulness to it. That, as artists, they needed their particular methods psychologically as well as intellectually (what a strange vision of the mind, where these aspects are so sundered!) only circles our point. One must remember that if what Seurat in particular and the impressionists in general wrote about their methods were to be taken literally, then their canvasses, when viewed from more than ten feet off, should suddenly look like Andrew Wyeth's! Similarly, the problems spelled out in Robbe-Grillet's *For a New Novel* (1965), while they are certainly real problems, are not the ones his novels triumph over.

Since the literal interpretation of neither of these artists' written theories appears, after an encounter with their works, as a literal description of their aesthetic undertakings, we are in the somewhat tricky position of asserting—in a work that is essentially a written theory of our own—that artists writing about their own theories are constructing not a description of their work, but a metaphor to take with one into the orderly chaos of that work as a tool for making one's own, personal map.

As Seurat's paintings create their stunning impression of stylized light and life by the power of paint placed so systematically on canvas, so Robbe-Grillet's novels gain their hypnotic quality through the strength of systematically disciplined words.

(10) The sexual/social myth that the good society takes its form from the most socially condoned sexual act is a result of two factors that, here, need only be mentioned, as elsewhere others have exhaustively described them. First, there is a mental template that was worked into the very form of fiction (among social entities) by the same industrial forces that contoured so much of the rest of the rhetoric of the nineteenth-century novel—forces that compelled all people, to the extent of their identification with, or even their contiguity to, the white male, middle-class nodes of power, to see the working class in general, racial and religious strangers in particular (as they represented, in large amounts, possible additions to the labor market), and the unstable (do they work or don't they? are they property or aren't they?) status of women in a radically revalued patriarchal society, as perennial threats to the order of things. The second factor—the twentieth century's

addition—was to lay over this basic template a muzzy misreading of Freud, that saw "...sex as the source of all things." (What Freud said, of course, was that, in a society which represses and/or sublimates it, sex is still very strongly at work, even in places where the repression and/or sublimation appears successful—which is another thing entirely. And though the mechanics of the workings are different, the same can be said of anger, pleasure, sadness, fear, grief, joy, pain, and intelligence.)

Lay over this the general aesthetic laziness of most modern novelists before the admittedly immense task of untangling the significance of the dense surround of human signs that is our life in the modern world, and you have the limits on the "impoverishment" of modern fiction.

One of the failures of Robbe-Grillet's method, for example, is that when he embeds all these objects in such textureless discourse (or, at least, discourse of such limited texture), rather than our reading the true message that flashes out from their syntactical-interaction-as-objects, it is too easy for us to read the style itself as saying, "None of these objects means anything other than the amassed, inarticulate presence it achieves through the repetition of names, attributes, dimensions—the stuff of terror and despair." The cumulative force of a Robbe-Grillet novel is, essentially, a negative one: the reaction of the reader to the text is best taken as a metaphor for despair before the task of ever untangling meaning from a complexity of objects—which is why his books that work best are the books that are about, in the most nineteenth-century way, "characters" for whom such despair is an appropriate reaction: a psychotic murderer, an obsessively jealous husband. And one cannot divorce the aesthetic success of these novels from the failure inherent in fictive discourse itself, which failure is emblemized by the "fact" that the "victim" in both the "successful" books is that terror and time-bomb which, in nineteenth-century fiction, must be gotten rid of, either by death or marriage, at any cost: the Female. (In a sense, *Lolita* [1956] can be seen as a novel struggling, both in its textures and its plot/structure, with precisely what defeats Robbe-Grillet in *Le Voyeur* [1955].) What one is looking for is a novelist who can make sense out of the plethora of semiotic associations our world yields throughout every arc-second of its field, whether or not her or his "plot" dramatizes the "success" or "defeat" of a "character" before the same task.

(11) To return to the end of the nineteenth century: The general despair of novelists at negotiating the recomplicated language of signs produced a fiction that responded, in historical terms, by becoming highly subjective and/or psychological. Between the seventeenth century and the end of the nineteenth century, the convention was established that a certain proportion of sentences in serious fiction must be devoted to récit—commentary on the subjective world of the characters or the sociological significance of the situation. To conform to this proportion was a way of meta-fictively signaling that the fiction was, indeed, serious.

It is just after the turn of the century that the myth of the sexual source of everything becomes an articulate force in modern fiction. It allowed the modern novelist (most specifically and successfully, D.H. Lawrence) to recharge these récit sentences, hitherto devoted to psychological analysis, with a certain energy that comes as much from the repetitions of real speech as it does from real speakers' ever-present topical interest in the passions. Before Lawrence, those récit sentences had to stand or fall on pure wit and socio/psychological insight. These sentences were not so much to "present character" (though this was how their task was referred to) as to present what the novelist knew of the workings of human psychology in interface with society—the task of the light essayist. (Yes, they knew this was not the "character" itself: in the nineties Wilde had quipped: "The more one analyzes one's characters, the more they come to sound like everyone else." Yet the whole history of the novel had shown the form committed to presenting the distinctions between human beings within the coherent matrix of society. The modern task of the novel, to show that all human beings are essentially the same while at the mercy of the flaws and contradictions of an incoherent society [a Durkheimian entity which, as Saussure's langue claims for itself an ontological status apart from parole, claims for itself an onto-logical status apart from the social behavior of any given individual], does not emerge until later.) But, at the same time, psychology itself, at the hands of Freud and others, was becoming a science. Lawrence's sentences of repressed sexual rhapsody implied, in the background social space of the novel, just as strongly as Balzac's descriptions of furniture et al. had accomplished an implication of economic commentary before, the entire discourse of that science. How could this implied discourse of a branch of medical science fail to triumph over those merely clever observations by amateurs who stated in their texts that psychology was a matter of verbal paradox, mental contradiction, step and misstep through the social dance, knowledge and ignorance of What Is Expected? At this point in the development of the novel, insightful and/or witty analysis of social and psychological situation was replaced by subjective rhapsody. Subjective rhapsody implied the entire discourse of a science—psychoanalysis—just behind it; novelistic psychological analysis suggested a competition with that same science that the novelist, as amateur, could not possibly hope to win in the face of the new erotics. Looking slightly askance at this development, one also notes that such rhapsodies are certainly easier to read, if not write, than the rhetoric it replaces.

I have written elsewhere (as have a number of others) that science fictional discourse redistributes the fictive attention between character and landscape (i.e., between subject and object) in a manner different from mundane fiction. Science fiction makes the attention on the landscape much higher. To work within this reorganized fictive frame gives us, first of all, a basically better matrix in which to deal with the recomplications of modern "sign" language. And I can think of no better place than science fiction in which to avoid "certain conventions of fiction" that make so much fiction such a political disaster.

I am attracted to those areas that most fiction handles with both textual and structural clichés—blacks, women, the mentally ill, the socially marginal, the relationship between society and sex—because I have had firsthand experience with many of the situations they imply: I am black, I have spent time in a mental hospital (three weeks as a patient and, before that, many visits to a friend at Hillside Hospital's Pavilion for Adolescents), and much of my adult life, for both sexual and social reasons, has been passed on society's margins. My attraction to them as subject matter for fiction, however, is not so much the desire to write autobiography, but the far more parochial desire to set matters straight where, if only one takes the evidence of the written word, all would seem confusion.

One of the most pernicious things about the myths—for that is all one can call them—shadowing these areas is that they preclude any possibility of envisioning a different social order whose members, in response to it, might grow up reasonably to seek and expect, for example, quantitatively more sexual encounters and/or who might foster a more reasonable and relaxed attitude about those sexual encounters they do have. The view of sexual encounters as affected and affective processes is abolished from possible consideration by the kernel of illogic at those pernicious myths' core: sexuality is a substance, and what is more, some individuals possess more of it than others, in measures entirely proportional to their distance from certain centers of bourgeois power.

To deny this whole set of prejudices, kernel and superstructure, is to affirm that, from the inside, all people experience their own surface behavior, sexual and otherwise, as a negotiable dialogue of response, reaction[14], desire, and control: not to experience the generation of one's own behavioral signs in this manner is the subjective experience of madness.

(12) So we will always recognize it, let us have this model one last time in all its raw absurdity: All peoples who are not by heredity and/or active bonds of control fixed to the centers of bourgeois power are seething masses of dull, inarticulate sexuality. The man's is completely identified with jealousy and aggression, the woman's with jealousy and acquisitiveness. Take, as an example, the bulk of men (one could as easily take their wives, sisters, and daughters with very little translation in the ensuing description) that statistically form the plurality of unskilled and semi-skilled labor in this country—traditionally referred to once as "The Working Class Male" and now as "The Lower Classes" (this social group is not to be confused in any way with any revisionary or other Marxist view of "the proletariat"), the "Under Class," or most recently by ironic European sociologists as "The Fourth World." In him, sex and aggression are one. The appalling and inhuman conditions under which he lives barely keeps this sexuality/hostility under control. Conceivably, if he could ever lower his persistent and dull anger enough, he might be able to employ enough intelligence to exert some beneficial influence over his own life as an individual or over the lives of his fellow men. (The obliteration of women and their labor, within the home and without, from this model is pivotal to its working efficacy.) But since this dull and disfocusing rage is fed by that inexhaustible and ever-brimming pit of

---

14. I intend these first two categories to cover habitual reactions that may run counter to more recently manifested desires.

sexuality (with which it is one), this lowering is not very likely—except now and then, when a particular lower-class male is able to exert great self-control, repress all primitive urges (which, for him, will be a nearly killing effort and cannot help but cause some great psychological crippling) for the rest of his days. And should he ever fail to repress, and that sexuality/anger should break free, he will destroy himself and all he has achieved in a single sweep, probably taking the odd bourgeois-born woman with him. On the one hand (the myth continues), it is mildly sad that the conditions under which the majority of such men live are so oppressive; and it is sighed over that things don't get better for them—so that the lower-class male could blossom forth, while sticking to his place. But any logical assessment of the situation makes it perfectly clear (declares the myth) that if the restraints of inhuman labor and/or inhuman conditions over inhuman hours were removed for more than one or two days a week, the sexuality/hostility would erupt and run berserk, and lower class males would destroy everything, more than likely including themselves.[15]

One can find this myth in all its quintessential absurdity in the portrait of Carlton Walpole, the migrant fruit picker, at the beginning of Joyce Carol Oates's 1967 novel, *A Garden of Earthly Delights*. It contours the portrait of all the prole-origined soldiers in Norman

---

15. In a depressingly real sense, the Marxist glorification of work for its own sake, coupled with the naive assumption that as long as everybody is working hard, all sexual "problems" will disappear, i.e., reduce to a pastoral (and suspiciously bourgeois) vision of respectful, shy, young working men getting up the nerve to propose to respectful, shy, young working women, who must get up the nerve to respond, quiveringly, "Yes..." (both, finally, taking courage from the fact that they are serving the state—the Marxist equivalent of "doing it for Old Glory"?), is historically, if not archetypally, one with the nineteenth-century industrial mythos: "Keep the proles working hard enough and they'll be too tired to break out into the orgies of lust, rapine, and [incidentally] economic devastation [the absent text supplies for this term, "looting"] we know seethes just below the surface of every prole soul. Under industrial containment [read: exploitation/exhaustion] their sex [read: aggression] can be limited to the most conventional and tepid expressions." The entire template, Marxist and Capitalist, is a pre-Freudian disaster area which Freud's own inability to distinguish between sensuality, sexuality, biological gender, and sex role socialization has done as much to perpetuate in the West as his basic discovery of the unconscious, sexual repression, transference, and infantile sexuality have prepared the groundwork to alleviate.

Mailer's 1948 novel, *The Naked and the Dead*. One tries to give these novels liberal readings— of a sort any contemporary social worker or psychologist might be expected to bring to the situations the novels portray: "The hostility here is a response to the inhuman conditions. If these men cannot seem to get it together to do anything about the conditions, the best explanation is what behavioral psychologists call 'psychological generalization,' an inescapable process that is a response to emotional overload—a process that occurs on all social levels; as well, the pressures to be dealt with, from inside the situation, are more complicated than they could possibly appear from outside, since they include the conditioning of these men and our conditioned view of the situation." But one can no more find emblems for this reading in the fictions than one can find emblems of the knowledge of the existence of the moons of Jupiter in *Don Quixote*.

The existence of the moons of Jupiter was simply not part of the aristocratic and upper-middle-class Spanish fifteenth-century épistémè.

What makes the situation of the modern novel so appalling is that the liberal reading was, more than likely, very much part of the épistémè of twenty-five-year-old Mailer in 1948 and certainly part of the épistémè of twenty-eight-year-old Oates in 1967. But it is not part of the épistémè that generated the nineteenth-century fictive discourses they write. And to write nineteenth-century fictive discourse, precisely to the extent that given examples of such discourse are recognizable as fiction, is to doom oneself to projecting the nineteenth-century épistémè of which such appalling myths as the one above are part and parcel.

Fictive discourse's treatment of women, blacks, Jews, homosexuals, etc., takes off from the same point as the myth we have outlined and moves along similar trajectories—with women's fictive treatment having a couple of particularly frustrating contradictions, which, to understand, we must begin with the understanding that women are not, as even my list might suggest, a category among four, but rather marginally more than half of the other three, and are just as exploitable within the work force (as that phrase is traditionally read) as they are "outside the work force" (i.e., at work in home for a father or husband), and that the two modes of exploitation are intimately connected and endlessly and mutually supportive. What all these fictions do is, first, take only a novelistically valorized set of visible elements (never an individualized totality: everything done by one woman, one working man, one Jew), and, second, suggest causal arrows between these elements in absurd directions. What makes modern fiction so uninteresting is that the causality and analysis implied by the fiction is demonstrably not the matrix of causality and analysis that the writers themselves could possibly believe in. We are at a point in history where the basic models proposed by the objective discourse of sociology and psychology—even in their most vulgarized, cocktail party versions—are more accurate and interesting than the basic models that underlie most "serious" novels.

Let the above galaxy of twelve be the readings which anchor all our subsequent statements to this text as we put our toe over the brim into the oceanic text of *Dhalgren*.

Here, on the edge, we note that some of the most disappointed readers were those who tried to read the "city" as a "projection" of the protagonist's (or, heaven forbid, the author's) "fantasies." I suspect these are the people who see the récit/foreground (subjective/objective) proportion of sentences as a fixed sign evoking an interpretive judgment that—for the SF reader, at any rate—such a proportion simply doesn't call up. The logic runs: If there are too many subjective-sounding sentences, this is a sign that some objective mystery exists to be solved; it is a sign that there is some objective correlative which will clear up the mystery and make "sense" of all this confused "subjectivity." (One recalls the more naive critics of books like *Finnegans Wake* demanding to know what it was "really" about, or those even more naively claiming to have "discovered" its "plot.") Such readers simply assume that every book must have a clear and linear reading that "explains" the "story"; for them the sign of its existence is the distortion of that proportion of sentences away from the objective. By the same token, too many objective sentences, again violating that proportion, for these readers is a sign to take all this objectivity as a projection of some traumatic, inner, subjective state-of-character: dream, guilt, psychosis... (One recalls the equally naive readers of *Le Voyeur* at this point.) *Dhalgren* is almost all foreground—as I have mentioned. One can only speculate that these readers took this as a sign for some great and inner subjective distortion (above and beyond the description and analysis of psychological distress the text supplies) which would "explain" it all.

They were, understandably, disappointed when the text did not supply one.[16]

And I suspect these were readers who, on the deepest level where it counts, simply could not read the book as science fiction—a practice of writing which has familiarized its readers with another proportion weighted toward the objective.

I would like to make the following suggestion humbly, but perhaps I have already crossed a limit, a line, into a landscape where humility has no existence. I may well be already in the city of the unacceptable:

Anyone who finds it helpful may approach *Dhalgren*, without fear of misreading the text because of the approach (though there is, alas, no way to insure a "proper" reading: it may have none) as (and in) an attempt to explore and respond to a small sector of the grammar of the language of human signs. It tries to focus on the grammar of that language by a science fictional reorganization of these signs' textual production/reproduction. Kid's sanity remains in question (and hopefully is never fixed to the circumscribed area of meaning that respectively overshadows the officially "sane" or the officially "insane") for the same reason the disaster of the city is unexplained: such explanations would become a fixed signified straiting the play and interplay of the signifier—the city of signs—that flexes and reflexes above it. To "clear up" either question (that of the Kid's "sanity" or that of "what happened to the city") would prevent us from apprehending *Dhalgren*'s real/true(?) topic: the organizing and reorganizing transformations we are free to view and experience once these restraining models are tossed aside.

—New York
September 1975

16. All possible readings of a book, naive or otherwise, are of course in dialogue with one another—but in different modes and at different intensities!

Some Remarks Toward A Reading of Dhalgren

by K. Leslie Steiner[17]

Dhalgren, by Samuel R. Delany, belongs to that scant handful of science fiction novels with obvious aesthetic range and clear seriousness. At our most cynical, if we cannot state that a full appreciation of that range and seriousness is the reason for the book's near three-quarters of a million sales to date (among paperback original science fiction where a hundred thousand is considered notably successful), we can reasonably maintain that such sales are due in large part to a curiosity over what such range and seriousness look like in a science fiction novel.

Sex will not account for it.

Thirty-five odd of *Dhalgren*'s near nine hundred pages do deal with copulatory mechanics, but this is simply not a high enough percentage—especially with the real and near-real pornography seldom more than a bookrack away. Also the "sex" in *Dhalgren* is too psychologically portrayed for real arousal. From the beginning to the end of it the characters never stop thinking.

It isn't publisher promotion.

Besides a somewhat more elegantly designed cover than is usual for paperback original science fiction[18], there's been none. Also, three-quarters of a million sales in any field outside science fiction is just not that spectacular—especially from the publisher of *Jaws* and *Day of the Jackal.*

---

17. By the time this piece was first published (but not at the time it was written), K. Leslie Steiner was known as a more-or-less playful critical alter-ego for Samuel R. Delany. She appears as a character and as a critic, complete with a biography and an occasional written text, in his series Return to Nevèrÿon. See *The Straits of Messina* for a full account of her genesis. (The "K" stands for Karen.)

18. Not until a few years later, did I learn that the cover for *Dhalgren* had won a design prize in its first year.

What has made *Dhalgren* a phenomenon at Bantam Books is not the sales so much as that those sales have come without one advertisement in prozine, fanzine, or general readership newspaper—a distinction neither *The Dispossessed* on the one hand nor *The Mote in God's Eye* on the other (both books which have sold less well by respective factors of three and four) can claim. Sales in the multiple millions helped on by hundred-thousand-dollar ad campaigns are not uncommon at Bantam. Sales of over half a million with only the standard seventy-five review copies are.

Dhalgren is a novel that has achieved its readership entirely on garnered reputation. To the extent that reviewer response contributes to such reputation, we must note that not one such response we have seen, whether the praiseful *New York Times Book Review* piece by Gerald Jonas or the hyperbolically glowing appreciation by Theodore Sturgeon in *Galaxy*, whether the vitriolic reaction of Ellison in *The Los Angeles Times* or the outrage of Del Rey in *Analog*, has even suggested that the book was traditionally "entertaining" or a "good read." In fact it has probably been the most appreciative reviewers, like Barbour and Lupoff, who have been the first to warn the general reader that the book, besides long, is involuted, obscure, and difficult—if not downright tedious.

Yet today, just over a year and a half after these first critical reactions, the tremors of one sympathetic reviewer concerned with whether or not Delany could continue to find publishers for such obviously uncommercial work, or the philistine remarks that, for a few months, littered both prozines and fanzines on the stupidity of the publishers for taking on such an obvious bomb, today seem like natterings from a parallel universe quite out of touch with our own. *Dhalgren* has found its audience. It is not the runaway audience of the manufactured bestseller. It is not the all too swayable and, finally, all too naive audience of hardcore science fiction readers. Because it is neither of these, we may speculate that it might well be the basis for that most important of audiences, the vertical audience of concerned and alert readers interested in the progress of American fiction. For it is our sincere belief that only this audience could find such a novel truly absorbing.

Among *Dhalgren*'s array of poets and priests, astronauts and engineers, lay analysts and leather queens, outlaws and oligarchs, all interlocked in a daymare plot sired by Borges out of Genet, each in intracranial trajectory across the deliquescent and quintessentially

American cityscape of Bellona—a 'scape duplicated in how many photos of burned-out central Harlem, depopulated Buffalo, dying Detroit and half a dozen other towns for which the book presents the fantastic calculus that, despite (or even because of) its avoidance of specific economic and political explanation, nevertheless demonstrates with exhaustive accuracy the workings of such images within the meaning codes that form and inform our epoch—we can only touch, in an essay of this scope, on the novel's most formal and framing structures.

As formal and framing as our exploration will be, we feel it is justified: *Dhalgren* does not yield up its center easily on first reading—at least not to this its first wave of readers. Our own attempt to illuminate that center, in all its dislocated play, is formed by highlighting elements on the borders of its vast tapestry: the center itself, which is not so much a location as a set of optical strategies to refract their glimmer, this essay must largely leave out; for that is something only a careful reading of the text itself can supply.

The simple key to *Dhalgren* is an old and familiar one to serious novel readers: *Dhalgren*'s central character, the Kid, has great charm. Unless one is prepared, however, to find a meticulous and exhaustive portrait of a somewhat shy and dubiously honest (if well-intentioned) ex-mental patient charming, *Dhalgren* cannot be a pleasure to read.

But one must find doughty old men charming to enjoy *Don Quixote*.

And one must find high spirited if somewhat naive young women charming to enjoy *Emma*. Indeed, if one does not find high spirited if somewhat naive young women charming, all Austen's extensive art, inexhaustible wit, and moral fervor will seem pretty cold fare. Similarly for Cervantes'. And one must find Delany's wandering madman charming; if one does not, the great net of verbal resonances Delany sets up around him, the glimmer of evanescent experience half comprehended in the burning city, the metaphoric superstructure of language and logic as well as the precision and energy with which Delany propels the Kid through them will seem pretty rarefied stuff.

The Kid, of course, is much more than a charming wastrel. He is deeply sensitive, sharply observant; he is very brave and sincerely—almost agonizingly—modest. But our approach to these qualities must be through a sense of his charm. If it is not, these other qualities will seem quite disembodied, and the structural complexities of the novel which support Kid's tragedies—tragedies which are the tragedies of our epoch underlined and highlighted by an extraordinary fictive surround—will seem mere cleverness or less.

Over a wide field of reading we can locate two categories of successful character. Characters of one category, on our first exposure, wrench at our sympathies, frequently overcoming seemingly insurmountable odds, to push us toward laughter or tears. One thinks of Salinger's Holden Caulfield, of Osborne's Jimmy Porter. Characters of the second category are presented usually at much greater length and always with greater analysis—frequently too much analysis for even a diligent reader to absorb at a single reading. Though the author, by this analysis, compels us to think about the character more, our initial emotional responses are much cooler. If we must watch such a character suffer or despair, we watch as we would a real person suffer in the street: it is sad, yes; but we do not get involved. One thinks of Stendhal's Julien Sorel, of Eliot's Dorothea Brooke. The characters in the first category, on repeated reading, pall. Their play on our emotions begins to appear too calculated, too strident. At worst, they dissolve, on fifth or sixth reading, into the various rhetorical postures out of which their authors cobbled them together but which adhere, finally, to no rich organization of psychological veracity. At the same time that we must now make an effort of will to experience these collections of verbal tropes as human beings, much less respond to them humanely, we realize that the intensity of our initial response was basically due to safety: we could cry and laugh so easily because, finally, we were not crying or laughing about anything very much. Characters of the second category, if we are lucky enough to indulge multiple readings of the works in which they occur, we find gaining an intense presence. Though we still may not cry at their suffering, frequently we are deeply moved by it, if not truly frightened. We begin to know in our bones why their insoluble problems are, for them, insoluble. Against this, their triumphs, however minor or momentary, present for us all we can know of our own human possibility, or the possibility of humanity for humanity. As their significance becomes for us more and more universal, our picture of them becomes more specific, more individual, unique. Without further denigrating the pleasure or importance of characters in category one, those in category two are the indisputable triumphs of the writing art.

In the eighteen months since its publication, we have read *Dhalgren* cover to cover six times. Though this suggests an enthusiasm of a sort usually associated with works containing category one characters, our own experience of the Kid is far closer to what we have known of category two.

But if the simple key to *Dhalgren* is character, the complexities it unlocks, like Austen's complexities, are structural. And it is finally an aspect of structure that we shall here explore.

In the second half of *Don Quixote*, the errant Don encounters men and women who have read of his adventures in the first half—which, in concert with the Don's literarily mediated ideals of chivalry from the first half, justifies the interpretation current among a number of critics that the *Quixote* is, among other things, an allegory of the progress of the text.

In the first chapter of *Dhalgren*, the Kid encounters a notebook which, though he only recognizes it in dim flashes, could only have been written by himself. The text of this notebook sweeps up the text of the novel proper and, in the last chapter, comes to replace it. We do not need to be critics, then, to assert that *Dhalgren*, in its foreground, deals with a theme others have found buried in allegory in Cervantes. What it does perhaps require a critic for is to trace out the organization of the numerous variations on this theme. For this organization recalls, in its complexity, one of Austen's minuets of affection and self-deception, if indeed it does not go beyond that complexity into a new mode altogether. Let us leave Austen and Cervantes and explore the play and progress of texts in the text of *Dhalgren*.

Dhalgren makes constant reference to, and/or quotes extensively from, three inner texts: the poems written by Kidd (his earlier onoma) which eventually form the booklet *Brass Orchids* (as well as the mysterious "second collection"); the newspaper published and edited by Roger Calkins, *The Bellona Times*; and the journal which appears in fragments throughout the novel and which, with Chapter VII, becomes one with it.

The most traditionally privileged of these texts is, of course, the poems—i.e., literarily privileged. The sign of their privilege, in the novel *Dhalgren*, is that they are not anywhere quoted in the text—at least not in final draft. We see (and experience) Kidd write them, revise them, correct them; we watch others read them, recopy them, and miscopy them. But whenever we are given any phrase from their text, almost immediately we are informed that the phrase is to be deleted or rewritten. And the once Denny reads a line aloud from the printed version (p. 510)[19], and we

---

19. All page numbers in parentheses, e.g. (p. 568), refer to *Dhalgren*, by Samuel R. Delany, Vintage, New York, 2001.

In February 1985 on the occasion of the 17th printing of *Dhalgren*, which marked the book's first decade in print, in *Locus, The Newspaper of the Science Fiction Field* (edited by Charles Brown: Oakland, 1985), Delany published an article on the textual history of his novel since its publication in January 1975. According to his article, some sixty-odd typographical corrections were made in the 6th printing in 1975. A further set of c.150 were incorporated in the 16th seven years later in 1982, with a dozen more incorporated into the 17th, at the end of 1984. That printing also included what appeared to be an error on the copyright page: a list mid-page citing the month and year of each of the sixteen previous printings fails to include the present, 17th, printing. But a row of descending numbers at the page's bottom, beginning at 25 and ending at 17, gives the printing's proper designation. This designation method holds true for *Dhalgren*'s 18th and 19th printings as well—printings which are textually identical to the 17th. As this essay goes to press, the 19th was *Dhalgren*'s last printing. For the first time since it reached print almost fifteen years ago, the book is now *out* of print—and has been for more than a year. Though now and again a great deal has been made of them, everyone who has actually taken the trouble to examine the corrections has judged them of a minor, if clarifying, nature.

Some months afterwards, Delany circulated a short list of further corrections still remaining to be made. They are, indeed, typical of the others.

The most major of these is the removal of Madame Brown's name from a scene in which obviously she does not appear (304/9/1). The name endured, Delany states, through a late, hasty retyping of a former version in which she was present.

As this terminal list is brief, with Delany's permission I reproduce it in full. The numbers indicate page/paragraph/line-of-paragraph, followed by the correct line reading and/or a typographical instruction in square brackets. This list, used on the 17th printing and beyond, Delany says, will produce an all but error-free text.

CORRECTIONS REMAINING TO BE MADE IN *DHALGREN*
17th printing & ff

16/1/1:
ception to pass it by. Rumor says there is practically no

36/9/3:
tresses cowling at light-ringed mirrors and freight

61/5/3:
Where was Dad now? In one of three cities, in one of two

85/2/4:
country, stitched with lightning, somehow there

94/2/2-3:
ing hard. After a moment, he straightened out the paper
and, on a fresh page, began to copy again:

100/2/1:
("Muriel! Now, Muriel, be quiet!"

131/9/1:
[Typesetter: This should be reset as two lines, both of them centered:]
MYSTERIOUS RUMORS!
MYSTERIOUS LIGHTS!

132/8/2:
We are sure *something* happened in the sky last night.

304/9/1:
"What is that?" the man on Mr Richard's left

339/3/21:
since he was in the area, why didn't he stay there. So the

367/2/4:
[Typesetter: Note this is in a different font from the main text. Observe the spacing:]
T E   G TA   Y

389/7/1:
It fell open in Kid's hands:

384-412:
[Typesetter: In these pages, change the spelling of "Tayler" to "Taylor" throughout.]

414/3/3:
international spies—I mean, maybe the whole city here

643/1/2:
the blowout George gave for the Reverend Taylor in Jack-

693/6/4:
Pure Reason, The Phenomenology of Mind, and *Being*

think we have at last heard a true fragment of these most privileged utterances, we learn two sentences on that he has misread the line. The astute reader will recognize that misreading as a combination of two rejected versions of the same poem (p. 242), which perhaps explains Kid's extreme anxiety at Denny's mistake: for a moment Kid must believe he did not make the corrections he remembered making, which corrections make the text of the poem authentic for him—and inaccessible to us.

But if we stand back from all three inner texts—poems, newspaper, and journal—and the text of the novel in which they are embedded, we notice what a substantial amount of the machinery of this very long book (far more than is devoted to the too often mentioned "sex") is given to

---

729/2:
[Typesetter: Retaining its present placement on the page, reset this paragraph so that there is no widow at the end and the last line ends flush right with "actual—"]

749/5/6:
chin toward Glass and Risa. "That nigger can fuck!"

767/4/2-3:
the pussy. Despite George, and a city consecrated by twin
moons, I know there must be some greater, female deity

785/2/21:
the Emboriky for

795rubric/l/l-2:
The active ones (of whichever sex) are denser
and crueler. The passive ones (of whichever

805/14/7:
funny things about me, and what had happened on the roof

820/5/3:
the train-tracks, boy. Apocalypse has come and gone. We're

835rubric/10/l:
She: "Madame Brown took me to the

838/6/1:
Mrs. Arthur Richards

debunking the traditional authority on which their various textual privileges are founded.

Thus, the newspaper's traditional authority of accurate public pronouncement is thrown into question by its shifting dates, its absurd headlines, and even its highly affected style. There is the suggestion that many of the articles assumed to be written by Calkins are really written by Bill. *The Bellona Times* has dealt in scandal, muckraking, and libel. It announces the publication of the "second collection" without Kid's agreeing to it, exaggerates the number and nature of the scorpions and their runs, and we catch it in at least one specific error of fact that is typical:

We would much prefer to give our opinions on Lower Cumberland Park [...where apparently all power has gone out with the breaking of the water main on my last Thursday...]. But another writer (page one, continued page seven) has already rehearsed his eyewitness, first-hand account. And, anyway, in his words, "...chances are, no one lives there anymore." (p. 490)

It is in Lower Cumberland Park that Dragon Lady has her nest and that George Harrison lives with his populous entourage of blacks.

The traditional authority of poetry is its claim to aesthetic integrity. This is thrown into question at the party given for Kid by the publisher Calkins—with Thelma pro and Frank con: and before the party ends, the poems' very authorship is put in doubt. During the party, the specifically social de-privileging of art and the art-text, for which the poems are a symbol, becomes explicit in the novel:

> Lanya sighed. "I guess that's why I'm glad I'm not an Artist... I mean Artist in the way this party presupposes... I don't just think you can be that kind of artist any more. Lots of people do things lots better than lots of others; but, today, so many people do so many things very well, and so many people are seriously interested in so many different things people do for their own different reasons, you can't call any thing the best for every person, or even every serious person... This party —it's ritual attention, the sort you give a social hero. I

> guess that can be an artist if there're few enough of them around—"
>
> "—like in Bellona?"
>
> "Bellona is a very small part of the universe. And this party is a very good place to bear that in mind..." She glanced down under her brows. "Maybe that's what Mr. Newboy was trying to tell you?" (pp. 624)

The journal, which is found in the novel's first chapter and quoted in fragments throughout *Dhalgren* (and was therefore written, at least in part, "before" the novel's action begins) is given in substantial portion as the last chapter. We reread a number of the same quotes we have read before, only this time in context. (This identifies what we are reading as the "same" journal.) Nevertheless, the journal seems to continue the story of the characters and events "forward" through time from where it takes up at the end of Chapter VI. Also, Kid claims never to have seen the journal before Lanya finds it in the park (p. 33), and yet when we are finally presented with the journal text, it certainly appears to be narrated by Kid—all of which undermines the traditional authority we grant a journal: that of a real recounting of real happenings written by a real person in real time. Even the variorum apparatus with which the opening section of the journal chapter is encumbered seems to be there essentially to point out its own inconsistencies, flaws, and generally to deflate itself (p. 651 & pp. 662–663).

As we stand back, however, we must also notice something else: the multiplicity of places these texts-within-texts connect with one another; and that the connections are most unlinear. We hope to show that these texts connect in such a way that their various privileges/deprivilegements form an interlocking and interdependent structure. A section of this structure, which we feel is indispensable for the true appreciation of the novel and a key to much that is in it, is what, in this essay, we shall explore.

We have already used once in this essay that most privileged of critical terms: symbol. The sin of privilege is that it allows what we grant it to pass without closer examination. But we shall not, I hope, indulge such a sin here.

Modern Active symbolization is semantic and plurally metonymic—rather than allegorical and globally metaphoric. If, for example, one character robs another in an alley, and we read at the incident's conclusion, "The buildings stared down with blind, accusing windows," the way to retrieve the symbolism of this (admittedly hackneyed) sentence is by imaginative metonymic extension and semantic substitution: by metonymic extension, the "buildings" and the "windows" symbolize the landscape in which the crime occurs. By semantic substitution, then, the landscape in which the crime occurs is "blind" and "accusing." The windows are blind because presumably (by metonymic extension) no one is looking out of them. The windows are accusing because (by metonymic extension and semantic substitution) people were looking out the windows, they might proffer an accusation. In another mood then (i.e., conditional subjunctive) the inhabitants of the landscape are symbolized by the sentence. We may also say (continuing the semantic substitution that allowed us the previous statement) that the symbol sentence symbolizes the material of the landscape and the inhabitants of the landscape in different moods. The double pair "buildings/windows" and "blind/accusing" symbolizes (again by semantic substitution) alternation in properties of the landscape, i.e., opacity and transparency, efficacy and ethics. We can say, by semantic substitution, that the alternation symbolizes the complexity of the landscape. We can then go on to discuss these various complexities of landscape, remembering that they are organized around a crime, and organized in relation to one another by the symbol sentence. We might return to other parts of the text to retrieve the trajectory at which we enter this symbolic structure (i.e., the web of signifiers that is our only expression of this symbol's signified): Was the crime recounted from the criminal's or the victim's point of view...? This will ultimately play a part in organizing our symbolic elements and their referents.[20]

---

20. Three further points may be of interest in our discussion of our symbolic model:

One) Imaginative metonymic extension and semantic substitution may of course proceed out from the symbol sentence in several "directions." The further they move from the initial symbol sentence, the more likely any two extensions are to diverge—though there is always a possibility of later intersection.

Two) Some ideas (and the words expressing them) are more strongly associated than others. (Here we see the power of the Saussurian concept of sound image over word.) There will frequently be, therefore, a stronger disposition to begin the journey out from the symbol sentence in one direction rather than another.

But the way not to untangle the symbolism of such a fictive sentence is to say: "The buildings, with their blind, accusing windows, are an allegory for the forces of society and justice." The metonymic leap here is too great and the semantic collapse too complete to be useful.

The first method explodes (as with a microscope) the elements of our awareness as we experience the symbol sentence itself, retaining those elements in their various moods and in their various structural relationships. The second merely takes one symbolic structure and replaces it with another, which, despite any accuracy of intuition, puts too little analytic energy to the task.

We have already said, rather conservatively, that the poems in *Dhalgren* symbolize the art-text and, by extension, art. We also say that the situation of Kid, his poems, and Bellona, symbolizes the situation of the modern artist, his art, and his landscape. But though we note that one situation might be considered an allegory (or metaphor) for the other, still we reiterate that we have arrived at the various symbolic correspondences not by intuitive leap, but by an extensive semantic/metonymic matrix which orders the symbol in the way it is experienced while reading the text. It may be assumed that such a matrix is constructible behind any subsequent use of the word "symbol" in the text at hand.

We have gone on at such length about our method here because it is precisely such a method that will most aid a reader in retrieving what, symbolically, is occurring around those sections of fictive discourse that so many have found nearly impenetrable, and which *Dhalgren* presents

---

Our point One) accounts for the richness and multiplicity of symbolic retrievals, while still keeping what is retrieved in some sort of order. Point Two) accounts for the fact that while two individual retrievals may be arrived at by the same number of steps, one may still be a more "obvious" retrieval than the other.

Three) is an answer to a possible question our model for symbolic retrieval may elicit at this point: Do we then say that in fiction something is always a symbol for whatever it is an example of! Briefly, yes. But examining our example should make it clear that not all symbolic retrievals may be accomplished merely by asking what various images in the text are examples of. Consider the mode in which "The buildings stared down with blind, accusing windows" symbolizes the landscape's inhabitants, or the complexity of the landscape, or the relation between opacity and transparency. We could not say our symbol sentence was an (or contained any) example of these without indulging catachresis in its most pejorative sense.

us with again and again—for example the following from Kid's musings as he approaches the city of Bellona:

> This parched evening seasons the night with remembrances of rain. Very few suspect the existence of this city. It is as if not only the media but the laws of perspective themselves have redesigned knowledge and perception to pass it by. Rumor says there is practically no power here. Neither television cameras nor on-the-spot broadcasts function: that such a catastrophe as this should be opaque, and therefore dull, to the electric nation! It is a city of inner discordances and retinal distortions (pp. 14).

We shall return to this passage to show how it is symbolically related (i.e., lies a mere step away in the symbol matrix) to another passage further on. That connection will strongly suggest one aspect necessary to the theme cited—i.e., the progress of the text. But we cannot leave the general problem of symbology without touching, in Delany's work, on its sister problem, the problem of mythology.

Our approach to the mythological allusions in *Dhalgren* is this: While there are mythical fragments scattered throughout the novel, we suspect that their symbolic significance (by semantic substitution) is precisely that they are fragments and not wholes. To locate a single myth with the same "plot" as *Dhalgren* and say that one symbolizes the other would be to commit, on a grand scale, the allegorical error that, on a small scale, we have analyzed above. At least one of *Dhalgren*'s explicit themes is the fragmentation of modern social myths (p. 249ff); the fragmentary nature of the mythic allusions merely dramatizes in privileged literary terms what the foreground of the novel dramatizes in action.

The novel begins with a clear recall of the myth of Daphne.[21] But when, in the next scene, Kid, about to discuss the incident with the truck-driver who

---

21. There is an intriguing paragraph on page 4 of Ernst Cassirer's *Language and Myth*, translated by Susanne K. Langer, Dover Publications, 1946, reissued 1953, which connects the mythical name Daphne, through the Sanskrit, with the word "sunrise"—intriguing in terms of Delany's setting his Daphne scene in the moonlight, and the subsequent rising of the giant sun that apparently bears some

has given him a lift, thinks, "No, the Daphne bit would not pass—" (p. 10), we suspect Delany is also telling us that we cannot discuss this novel as though it were a contemporary *Ulysses*, i.e, a novel with a coherent referent myth in place of a traditional foreground structure or plot.

It won't pass.

The Daphne encounter takes place outside the city of Bellona. The myth fragments are encountered after we cross the bridge into Bellona proper. We think the symbolism here is: clear, recognizable myths—not only literary, but (by metonymic extension) social ones as well—are to be found outside Bellona. Inside the city all myths/fictions/signs—literary and social—are shattered, revalued, and recombined.

We have spoken of connections between texts in *Dhalgren*. Let us examine one such connection—between the text of *Brass Orchids* and the text of the novel proper.

In Chapter II, Kid is walking up Brisbain Avenue, looking for Calkins' mansion. He is carrying the notebook; recently he has broken into a house for something to eat. When he is on the street again, continuing his search, we come across the following description:

> Charcoal, like the bodies of beetles, heaped below the glittering wall on the far corner. The sharpness of incinerated upholstery cut the street's gritty stink. Through a cellar window, broken, a grey eel of smoke slithered the sidewalk to vaporize in the gutter. Through another, intact, flickerings... The singular burning among the dozens of whole buildings was the most uncanny thing he'd seen.
>
> He crossed quickly to the next block, (p. 77)

---

ineffable female name (p. 693). Delany is obviously something of a Langer admirer (see *Nova*, p. 25, Bantam Books, New York, 1969, and also *Triton*, p. 352, Bantam Books, New York, 1976, both by Samuel R. Delany); so it is not so farfetched to suspect he is familiar with the Cassirer. For the import of those myths that connect human beings with vegetation in general and trees in particular there is of course all *The Golden Bough* (Frazer) to browse over. And it is not forcing the basic plot structure of *Dhalgren* to describe it in terms of one of the most elemental myth plots: The hero, after an encounter with the Goddess, is struck with madness and poetry. But as we have said above, to specify any more than this is to violate the book.

Kid continues up the avenue, writes his first poem ("Brisbain") on the blank verso of a notebook page, finds the Calkins mansion and, while he is trying to look over the wall, is set upon by three scorpions (who will be revealed later as Copperhead, Glass, and Spitt); he is revived by Newboy the poet and Fenster the black liberal, but is not allowed within the mansion gates. He starts back down Brisbain Avenue; and, after he sees some people down the block who might be more scorpions, he responds to his terror by sitting down against a lamp-post to write again:

> His heart pounded.
>
> His armpits grew slippery.
>
> Breathing hard, he sat with his back to the post's base.
>
> He took the pen from his pocket.... "Charcoal," he wrote down, in small letters, "like the bodies of burnt beetles, heaped below the glittering black wall of the house on the far corner." He bit at his lip, and wrote on: "The wet sharpness of incinerated upholstery cut the general gritty stink of the street. From the rayed hole in the cellar window a grey eel of smoke wound across the sidewalk, dispersed before" at which point he crossed out the last two words and substituted, "vaporized at the gutter. Through another window," and crossed out window, "still intact, something flickered. This single burning building in the midst of dozens of other whole buildings was," stopped and began to write all over again:
>
> "Charcoal, like the bodies of beetles, heaped below the glittering wall. The sharpness of incinerated upholstery cut the street's gritty stink." Then he went back and crossed out "the bodies of" and went on: "From a broken cellar window, a grey eel wound the sidewalk to vaporize at the gutter. Through another, intact, something flickered. This burning building," crossed that out to substitute, "The singular burning in the midst of dozens of whole buildings," and without breaking the motion of his hand suddenly tore the whole page from the notebook.

> Pen and crumpled paper in his hand; he was breathing hard. After a moment, he straightened out the paper and, on a fresh page, began to copy again:
>
> "Charcoal, like beetles heaped under the glittering wall..."
>
> He folded the torn paper in four and put it back in the notebook when he had finished the next revision. (pp. 83–84)

What Delany has done here is construct a purely verbal perspective that begins, broadly, below the baseline of the novel's text, then rises through it until it converges somewhere above at the vanishing point—at the "next revision" we never see—that is, presumably, the poem. The history of poetics gives us the reading for those perspective lines. They progress from the direction of prose and in the direction of poetry. From Coleridge's "Prose is words in the best order; poetry is the best words in the best order," through Flaubert's rhetorical inquiry of George Sand in a letter of 3 April 1876, "Why is there a necessary connection between the right word and the musical word? Why does one always end by writing a line of poetry when one condenses one's thoughts too much?" to Marianne Moore's "In poetry, the instantaneous solution to almost any problem is to delete," the history of poetics is littered with topoi that leave the reading clear. And these perspective lines establish a clear connection between the text of the novel and the text of Kid's poem—though in such a way that we cannot say for sure that any word in the novel text, including "charcoal" or "beetles," survives into that final draft.

Here we refer the reader back to the paragraph quoted on page 95 of this essay, and particularly the sentence: "It is as if not only the media but the laws of perspective themselves have redesigned knowledge and perception to pass it by." It, of course, is Bellona. The first clear appeal to perspective we encounter in the novel is in this purely verbal illusion of perspective. At this point we should also recall that historically the "laws of perspective" arose as an essentially ironic two-dimensional commentary on a ponderous, three-dimensional real: lines that met were suddenly signs for lines that no less than Euclid had claimed would never touch; one angle was a sign for another; ellipses were signs for circles; in short, systematic distortion was a sign for the organically undistorted. And what facilitated the codification of these laws in the west? A specifically ponderous architecture! Japan, despite a solid tradition of highly representational painting, never developed these "laws," and there are numerous examples of Japanese, till the beginning of the twentieth century, reporting that Western painting was "curiously distorted."[22] All this metonymic interplay between perspective, perception, distortion and architecture, as well as *Dhalgren*'s precise rendition of the first of these (and its overwhelming rendition of the last) as language, is the first clear, symbolic suggestion that Bellona is a city of words, on a far deeper level than we might have suspected—indeed, on a level that recalls nothing so much as that astonishing Chapter II in Book V of Hugo's *Notre Dame de Paris*, "This Will Kill That," where Dom Claud outlines, in a way that, to the modern ear, casts forward to McLuhan far more than it recalls anything medieval, how the birth of printed language signals the death of architecture.

But there are other junctures between text-and-text within *Dhalgren* which, when we begin to trace out their pattern, reveal even more interesting symbolic structural exfoliations.

The Necker cube is a visual illusion with which we are all familiar. As we regard the two-dimensional projection of the three dimensional object, spontaneously what was the back face leaps forward to become the front, and what was the front face drops away to become the back. Planes seen from above are suddenly seen from below; outsides are now insides and insides outsides:

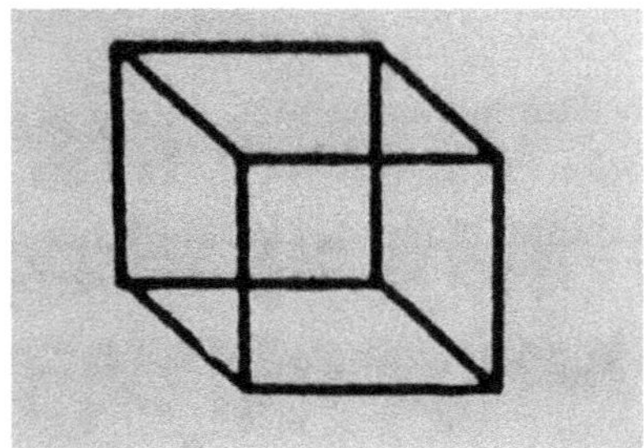

22. For a discussion of this phenomenon, see *Art and Illusion*, by Ernst Gombrich, Princeton University Press, 1960, a book which Delany discusses briefly in his article "Shadows," §30, page 275, in *Longer Views*, Middletown: Wesleyan, 1996 (Appendix One) or "Shadows," page 63, in *The Jewel-Hinged Jaw*, New York: Berkley Windhover, 1978. (It is not in the current edition of *The Jewel-Hinged Jaw*.) Delany's use of "perspective" to project these never-uttered utterances is, we feel, also ultimately ironic.

To some extent, once we know how the illusion is supposed to affect us, we can control the switching back and forth—the alternation of "readings" for its interlocking junctures.

Dhalgren is a novel that is frequently described as circular—because the last non-sentence in the book ("Waiting here, away from the terrifying weaponry, out of the halls of vapor and light, beyond holland and into the hills, I have come to") can be read as the first part of a sentence completed by the book's opening non-sentence ("to wound the autumnal city."). But we must point out that a circle is not the only closed figure possible to inscribe on a plain sheet of paper. A careful reading of *Dhalgren* shows that the connecting nodes of various textual modes of discourse give rise to a figure more closely resembling a Necker cube than a simple circle. The resultant shifts in authority of the various fictive planes, leaping back and forth as we observe them, are, we feel, crucial to the appreciation of *Dhalgren*.

We take the trouble to describe these shifts in the hope that, once the reader can bring them more or less under control, she or he will appreciate the structural beauty and complexity of the novel Delany has architected.

The first movement of *Dhalgren*'s Chapter I begins with subjective rhapsody:

> to wound the autumnal city.
>
> So howled out for the world to give him a name.
>
> The in-dark answered with wind.
>
> All you know I know: careening astronauts and bank clerks glancing at the clock before lunch; actresses cowling at light-ringed mirrors and freight elevator operators grinding a thumbful of grease on a steel handle; student riots; know that dark women in bodegas shook their heads last week because in six months prices have risen outlandishly; how coffee tastes after you've held it in your mouth, cold, a whole minute, (p 1).

The second movement of Chapter I begins:

> It is not that I have no past. Rather, it continually fragments on the terrible and vivid ephemera of now. In the long country, cut with rain, somehow there is nowhere to begin.... (p. 10)

In the fourth movement of Chapter I, the harmonica player (who will later be identified as Lanya) brings a notebook up to the park commune's campsite. And when Kid reads this notebook, it begins on its own page one:

> In Palmer-perfect script, an interrupted sentence took up on the top line:
>
> to wound the autumnal city.
>
> So howled out for the world to give him a name. That made goose bumps on his flanks...
>
> The in-dark answered with wind.
>
> All you know I know: careening astronauts and bank clerks glancing at the clock before lunch; actresses cowling at light-ringed mirrors and freight elevator operators grinding a thumbful of grease on a steel handle; student (p. 32)

But here, apparently, the text alters. For when Kid picks up the notebook again to show Lanya the mention of student riots:

> He reached for the book (she pulled back sharply from the orchid), spread his free hand on the page (she came forward again, her shoulder brushing his arm. He could see her breast inside her unbuttoned shirt. Yeah) and read aloud:
>
> "'...thumbful of grease on a steel handle; student happenings with spaghetti filled Volkswagens, dawn in Seattle, automated evening in LA.'" He looked up, confused, (p. 33)

And the next day when Kid is looking for Calkins' mansion, he discovers (shortly before the writing scene with which we examined our—but not the novel's—first textual juncture) the following passage in the notebook:

> It is not that I have no future. Rather it continually fragments on the insubstantial and indistinct ephemera of now. In the summer country, stitched with lightning, somehow there is no way to conclude… (p. 76)

Whatever the significance of the correspondences between the text of the narrative and the text of the enclosed (and enclosing) journal, in terms of "plot" or "symbolism," what we can say unequivocally is that such correspondences do exist and that they exist between texts of differing modes—modes that differ even though some of the words shared by these differently moded texts are identical.

The correspondences are furthered in more generalized, semantic ways as well: in the scene at the commune, from which we have already quoted, the two young women, Milly and Lanya, discuss the notebook's contents:

> Milly had taken the book, turned to a later page. The green-eyed girl leaned over her shoulder:
>
> "Read that part near the end, about the lightning and the explosions and the riot and all. Do you think he was writing about what happened here—to Bellona, I mean?"
>
> "Read that part at the beginning, about the scorpions and the trapped children. What do you suppose he was writing about there!"
>
> They bent together in firelight, (p. 34)

Chapter VII, which is the text of the notebook itself, indeed begins with some entries concerning the scorpions and the five children who had been trapped in the burning house (and rescued by George and the Kid); and, indeed, it ends with a description of catastrophe in the city, involving lightning, riot, and explosions. The notebook, which will begin in the middle of a line, will not, however, begin with "to wound the autumnal city." But there is internal justification for this. We shall read among the journal entries:

> I've read some pages so many times they've pulled loose from the wire spiral. Some of these I've caught before they ripped completely free, folded them up and put them inside the front cover. Carrying the book around, though, I must have let them slip out. The first pages—poems and journal notes—are all gone, as well as pages here and there through the rest. (p. 686)

We have seen how Delany has connected the text of the novel proper with the poetic text: a section of text is condensed until it is one with the novel's, then that text is condensed and recondensed until it disappears into the (inviable) poem, via the verbal perspective lent by poetic tradition. What is the nature of the correspondence between the novel text and the journal text?

From an examination of the above examples, we see that sometimes the texts are identical and sometimes they are substitutive variants, one for the other.[23] What do these correspondences accomplish within the novel's

---

23. One of the most interesting correspondences between novel and journal text is found between the scene in Chapter IV where Kid is searching for Lanya at the mysteriously abandoned commune site (p. 317) and the end of that mysterious journal section (that begins p. 756) in which Lanya, again in her glittering dress, exhorts Kid over Fenster's murder and the burning of the "second collection"—and there is the hint of a tree beginning to turn back into... something! This entry, after Lanya disappears and Kid, hiding from the marauders, sleeps in the park, finally degenerates (as he returns to the commune site) into a page of schitz-talk—the first of three such in the journal.

The novel section we would consider (p. 317) begins:

> "Lanya?"
>
> He turned, waiting, for her answer, uncomfortable at any noise in this ringed, misty clearing. Even at the height of the project period, there were... etc.

The corresponding journal section (p. 761) begins:

> "Lanya?"
>
> They squatted to the furnace, simulatable in every break on those fenestrated, rusty fill-ins. Only for a distance in civet furrow, here hid... etc.

foreground space? Besides unequivocally connecting two modes of discourse, they hint, whenever, as in his stopover en route to Calkins' mansion, Kid becomes aware of one, that "he pay attention to part of his mind he could not even locate" (p. 76). We might let this phrase pass without comment were it not for another passage earlier in the book, in which Kid, referring to his stay in a mental hospital, tells Tak what it's like to be insane:

> "Look, about... being nuts." He felt self-righteous and shy, looked at the doubled fist of flesh, hair, horn and callous pressed into his groin; it suddenly seemed weighted with the bones in it. "You're not, and you never have been. That means what you see, and hear, and feel, and think... you think that is your mind. But the real mind is invisible: you're less aware of it, while you think, than you are of your eye while you see... until something goes wrong with it. Then you become aware of it, with all its dislocated pieces and its rackety functioning, the same way you become aware of your eye when you get a cinder in it. Because it hurts... Sure, it distorts things. But the strange thing, the thing that you can never explain to

---

With the exception of the participle "waiting," the article "the" (before "height"), and the possessive adjective "his," the one is an almost perfect morphological rhyme of the other: pronoun/pronoun, verb/verb, participle/—, preposition/preposition, adjective/article, noun/noun, adjective/adjective, preposition/preposition... etc. The correspondence, with perhaps half a dozen exceptions, is perfect for one hundred eighty words. To discuss the significance of this correspondence in detail would require an essay almost as long as this one. But for those searching out "plot" in *Dhalgren*, we suggest that here is a clue to some of what transpired during Kid's missing five days. The vanished time obviously must have started somewhere around Lanya's (and the commune's) disappearance. This suggests that the fight in the park with the man from the Emboriky, recounted in the journal (p. 711), might have occurred some time within the "forgotten time," as Jommy claims it was the people from the Emboriky who'd already "run them from one side of the damn park to the other" (p. 711); which may also, given the correspondence, be the explanation of why the commune was abandoned in Chapter IV. There is internal evidence in the journal not only that it was written before the novel and after the novel, but during the novel as well.

> anyone, except another nut, or, if you're lucky, a doctor who has an unusual amount of sense—stranger than the hallucinations, or the voices, or the anxiety—is the way you begin to experience the edges of the mind itself… in a way other people just can't." (p. 48)

Though Kid cannot "locate" the "part" of the mind where these correspondences are significant, he is at least aware that its "edges" exist, because he has had some firsthand experience of them, thanks to his bout with mental illness.

I suspect that these places in the mind, "dislocated" and functioning in a "rackety" way during mental distress, are nothing less than the unconscious itself—though they are not the "Freudian" unconscious (i.e., the popular misconception of Freud's discovery), filled with lurking monsters, repressed terrors, and archetypes. Rather, it is a very specifically Lacanian unconscious (i.e., the concept of the unconscious Lacan has retrieved from a close examination of Freud's original work), an unconscious composed of the infrastructure of language itself, where such syntactic substitutions may be made, and where the reality-model is stored "as a language."[24] The circularity that so many elements of *Dhalgren* suggest is, symbolically, not so much a circularity through time as it is a circularity through the great, unconscious storehouse of language itself, where modes of discourse are stacked, helter-skelter, up against one another—as in the great MSE Warehouse, in which are stored all the inventions in (and the inventions of) the novel. Here is the prokaryotic magma of speech itself, which erupts the words actually composing the

---

24. See "Of Structure as an Inmixing of an Otherness Prerequisite to Any Subject Whatever," by Jacques Lacan, in *The Structuralist Controversy*, edited by Macksey and Donato, The Johns Hopkins Press, Baltimore, 1972, and particularly Lacan's comment in the discussion afterwards on how reality is stored in the mind, page 198: "I said like language, French, English, etc." See also *The Language of the Self*, by Jacques Lacan, translated by Anthony Wilden, Delacorte Press, Delta Books, New York, 1975.

novel,[25] as well as, presumably, those words that make up the journal, the newspaper, and even the final, unuttered utterances of Brass Orchids.

We may reasonably assume Delany is aware of the differing weights of varying modes of discourse—reportage, fiction, fantasy, etc. On the final page of *Dhalgren*, we read that work on its immense text was begun in January 1969 (p. 801). Just a week or so before, on 27 December 1968, Delany delivered a talk at the MLA Seminar on Science Fiction that grew into the paper "About Five Thousand Seven Hundred and Fifty Words,"[26] which deals with the various levels of subjunctivity that inform various types of discourse—reportage, fiction, fantasy, and science fiction. It is therefore reasonable to assume that in the novel he began work on between four days and four weeks later he may well have been interested in exploring the fictive possibilities resulting from juxtaposing one discourse with another, embedding one in another, transforming one into another. (If the paper cited—which begins with an appeal to an extremely close reading of fictive sentences, literally word by word—does not precisely announce the theme of the novel [and a reasonable argument can be made that it does], it is nevertheless closely related to it.) As we have seen, *Dhalgren* is lush with such juxtapositions, embeddings, and transformations.

If we read across the book's final circularity, we see one of these transformations accomplished: as we reach the final pages of the last journal entry, in which the diarist has been describing his exit from Bellona, suddenly the entry loses narrative coherence and becomes—for the third time in the journal—schiz-talk. The schiz-talk joins with the subjective rhapsody which begins the book, out of which, phoenix-like, emerges the jeweled and polished prose of the novel's text, describing the initial encounter between the Kid and the strange tree-woman, just before

---

25. See "Thickening the Plot" by Samuel R. Delany, in *The Jewel-Hinged Jaw*, op. cit., pp. 147–154. Compare Delany's description of the continual inter-effect of words and mental images with Lacan's description of the inter-effect (or "intrusion") of the signifier into the signified in "The Insistence of the Letter in the Unconscious," by Jacques Lacan, included in *Structuralism*, edited by Jacques Ehrmann, Doubleday, Anchor Books, New York, 1970.

26. Included in *The Jewel-Hinged Jaw*, *op. cit.* See note 21 on page 99.

Kid's entry into the city. But let us look a little more closely at what is going on around the juncture of these modes.

At the beginning of the book, Kid (then nameless) encounters an Oriental woman (with a Midwestern Standard accent) in the woods. They make love. He asks her to tell him his name; instead of answering, she shows him where to get a strange chain of prisms, mirrors, and lenses. While he is taking it from the cave, she runs away. He follows, to find her in the middle of a field, whereupon she turns into a tree. *He* runs away.

Going only so far into the novel, we note that there are two possible modes in which this opening incident can be read: either it is one with the base-line reality of the novel, i.e., we are to take it as something that really happened and assume there is some implicit or explicit fantastic/science-fictional explanation for it, an explanation that goes along, as it were, with the mode; or it happens against the base-line reality of the novel, i.e., we are to take it as a dream, a hallucination, or a fantasy (in whole or in part) of the character, a mental fiction that Kid reads, as it were, in the wrong mode.

These are the two modes of fictive authority that such fictive discourses —especially that discourse labeled science fiction—present us with.

Kid runs away from the meadow and, on the highway, is given a lift by a trucker:

> The driver, tall, blond, and acned, looking blank, released the clutch.
>
> He was going to say thanks, but coughed. Maybe the driver wanted somebody to rap at? Why else stop for someone just walking the road.
>
> He didn't feel like rapping. But you have to say something:
>
> "What you loading?"
>
> "Artichokes."
>
> Approaching lights spilled pit to pit down the driver's face. They shook on down the highway.
>
> He could think of nothing more, except: I was just making love to this woman, see, and you'll never guess... (p. 10)

This is their only exchange. Later, when the ride is over, most of the actual ride—so various sentences in the ensuing text would indicate—slips from Kid's mind; the only thing that remains with him is the word "artichokes" (that plant of many leaves and many layers, its own exfoliation of its most sumptuous heart), which rings here and there in his mind throughout the novel, an absurd emblem from the gap in the Kid's memory[27]—a gap that the text of the novel has traversed and retrieved for

---

27. In connection with memory-gaps, so significant in the action of *Dhalgren*, we quote the following text-plus-text-within-text from *The Prison-House of Language*, by Fredric Jameson, Princeton, 1972, page 51:

> Shklovsky's famous definition of art as a defamiliarization, a making strange (os-tranie) of objects, a renewal of perception, takes the form of a psychological law with profound ethical implications. The passage of Tolstoy's journals which Shklovsky quotes in illustration is as close as he ever comes to taking an actual metaphysical or ethical position:
>
>> I was cleaning a room and, meandering about, approached the divan and couldn't remember whether or not I had dusted it. Since these movements are habitual and unconscious, I could not remember and felt that it was impossible to remember—so that if I had dusted it and forgotten—that is, had acted unconsciously, then it was the same as if I had not. If some conscious person had been watching, then the fact could be established. If, however, no one was looking, or looking on unconsciously, then such lives are as if they had not been lived.
>
> Art is in this context a way of restoring conscious experience, of breaking through deadening and mechanical habits of conduct... and allowing us to be reborn to the world in its existential freshness and horror.

Three points are to be made here in terms of *Dhalgren*.

First, we note that art, forgetfulness, and strangeness have a venerable tradition of intellectual juxtaposition, which is not begun, but only developed, in *Dhalgren*. Some familiarity with that tradition, however, will make us more appreciative of the intensity and originality of Delany's development. Second, we note that Tolstoy's "couldn't remember whether or not I had dusted it" is a signifier which has collapsed a much more complicated process beneath it than first appears. Taken literally, the phrase contains a nonsensical double negative. (How much of this is translation, of course, we do not know.) One cannot "remember not doing something." One can only remember deciding not to do something. In his preoccupied meanderings around the room, obviously Tolstoy came upon evidence that the divan had been dusted, i.e., it was probably free of dust. Also Tolstoy had no memory of dusting it.

Yet there was probably other evidence to suggest that the duster had been, indeed, himself, e.g., perhaps he had a dust rag in his hand; perhaps he had memories, only seconds old, of dusting other pieces of furniture in the room; possibly he also knew no one else was in the house; possibly he also had memories of being preoccupied; or perhaps he realized his mind had not been on much of anything because what memories he did have of dusting some of the objects in the room were so hazy. Presumably, however, if his wife or a servant had run into the room just then and explained that only minutes before Tolstoy had come in to dust, she had been in and dusted only the divan, Tolstoy would probably have been quite happy with the explanation. In other words, it is the apprehension of evidence that things have gone other than one remembers them that sparks a certain sort of personality to "be reborn to the world in its existential freshness and horror." The strange thing encountered is both the stimulus to be reborn as well as part of the freshness and horror one is reborn to. (This rich strangeness, I suspect, is the be-all and end-all of that so elusive "difference" that is such a central concept in Delany's *The Einstein Intersection*.) But it is not some impossible memory-of-something-not-remembered. Certainly the Kid's world is composed of practically nothing but such evidence of things gone differently. But what is, by implication, analytically muzzy in the Tolstoy passage is, by the same implication, analytically clear in Delany. The progression from one to the other presents a true diachronic development, however minor; and it is not insignificant (if the reader will forgive us our single litotes for this paper) that such analytical clarity should be manifested in a modern science fiction novel. Our third point is this: Tolstoy, Shklovsky, and Jameson would no doubt all agree that it is the habitual which dredges out the inland seas of forgetfulness, beneath which occur the slippages in the faults of the real that leave their evidence on the beach of perceived reality. Kid forgets, at least for a while, his last hitchhiking lift.

Is he then a habitual hitchhiker?

We quote:

> I recall and want this:
>
> Swinging up into the cab of a truck, miles north of Florida, and the driver asking how long you've been hitching, and the sunlight fills his lime-splattered lap and your rank jeans and he lets the radio play pop music for a while, for a while country; then twists the dial; your forearm burns on the door, your hair snaps and your cheek freezes, and the motion is spindled on the rush of music. So you sit, just breathing, to hear and to move through the red and green country, with the sun in the tree-tops a stutter of bright explosions.
>
> The City suffers from the lack of it.
>
> But most of us have come here by way of it. (pp. 661–662)

It is easy to read *Dhalgren* as a response to the horror of the world. But we must remember that it also contains some marvelous and lyrical responses to the freshness.

the reader. For the character, it is an emblem of ignorance and absence; for the reader it is both an emblem and a reminder of privileged knowledge, of the sort only third person narrative fiction can supply.

Kid, at any rate, is let off by a river and starts across a bridge into the bizarre and shifting city. At this point, however, the conversation with the women he meets while crossing the bridge must be reviewed in full. Rather than quote three entire pages, however, we urge our readers to open their own texts of *Dhalgren* at this point and re-read pages 10 through 13 before continuing.

Other parts of the novel supply us with more information about these "characters." It is very easy to identify the small, pregnant black woman with the black, pregnant fifteen-year-old Gladdis, whom we meet in the scorpion nest during the journal chapter. As well, the woman who has the fever could easily be the nameless girl who is referred to as "Denny's girlfriend." Also, we will hear that at the woman's commune there is a Eurasian woman sculptor who made a lion out of scrap metal and old car parts.

Let us now skip to the closing entry in the final journal chapter—but we must note that our first encounter with this section of text is not in the closing pages of Chapter VII, but rather in Chapter III, when Kid is visiting Newboy at Calkins' mansion. At one point, the notebook falls from Newboy's knee while the elder poet is reading the poems:

> The poet bent, but Kidd snatched it up first.
>
> Its back cover had fallen open. Kidd frowned at the final block of handwriting that ran off the page bottom:
>
> ...The sky is stripped. I am too weak to write much. But I still hear them walking in the trees; not speaking. Waiting here, away from the terrifying weaponry, out of the halls of vapor and light, beyond holland and into the hills, I have come to
>
> ...Kidd's hand fell on the page. He looked up slowly. (p. 262)

Again, this suggests strongly that this entry—which in Chapter VII we get in full and to which the above lines indeed form the abrupt conclusion—was written before the action of the novel proper, i.e., before the action recounted in the first six chapters begins.

At this point, we must look closely at what happens in this final entry: it begins with a description of a strange catastrophe, from which Kid, along with a handful of scorpions, flees to the bridge. As the little bunch are crossing the bridge, they encounter an Oriental woman coming into the city. At this point we again urge our readers to open the novel and review the exchange that begins on page 798, and continues on to the "end."

Our general tendency to exercise fictive coherence makes it very easy to read the Oriental woman who enters over the bridge as none other than our lion-sculptor, coming into the city to begin her stint at re-education within the city of revalued signs. (It is equally easy to identify her with the tree-woman Kid first makes love to. We note in passing: if the woman is, as Lanya elsewhere describes her, Eurasian, that means she is half Oriental and half Caucasian. Kid is half American Indian: the American Indians are traditionally considered a Mongoloid race.) As Kid was given the orchid by her on her departure and his entrance, now he gives the orchid to her at his departure and her entrance—and it is precisely at this point in the cyclic completion that the journal's narrative coherence breaks down and becomes babble.

Coming out of the journal text (and the novel) at this particular trajectory, we note that there are two possible modes in which the closing incident may be read—as there are two possible modes in which any first person account, found in a notebook, may be taken: either it is real; or it is invention. One recalls Cecily's diary of her non-existent romances in Wilde's *The Importance of Being Earnest*: "These are merely the innermost thoughts of a young girl and consequently meant for publication." What presses a diarist to fictionalize, however, need not be so cynical. More to the point, one recalls the occasional chimerical or fantastic occurrences that appear in Kafka's, Rilke's, or Nijinsky's diaries, without comment, among the more quotidian concerns, and the occasional account of what could only have been a dream, notated exactly like some diurnal happening.

We have already pointed out that the opening of the novel avails us two possible modes of interpretation—reality or hallucination—just as the closing journal entry avails us two possible modes—reality or invention.

We maintain, in this essay, that the amazingly close correspondences between both dialogue and description in the two texts—novel and journal—strongly suggest that one or the other of the two passages must be read in a non-reality mode: Two real events are just *not* likely to occur with such extended similarities!

How one reads the temporal relation of the journal to the novel determines which passage we take as real and which passage we take as hallucination/fiction.

If the journal does precede the novel and does recount an actual exit (of Kid's) from Bellona, then the novel's opening, i.e., everything that happens outside the city—the tree woman, possibly the driver, and definitely the women on the bridge—are most likely some sort of hallucination; moreover, the hallucination of the women on the bridge is probably based on the real encounter recounted at the journal's close.

If the novel precedes the journal, however, and the meeting with the women on the bridge did occur when Kid first entered the city, then the closing account in the journal must be a fiction, extruded no doubt under some neurotic pressure, but based on the real experience of the encounter which occurred when Kid entered Bellona. ("Real" here means, of course, one with the novel's base-line reality.) It is under the pressure of this anxiety—the character's anxiety at producing such a fiction—that the narrative discourse breaks down into the babel that ends the book[28], and out of which, as we swing round to the beginning, the true Active discourse of the book arises.

Need we make it explicit?

These two readings are not to be chosen between.

They are to be experienced as shifts back and forth between possible textual authorities, like the shift between foreground and background of the vertical planes in the Necker cube.

The shift symbolizes the paradoxical frame of the novel itself:

---

28. At the end of Delany's more recent novel *Trouble on Triton*, op. cit., the protagonist, on being proposed to by another character, breaks down under the accumulated pressure of his/her life-lies to produce another such neurotic fiction, thence to retreat, under pressure of accrued guilt, into a near-psychotic mode. But in *Trouble on Triton*, unlike *Dhalgren*, the retreat is not sudden but is, rather, mapped out step by painful step over the novel's concluding seven pages.

If Kid really entered the city, then he never truly left it.

If Kid really left the city, then he never truly entered it.[29]

We have described two faces of Delany's Necker cube, flickering between background and foreground by the interplay of modes of fictive authority. We reiterate: to ask which of these two readings is "correct" is as pointless as asking which is the proper interpretation of an optical illusion that has been so carefully drawn to allow our interpretation to fall back and forth between them.

What the illusion does, of course, is maintain both readings while deprivileging the authority of each—and as such is in keeping with the theme of deprivileging certain textual authorities that runs through so much of *Dhalgren*.

In light of this fictive paradox, we turn to another which we shall only explore briefly: the death of June's brother—Did he fall, or was he pushed? Some readers have felt the book leaves the situation unresolved. But when Kid outlines both possible interpretations of the situation to George, in Chapter V, what George tells Kid in effect (p. 478) is that the asocial nature of George's sexuality deprivileges the traditional social value—June's innocence or guilt of the crime—that traditionally accrues to either reading of June's actions.

We have already mentioned the theme of deprivileging the art text; it is carried through the book by a host of ironic and symbolic machinery: the poems are written on the verso sides of totally impossible journal pages, or in the margins of a completely bogus newspaper. Such aesthetic deprivileging has been one of the major problems of art for the last eighty years (if not the major problem since Romanticism)—at least since Gertrude Stein first began to write in Paris.[30] There would seem to be two major sets of reasons for this. The first set are internal to the fiction itself: they are the reasons Delany discusses so lucidly in his letter/article "Of

---

29. See the discussion of the antinomies in "Shadows," §27–29, pages 266–275, in *Longer Views*, Middletown: Wesleyan, 1996 (Appendix One).

30. For an extended discussion of this problem, see Roland Barthes' *Writing Degree Zero*, Cape Editions, London, 1967. Delany cites Barthes in passing in a number of places, notably in his essay "Of Sex, Objects, Signs, Systems, Sales, SF, and Other Things," pp. 56–82 *supra*, and in his essay on Ursula K. Le Guin, "To Read *The Dispossessed*," in *The Jewel-Hinged Jaw,* Wesleyan University Press, pp. 105–165.

Sex, Objects, Signs, Systems, Sales, SF, and Other Things,"[31] i.e., the great tendency of fiction to be staunchly conservative even in the face of its writer's own liberal, if not radical, political sympathies. The second set of reasons are external, and Delany has discussed them in part in his essay "Popular Culture, High Art, and the SF Landscape,"[32] i.e., the various types of mystification that accrue to the art object and the artistic enterprise through the granting of social privileges by a critical public that, itself, will lose much of its social privilege should the mystification ever be dispelled. Delany treats the social emblems of the privileged art text with much irony in *Dhalgren*: the publisher has not read the poems, but publishes them purely on the mention (not even the recommendation!) of an establishment poet, who refuses to say if he thinks the poems good or bad; the publisher gives an elaborate party on the book's publication, at which he does not bother to show up because he is having a religious crisis. This is rare irony indeed! One reason the social emblems of artistic privilege are a problem is because there is no way today that they can possibly be doled out according to merit. As Lanya says, there are too many good artists around, and too varied a range of serious, public tastes. At best these emblems are a distraction and at worst they are a prison—a gilded prison the desire for which helps promulgate literature's internal conservatism. The traditional aesthetic response to this problem, beginning with writers like Stein, has been to write purposefully impoverished texts (frequently under the banner of social and psychological honesty; but as frequently with a sense of aesthetic purity), and to create works too bare to be considered political. But, as Lacan has demonstrated[33], a signifier (such as a work of art) always takes some of its meaning from the signified (such as the social response) that accrues to it. And since such works do indeed answer the aesthetic problems of the times, the establishment world of better-informed aesthetic opinion-makers frequently responds by turning all its traditional privilege-cum-

---

31. Pages 56–82 *supra*.

32. In *The Jewel-Hinged Jaw*, *op. cit.*, pp. 3–18.

33. See "The Insistence of the Letter in the Unconscious," by Jacques Lacan, in *Structuralism*, *op. cit.*; see also note 24.

mystification powers on these conscientiously impoverished works, granting Beckett a Nobel Prize, or devoting an official museum show to found-object art.

What Delany has done is construct not an impoverished, but a *rich* text, that deals specifically with the break-up of social signs (and, I think most readers will agree, treats of this break-up as a good thing), and in which the various social privileges of the text (in its various modes) simply cannot be held onto, because each is laid against a fictive foreground plane that, as we perceive it, vanishes into the background and is swallowed up in a concert of possible deconstructions.[34]

We have outlined one of the most important of these shifts. As we began by discussing a textual mode that was not vital to this particular shift, so we shall close by discussing another:

The journal/Chapter VII/novel closes with an entry we have already discussed in part, which deals with Kid's actual-or-invented exit from the city. Marginal to it, however, beginning (p. 787) immediately after the last, textual lacuna, is an entry which has Kid still in the city, still writing his poems, still living with Denny and Lanya. How are the marginal entries of the journal connected to the major entries? The editorial apparatus, as well as internal evidence, suggest a clear and coherent answer:

> *...The rubrics running pages left or right, which we print in slightly smaller type, are marginal (sometimes rather wide) entries made along the sides of our typescript at somewhat narrower spacing; most probably they*

---

34. It suggests Guy Debord's quoting (without attribution, in section 207 of *Society of the Spectacle*) from Lautreamont's *Maldoror*,"Plagiarism is necessary," or an explanation for why some critics, exhausted with the task of reading what is new in Sturgeon's *More Than Human*, or Nabokov's *Pale Fire* or *Pnin*, John Barth's *Sot Weed Factor* or Durrell's *Alexandria Quartet*, Robert Coover's *Public Burning*, or, indeed, an original mass-market paperback like *Dhalgren* "without a bit of pulp in it," and take refuge instead in the perfectly reasonable (but all too easy assertion since Shakespeare began to ransack his Hollingshead, his Golding translation of Ovid and his Montaigne, for plots and ideas for his cannon of 38) that all literature is about other literature. What's new is what it has to say about all those recognizable situations in light of what's going on at the time.

> *represent* "entries in quarter-sized, near illegible scrawl all over the margins"—*that is, entries of a later date than the one beside them we print in ordinary sized typeface. (Note also that the rubric which breaks off marginally to the last entry in the notebook continues as the major entry just two previous to this.)* (p.662)

We wonder how many readers who have been baffled by "what happens in *Dhalgren*" have stopped to make use of this extremely important note on ordering the events of the text.

The first implication of this note is certainly, at any rate, that the last marginal entry concerning Kid's, Lanya's, and Denny's stay at Madame Brown's (and Kid's finally getting to work on his new poems), is written after the entry about trying to leave the city.

The marginal entry concludes:

> Woke up loggy but clutching for my pen. Took some blue paper to the back steps, put the pine plank across my knees and wrote and wrote and wrote.
>
> Went back into the kitchen for some water.
>
> Lanya and Denny were there.
>
> "Hi."
>
> "Oh, hi."
>
> Went back to the porch and wrote some more. Finally it was (p. 792)

And the entry continues, a hundred thirty-eight pages previously, on page 659:

> too dark to see.
>
> So got up, stretched, put down my plank, went inside—and was suddenly bellowing and yelling and laughing....

Running marginally to the second half of this entry (which, now, is the major entry) is one of the entries concerning the rescued children—which suggests that the whole incident of the fire, rescue, and its aftermath happened even after Kid began to write again, which happened after the catastrophe with the lightning and explosions (during which Kid may or may not have actually tried to leave Bellona). If all this chronology is to be trusted, then the "second collection" that gets destroyed before being published would actually have been written before *Brass Orchids*, making the actual text of *Brass Orchids* his *third* collection....

We shall cease here.

But the point can be made that critics are simply not prepared to discuss *Dhalgren* until they have wrestled that last chapter into some sort of chronological order—or, more accurately, retrieved some of its possible chronological orders, for there are more than one and all are in dialogue. Delany has allowed several possible interpretations to the chronology of events. These alternate chronologies play as alternate signifieds beneath the fixed signifier of the musically satisfying order of the fragments as presented in the text. (The American reviewers who shout, with high-flung vitriol, "Joyce" or "tenth-rate Joyce pastiche"—most recently Barry Malzberg in a near-schizophrenic article in the September '76 issue of *The Magazine of Fantasy and Science Fiction*—are simply revealing that sad, abysmal, but typical ignorance of their country's literary production. If there is a source to be located for this technique, it is the opening movement of Faulkner's *The Sound and the Fury*. But Delany presents such a rational and effective development on this technique, bringing it into such a clearly autonomous mode, that no one could really make the accusation—as one can with the Brunner of *Stand on Zanzibar* vis-a-vis Dos Passos—of simple imitation. At any rate, the technique has no parallel in either the *Portrait, Ulysses*, or the *Wake*.[35]

---

35. To pursue beyond the development of a Faulknerian technique the literary precursors of *Dhalgren*, we note that the general template of the novel (a young man comes into a strange and isolated place where time seems to have lost all meaning and where a group of eccentric retirees from the real world put him through a series of educational and frequently disillusioning experiences) sits only a hair's breadth away from the general template of Mann's *The Magic Mountain* (that *other* seven-hundred-plus-page text also divided into seven further subdivided chapters). It is easy to see Kid as a sort of counter-culture Hans Castorp. In the two novels' use of psychotherapists and psychotherapy, in the general makeup of their respective social microcosms, indeed, there are too many parallels even to enumerate in a note that already threatens to be overlong. Nevertheless, one can reasonably argue that, for Delany, *Dhalgren* bears a relation to Mann's work similar to the relation that, for

---

Bester, *The Stars My Destination* bears to Joyce's. To retrieve the former relation, then, let us outline the latter: During the 'teens of the century, Joyce noted that the single, classic plot-structure he was assuming for *Ulysses* actually covered a number of tales. As Hugh Kenner puts it in *The Pound Era* (University of California Press, Berkeley & Los Angeles, 1971, p. 147): "In Zürich James Joyce was drawing the 18 hours of Leopold Bloom through a patterned integrity defined by Homer: a tough self-interfering pattern through which, he discerned, Shakespeare had already drawn the skein called Hamlet (Telemachus, Stephen), and Mozart his Don Giovanni (Antinous, Boylan) and even the elder Dumas his Monte Cristo, returned avenger (Odysseus at Ithaca, the stone guest at the banquet, the ghost at Elsinore). Time, place and personnel alter; the pattern remains."

"In 1941," Paul Williams continues the tale for us in his introduction to the Gregg Press edition of Bester's *The Stars My Destination* (G.K. Hall & Co., Boston, 1975, p. vi), "Mort Weisinger and Jack Schiff, the editors who had purchased Bester's first story and with whom he had held running discussions of James Joyce's *Ulysses* for several years, invited him to write scenarios for them at Superman Comics, their new employer." (Delany, in the early '70s, briefly scripted *Wonder Woman* for Superman Comics' corporate descendant, National Comics.) "For some time," Williams goes on to quote Bester directly from his article "My Affair with Science Fiction" (written in 1972 and published in *Hell's Cartographers*, edited by Brian Aldiss, Harper and Row, New York, 1975), "I'd been toying with the notion of using the *Count of Monte Cristo* pattern for a story. The reason is simple: I'd always preferred the anti-hero and I'd always found high drama in compulsive types," (op. cit., p. ix). When Bester got to the actual writing of his novel (begun in England, rewritten in Rome during 1955), he signaled his position *vis-a-vis* Joyce by paraphrasing on page 14 of his own text (the first page of Chapter One, after the prologue) the poem that Fleming had written on the flyleaf of Stephen's geography text (on page 16 of Joyce's) opposite Stephen's attempt (in *A Portrait of the Artist as a Young Man*) to record "himself, his name and where he was.

Stephen Dedalus
Class of Elements
Clongowes Wood College
Sallins
County Kildare
Ireland
Europe
The World
The Universe"

Fleming had rendered this:

"Stephen Dedalus is my name,
Ireland is my nation.

Clongowes is my dwellingplace
And heaven my expectation."

Bester's Gulliver Foyle, the wrong choice of an oxygen bottle away from death, in the midst of his struggles, prayers, and blasphemies, suddenly remembers "a nursery jingle:

Gully Foyle is my name
And Terra is my nation.
Deep space is my dwelling place
And death's my destination."

To recognize the Joycean source under Bester's jingle (as a piece of demotic folk doggerel alive in the Midwest it provided a title for Thornton Wilder's novel *Heaven's My Destination*) is to realize that Bester has flung down his version (with existential obliteration—"death"—replacing fundamentalist salvation—"Heaven") as a challenge that is merely intensified by the choice of the Monte Cristo version of the pattern that Joyce (and, presumably, Bester both—as Joyce states it in the text of *Ulysses*) knew was finally one with *The Odyssey*. For as Joyce's *Portrait* and its peripatetic sequel are, in our time, the novels of the privileged aesthetic sensibility, so Bester's book is the most resonant, intense, and reintensified image/metaphor/exploration of the "common man," the man who lacks precisely this aesthetic sensibility, the man "too easy for trouble, too slow for fun, too empty for friendship, too lazy for love," (*The Stars My Destination*, p. 14), the man with

EDUCATION:	NONE
SKILLS:	NONE
MERITS:	NONE
RECOMMENDATIONS:	NONE
	(p. 15)

the opposite of the privileged Joycean artist if ever there was one. And this is the man who becomes, not the fatherly supporter, drinking companion and somewhat bewildered admirer of the artist, but rather the vibrant, demonic, and implacable savior of humanity itself—in Bester's novel.

In the twenty years since its publication, no one in the science fiction community (with the possible exception of Delany himself; c.f., "About Five Thousand Seven Hundred and Fifty Words," cited in note 25) seems to have noticed this illuminating Joycean parallel in what has come to be regarded as the greatest of far-future SF novels. Let us not allow such a time to elapse before noting the Mannian parallel in what is no doubt the most ambitious S F novel to date, of futures near or far.

As Bester's novel of 1956 challenges the Joycean precept of privileged aestheticism, so Delany's novel of 1975 challenges the Mannian precept of decadent bourgeois centrality. (Mann's comment on the artist's knowledge of the value of his own work—"I cannot know and you cannot tell me."—is quoted by Newboy in

---

Dhalgren; and the Mannian passion for "the exhaustive" which was, Mann felt, the only thing that could be "truly interesting," is reflected in *Dhalgren* by the whole, massive and intricate text itself.) Mann's hero, the young engineer Hans Castorp, is a socially central naif. Delany's basic precept is that today there is no social center; and Delany's hero is a socially marginal naif, in a world where there are only margins. (Compare Delany's "young engineer," the oddly "Germanic" Tak Loufer—the first person to befriend the Kid when he enters the city—with Mann's: the contrasts between the two are a bouquet of exfoliating ironies.) Society for Delany is merely an interweave of social margins, with various economic privileges—magically invalidated by the novel, but nevertheless leaving their mythic detritus—but none with true social primacy. (Henry Hatfield, in his *Thomas Mann*, New Directions, New York, 1951 revised 1961, p. 40, recounts Trotsky's remark "that the German workers would not seize a railway station unless they had bought tickets first," in relation to Mann's comic description of the ill-fated German-liberal revolt of 1848 in *Buddenbrooks*. Delany's scorpions are far closer to the energized Gully than to Mann's bumbling workers.)

At intriguingly corresponding points in their respective novels, Proust's Mme Verdurin and Delany's Mrs. Richards express the conviction that the much more sophisticated Guermantes, in the one case, and the much more sophisticated Calkins, in the other, no doubt actually pay people to attend their parties. But if Mrs. Richards is a Mme Verdurin, think of how much more drastically, tragically, pathetically she is displaced in her particular illusions of social centrality.

Delany's Kid is a socially marginal naif, but he is streetwise; and his literary education is—as are all educations today, in light of what there is to be known—eccentric. He speaks Portuguese and has read Mallarme in that language. He is a long-time reader of *Poetry* (Chicago) but has never read *The New Yorker*, and he has never heard of iambic pentameter before, and the suggestion is made that trying to write in it may have hopelessly perverted his natural, Olsonian breath-line. Hans Castorp, after his epiphany in the snow, moves on to disillusion and flight from the illusions of Devos. In Delany's book, as we have tried to show in the discussion above, it is both the flight and the disillusion that are posited in themselves as "optically illusory." For the same structure that so playfully challenges the Kermode theory of fictive resolution (q.v. note 35 below) throws down the gauntlet before Mann's privileged bourgeois centrality as Bester threw down his own before Joyce's privileged aestheticism.

We end this note with two comments: first, science fiction has always been ambitious, and if we are not put off by its constant taking on of the problem of Humanity in the Universe, we cannot be too surprised by its taking on *en passant* the ethical (if not the aesthetic) challenges of a Joyce or a Mann—though even this suggests a self-confidence that would leave most modern mundane fictioneers quaking in their boots lest they be found out. That Bester and Delany have signaled their ambition so off-handedly without rippling the surface of their works (by, essentially, a rewritten quatrain and a plot choice in one case and by a mere chapter schema—but not a table of contents—and a line or so of quotation on the other), in what have proved to be two very popular novels, and with signs only readers likely to care are, finally, likely to notice, is itself a sign of

And if *Dhalgren* does borrow the technique of pastiche itself from *Ulysses*' "Oxen of the Sun"—for *Dhalgren* does contain pastiches of Auden, Rilke, and Valéry, as well as an amusingly covert allusion to John Ashbery's early poem "The Instruction Manual" (p. 164)—it does so in such an idiosyncratic way as to put the whole concept of "borrowing the technique of borrowing" (as does Debord's) into its necessarily dubious light.) Some have argued that nothing in *Dhalgren* is resolved. We maintain the specific contrary: practically everything in the book is furnished with at least two possible resolutions, one of which is in the foreground and one of which is in the background, the two always ready to change places at an eye's blink, depending on which way we choose to read Delany's complex Necker cube. "Most of the time," writes Flaubert in another letter, "conclusions seem to me acts of stupidity." One can only go back to the frequently quoted line from Delany's *Einstein Intersection*[36]: "...Endings to be useful must be inconclusive." But

---

the reticence, sensitivity, and intelligence of the field, as well as a sign of the aesthetic self-confidence of the respective writers. Our second point is simply that if those reviewers so miffed by *Dhalgren*'s popularity, such as Malzberg and Ellison, would cease to bandy about "Joyce" as a literary catch-all (that should have been the cry twenty years ago with Bester) and turn their attentions to Mann—whether to praise, denigrate, or merely explain Delany—they would quit the merely rhetorical and approach what is at least documentable.

36. See *The Einstein Intersection* by Samuel R. Delany, Ace Books, New York, 1967, reprinted 1973 (4th printing), page 137. In regard to this point, we note that Delany, in his article "Of Sex, Objects, Signs, Systems, Sales, SF, and Other Things" (q.v. notes 27 & 28), cites as an influence on *Dhalgren* Frank Kermode's excellent study in the theory of fiction *The Sense of an Ending*, Oxford University Press, New York, 1967. (One of Newboy's books of essays is called *A Sense of Commencement*.) In connection with this, let us simply juxtapose a passage from Kermode's study with a passage from *Dhalgren*.

Kermode writes, on page 45, "The clock's tick-tock I take to be a model of what we call 'plot,' an organisation that humanizes time by giving it form.... Tick is a humble genesis, tock a feeble apocalypse." In his journal (p. 710) the Kid observes: "People probably do hear watches go tic-tok. But I'm sure my childhood clock went tic-tic-tic-tic-tic-tic-tic.... Why do I recall this in a city without time?" We may answer the Kid's rhetorical question with Kermode's terminology: Kid recalls this because Bellona is a city (as *Dhalgren* is a novel) of perpetual humble genesis. And inconclusive does not mean unstructured. And the ending(s) of *Dhalgren* are organized into the most dazzling of fictive structures, to preserve even more purely that so necessary inconclusiveness.

The careful reader will note, on second or third reading of *Dhalgren*, that the book contains not two or three of these optical illusions, but dozens. Indeed, to trace out all their interconnections is to realize the novel is constructed of practically nothing else. *Dhalgren* accomplishes the Herculean task of presenting us with a totally coherent foreground which, by the fictive geodesies it establishes throughout the contours of its fictive field, allows not one plane of meaning to hold to any one single level. The task of treating the major problem of modern aesthetics in such a rich and recomplicated mode in the already deprivileged field of science fiction is certainly an impressive undertaking. Symbolically what the concert of *Dhalgren*'s illusions says is that we cannot trust too deeply in any socially privileged certain knowledge.[37] All we may trust are our own readings of

---

Dhalgren's "plot," which substitutes a continuous movement toward rebirth for the sense of closing finality that Kermode cites as one of the basic forms of literary expression, reflects this. Most modern clocks do not go tick-tock. And in Kid's sensibility, or the sensibility projected by the novel, tock is therefore unnecessary. For, as Calkins says, in Bellona "Apocalypse has come and gone... That simply isn't our problem any more." (p. 745).

37. The title "*Dhalgren*"—which so many readers have found baffling—is a symbol for the uncertainty of certain knowledge. It is a symbol for this in no more complicated a way than "A Streetcar Named Desire" is a symbol for human movement toward emotional catastrophe, or than "The Iceman Cometh" is a symbol for the inevitable arrival of death, in the respective works that bear those titles. Upon remembering his own first and middle names (and the first initial of his last one), Kid suddenly experiences certain knowledge of the last name of the newspaper reporter Bill, prompted by the double metonymy, no doubt, that Bill is the nickname associated with William and that William Dhalgren was a name on the list of names that pulled free from the notebook (pp. 782–783). Yet Kid has no logical reason to think he knows. The point is: the name is not mentioned anywhere in the scene. Yet the reader is just as certain in his or her knowledge of what the name in Kid's mind is as the Kid is certain to whom that name belongs—though there is as little logical reason for the reader to know as there is for the Kid. This is another of Delany's most striking optical illusions. What Delany is saying, symbolically, is that "certain knowledge" is really founded on the interaction of random encounter (the list of names, pp. 63, 530, etc.), accidental correspondence of phonemes (the name of the Oregon workman, p. 628), mythical resonances (Grendel/Grendal/Grendhal, p. 679), psychological propinquity (the one name he remembers from the list once it pulls free of

the paradoxes of the world, until we encounter evidence that things are not as we have thought, and our reading drops into the background and a new reading springs to the fore. In our quotidian rounds, all but philosophers (and certain types of madmen) tend to forget what a flimsy mental construct "certainty" is. As Wittgenstein says in the beginning of *On Certainty*, "If you can prove to me that 'Here is one hand,'" referring to a line in G.E. Moore's *A Defence of Common Sense* (a line Delany plays with in Chapter VI of his most recent novel *Triton*, Bantam Books, New York, 1976, p. 268), "I will give you the rest." Knowledge, even knowledge of the laws of logic or the facts of science, is a mode of belief. Belief is always a matter of faith. Faith is a mystical occurrence, whether it be in the existence of God or the existence of the external world. What is mystical is not that we have more evidence for one or the other, but that we are able to constitute whatever evidence we have—for either one—into belief in the first place. Human knowledge has only been able to grow to the staggering proportions it has reached in this century of technological advance because our belief in reality, as Delany's book symbolically suggests, must be like our belief in one reading or the other of the Necker cube: the earth may appear flat, or the scatter pattern through a pinhole may suggest light is made up of particles, but there is evidence waiting just over the horizon, or in the diffraction pattern through a fine mesh grid, for another reading of both phenomena. This symbolic evocation alone, we feel, is enough to judge *Dhalgren* science fiction. (It is certainly epistemological fiction!) And the skill, art, richness and complexity with which the work accomplishes its theme and themes, within its highly articulated structure, renders it science fiction of the highest order.

—Ann Arbor, 1975
[New York, 1975]

---

the notebook and is lost, p. 776), and aesthetically prejudiced expectation (the novel's title). Delany is saying—symbolically—that even this evidence is hugely scattered and only rarely encountered. For this is how we encounter the evidence— whether we choose to draw our conclusions from it merely by intuition, or we try to reconstitute it into the form of a scientific experiment complete with controls— scattered through life as widely as it is through the vast, paradoxical tapestry of *Dhalgren*.

From "The Semiology of Silence," an interview with Samuel R. Delany, included in Silent Interviews
[Wesleyan University Press, 1994][38]

SG: Of course, when your SF novel *Dhalgren* came out you had to deal with a lot of people claiming that you *weren't* writing SF, that you had gone outside the tradition.

SRD: Perhaps when a book sells seven- or eight-hundred thousand copies, the controversy contributes to the acceptance. You might even say the controversy *is* the acceptance—in which case the acceptance of *Dhalgren* was rather small. Most of the American reading public was quite oblivious to any controversy at all among the few thousand or, more likely, few hundred who, in that fanzine or this one, on one SF convention panel or another, expressed their conflicting opinions.

Myself, I never saw any *serious* controversy over whether or not *Dhalgren* was SF. When the idea was put forward at all, it was more in the line of name-calling. You know: "*That's* not science fiction! That's just self-indulgent drivel!" To me it seemed a much more modest argument—between the people who didn't like the book and the people who did. And my impression was that the contention centered mainly on discontinuities in the action and the lack of hard-edged explanation for the basic nonnormal situation… along with the type of people I chose to write about. This last is a point it's polite, today, to gloss over. But at least one academic (of highly liberal if not leftist tendencies, too) told me straight out: "I'm just not interested in the people you write about. I can't believe they're important in the greater scheme of things." What makes this significant is that the vast majority of fan letters the book received—many

38. Questions by Sinda Gregory and Larry McCaffrey. The full interview appears in *Silent Interviews*, pp. 21–58, Middletown: Wesleyan University Press, 1994.

more, by a factor of ten, than any other of my books have ever gotten—were almost all in terms of "...this book is about my friends." "This book is about people I know." "This book is about the world I live in." "This book is about people nobody else writes of...." These letters came from people in schools and people outside of schools. They came from SF fans and from non-SF fans. For these readers, the technical difficulties of the book, the eccentricity of structure, and the density of style went all but unmentioned. After all, if the book makes any social statement, it's that when society pulls the traditional supports out from under us, we all effectively become, not the proletariat, but the *lumpen* proletariat. It says that the complexity of "culture" functioning in a gang of delinquents led by some borderline mental case is no less and no more than that functioning at a middle-class dinner party. Well, there are millions of people in this country who have already experienced precisely this social condition, because for one reason or another their supports at one time or another were actually struck away. For them, *Dhalgren* confirms something they've experienced. It redeems those experiences for them. For them, the book reassures that what they saw was real and meaningful; and they like that. But there are many others who have not had these experiences. Often they are people who during their lives have been threatened by the possibility of their social supports all going, who fought very hard against it, and who have worked mightily to stabilize their lives in such a way that they will never have to endure these real social disasters. Needless to say, these readers do not like the book. For them, it trivializes real problems and presents as acceptable things (and I don't mean sex) they have specifically found unacceptable—and are to be avoided at all costs. But the arguments between those people who disliked the book intensely and those people who liked it exorbitantly helped it to become somewhat more widely known—and, presumably, to reach an even larger audience.

In the world of paperback sales, you know, 700,000 is actually a rather odd number.

The average paperback book still sells under 100,000 copies. To be a bona fide paperback bestseller, you have to get in sight of the solid 2,000,000 mark. So anything between, say, 250,000 and 1,500,000 is in a rather anomalous ballpark—especially if those sales are drawn out, as with *Dhalgren*, over ten years or more now. To appease the commercial anxiety that makes them want to name everything in case they need to sell it to somebody who hasn't seen it yet and doesn't want it, publishers have recently started calling such books "cult successes." So at Bantam I'm known as the author of a "cult" novel.

When you're passing an open door in a publishing company hallway, where people are talking in the offices, "cult" can sound close enough to "occult" so that, I gather, there's some small controversy within the company as to whether I write "cult" or "occult" books. But people who read me don't seem to have that problem. For them I'm still an SF writer. And my books are still SF.

SG: It's hard for me to think of a mainstream book as long and difficult and experimental as *Dhalgren* that has sold 700,000 copies. (I doubt if even *Gravity's Rainbow* has sold that many.) That seems to be another possible advantage to the SF field: An ambitious, serious writer who is interested in formal experimentation (even if this is part of the tradition) may have a greater chance to get his or her book out.

SRD: *Dhalgren* has outsold *Gravity's Rainbow*—by about 100,000 copies: we share a mass market publisher and statistics leak. But *Gravity's Rainbow* is a fantasy about a war most of its readers don't really remember, whereas *Dhalgren* is in fairly pointed dialogue with all the depressed and burned-out areas of America's great cities. To decide if *Gravity's Rainbow* is relevant, you have to spend time in a library—mostly with a lot of *Time/Life* books, which are pretty romanticized to begin with. To see what *Dhalgren* is about, you only have to walk along a mile of your own town's inner city. So *Dhalgren*'s a bit more threatening—and accordingly receives less formal attention.

Sadly, your description of a field of writing open to experimentation and ambition better fits SF when I began publishing in the early '60s than it does today. The period in the late '50s and early '60s known as the paperback revolution created a flood of books—and, with it, a relatively friendly climate for new writers. William Burroughs published his first novel, *Junky*, with Ace Books back in 1953. Those same economic forces probably account for why Vonnegut's books were, indeed, appearing as paperback original SF novels in the '50s and early '60s. Carl ("I'm with you in Rockland") Solomon, of *Howl* fame, worked at Ace as an "idea man." And when, in 1962, Ace became a publication possibility for me, I spent the odd minute smiling over the fact that names like Burroughs and Solomon seemed pretty good writerly company.

The economic crunch crunching through the last decade has left the publishing world far less accepting and more suspicious of the new and the vital than it was when the '60s dream of unlimited affluence and endless experimentation was about. Add to our economic hassles the current "block-buster" mentality that's infected the book business via the movies, as a hysterical response to that crunch, and you have a really nasty situation for any serious writer, in whatever field, trying to break in. And it strikes me as a very different situation from the particular style of endemic commercialism rampant in book publishing since it came under its present book distribution system just after World War II. (Most people are unaware that book distribution companies today are much bigger than book publishing companies. It's an open publisher's secret that the publishing companies work for the distributors, and not the other way around. But most readers can't name one distribution company.) Before, the court of sales was always there, at least as an ideal to talk about, no matter how difficult it was to get your work put before that court. Today, everybody in publishing is pretty well convinced that the court of sales itself has been hopelessly corrupted, by hype and other, nameless pressures, so that an editor who says, "I think there is an audience (however small or however large) that will enjoy this book," is no longer considered to be making a rational statement in business terms. The only statements considered rational in commercial publishing today are those which speak to the questions: "How can it be pushed? How can it be hyped? How can it be made bigger than it is?"—whereas *what* is being pushed is of secondary or even tertiary importance, save to the extent it's got a hot synopsizable angle. Today's publisher would much rather publish a book which, when described in three sentences, sounds catchy than a book which affects its readers so deeply and profoundly that, before speaking of it at all, the reader must pause. The desired book today is the one that prompts its readers to blurt, "Hey, it's about..." and go on with something snappy.

This not only ends up reducing everything to the lowest common denominator; it lowers the denominator itself, driving it constantly down. And in an already shaky capitalism when the quality of what you've got to sell is locked in a downward spiral, that doesn't leave you much to appeal to.

Of course, pulling together such a tenebrium of gloom-clouds is very easy from the Olympian perspective of 40-plus years—and always has been. It's not a bad idea to remember that 25 years ago the paperback revolution itself was seen by many, if not most, establishment critics (Bernard DeVoto's name comes to mind) as the end of Literature with a capital L. Well, it's always surprising how writers—the people actually writing—have managed to articulate something over the range of the writing practices available; even invent new ones if they have to. And those articulations have their own character in each age. The writing practices that were most exciting and vital between 1890 and 1920—say, in the novels of James, Bennett, Conrad, the early Lawrence, and Proust—looked very different from the writing practices that were most vital between 1920 and 1950—say, those of Joyce, Barnes, Woolf, Faulkner, and Ellison. And the writing from 1950 to 1980 looks very different still. Are we going to go on to another change of style, concerns, and structure, in which the realities of contemporary publishing, from computer typesetting to distribution monopolies, play a large if ill-understood part?

Probably.

But I think it would also be a good idea for historically sensitive critics to take a look at how one practice of writing, science fiction, was positively helped by a situation which, at the time, was assumed in most cases to be a moral and aesthetic disaster. It might be instructive in terms of understanding what's to come.

SF benefitted hugely from those early years of the paperback revolution. Joanna Russ, Thomas M. Disch, Ursula K. Le Guin, Roger Zelazny, R.A. Lafferty—the number of markedly exciting SF writers whose careers were strongly shaped by that revolution makes your jaw drop. In 1951, there were only 15 volumes published which, by any stretch of the imagination, could be called SF novels, while last year SF made up approximately 16% of all new fiction published in the US. When, by the mid-'70s, crunch-crunch was undeniable, there still seemed to be some factors built into the geography of our particular SF precinct (or ghetto, if you like) that kept the damages at bay a little longer than in some other fields—primary among them, the vitality and commitment of SF's highly vocal and long-time organized readership, whose most energetic manifestation is the complex and fascinating phenomenon, fandom. But by now, the material hardships have made their inroads even into SF.

A few intriguing details of that history scatter through some of my essays of the last half dozen years.[39] Am I concerned about what's going to happen to this lively field over the next half dozen? Am I ever! But I'm also sure that, though it will be intimately connected with, it will also be markedly different from, what happens to literature.

LM: I heard an anecdote that very early in your career, you self-consciously resisted jumping on the treadmill of quick-writing-for-quick-money that exhausted writers like Philip K. Dick and others. What gave you the nerve to say to the SF publishing establishment, "Look, I'm going to take my time and write a good book—not in six weeks or six months, but in however long it takes me"?

SRD: Anecdotes often reduce the primary reasons for themselves right out of existence—especially when you tell them about yourself. And I think I once wrote about that situation—briefly and anecdotally—in an essay you may have come across. As an anecdote, it sounds very brave and moral; and I'm willing to take a *modest* bow. But the simple fact is: I'm constitutionally incapable of writing quickly. I'm highly dyslexic. That means, among other things, I must write slowly and revise endlessly, if only to get right what are so cavalierly called, by the lexic, the "basic mechanics." With all the time I spend looking for the dropped, misspelled, and transposed words that litter my early drafts, I might as well, while I'm at it, X the odd adjective, apocopate some terminal preposition, clarify a parallelism here, or strengthen an antithesis there. It goes, as they say, with the territory. Any text I write, I'm going to have to stay with a while—longer, anyway, than the lucky talents who whip out journeyman-like first drafts, which, once glanced at by the copy-editor for styling, can be sent on to the typesetter. It behooves me to think about what I'm doing a little more, if only to make sure it's complex enough to hold my interest during the extra time I have to live with it. (An apothegm in the SF community I've heard leveled at a number of our high-

39. Collected as *Starboard Wine* (Dragon Press, Pleasantville, NY, 1984).

production moguls goes: "If he were a worse typist, he'd be a better writer"—meaning that such writers commit stylistic bloopers of the same blatancy as the mechanical ones automatically corrected by simply running the text once more around the platen. I've heard it said of both Harlan Ellison and Barry Malzberg—two dizzyingly talented writers, by the bye.) There've been a number of dyslexic writers, of course: Gustave Flaubert and William Butler Yeats are among the best known. Dyslexic writers tend to be slow and painstaking. The fascination of what's difficult, Yeats wrote, had dried him up and left him old. But for a writer who, like Yeats, didn't really learn to read until he was 16, more things are going to be difficult than most might expect. Such a writer has a push to substitute quality for quantity—which isn't entirely moral. A writer like Joyce, on the other hand, was as lexic as they come. And when he wanted to, he could write like a speed demon. Fully a third of *Ulysses* was written in galleys. That's over 250 of its 765 pages! Even in Paris in the '20s, you had galleys only for a couple of months, at the outside.

I could no more write 250 pages of fully realized fiction in two months—science or otherwise—than I could fly to the Moon flapping. And the more I'd thought about it and the more complicated a structure I'd planned it out to have, the longer it would take me actually to set down.

When I was 23, I wrote a long story in 11 days. The manuscript ran to 130 typescript pages—with wide margins: say, 75 pages of ordinary book type. But that was an endurance test I'd set myself, with mornings given over to first drafting, then, after a non-lunch, the rest of the day and a good bit of the night spent rewriting the previous day's work.

It's still moot whether I passed or not.

But that 11 days doesn't count the two weeks of notes on the early side to plan out a simple fabular structure that eschewed most of the complexities I'd previously (and have since) tried to work into fiction. (You could call it two weeks of testing the water before the plunge.) Nor does it take in yet another week on the far side for another retyping—in which much rewriting got done. As an anecdote, I'd like to say that the story—which was eventually published as a separate book, and has been called a novel—took 11 days. And certainly the hardest non-stop work was crammed into those 11. But I could as easily say that it took me 11 days plus two weeks at the beginning for notes, and a week of rewriting after. Composition times are almost as hard to individuate as propositional meanings.

SG: From early on, your books have explicitly dealt with some very controversial subject matter. Take, for example, your treatment of three-way or multiple sexual relationships, of gay and bisexual relationships (and all sorts of subgroups) in *Triton*, and your general call for the need to explore male and female sexual roles in all their guises. Do you think that working in the SF field has given you more freedom to explore these areas? I'm thinking of the controversy that surrounded, say, Mailer's *American Dream* or Roth's *Portnoy's Complaint*—books that are very mild in their sexual presentation compared with what you are dealing with in *Dhalgren* and *Triton*.

SRD: For a number of reasons, from my racial make-up to my sexuality to my chosen field of writing, SF—or even because, in this society, I've chosen to write at all—my life has always tended to have a large element of marginality to it, at least if you accept a certain range of experience that overlaps those of an ideal white, middle-class, heterosexual male as the definition of centrality. To write clearly, accurately, with knowledge of and respect for the marginal is to *be* controversial—especially if you're honest about the overlaps. Because that means it's harder to regard the marginal as "other." And at that point, the whole category system that has assigned values like central and marginal in the first place is threatened.

As to whether SF is more tolerant of what is usually called the marginal… Well, it would be nice to think that because SF itself has traditionally been considered a kind of marginal writing, it recognizes the problems of life on the edges and welcomes them with insight and compassion. But that may just be a somewhat naïve anthropomorphism.

Basically the idea that a genre, or even an age or epoch, *gives* a freedom (or, indeed, imposes restraints) that any old writer, once he or she plops down in the middle of it, can turn around and exploit wonderfully (or be totally stymied by) is one I've heard before—and distrust.

It's not that I don't believe in history. Rather, I believe the historical process is more complicated than it's sometimes given credit for. The play of social forces lays down constraints (in sexual matters, say) that are internalized by individuals. Because society is not monolithic, these constraints are not necessarily the same for everyone; there may be class patterns, but even that's a reduction. There are going to be lots of variations, even individual to individual—which variations, if you squint at them from other angles, will make other kinds of patterns which aren't going to respect class boundaries at all.

The same play of social forces also lays down constraints for the various practices of writing—what, in practical terms, is generically acceptable, and what isn't.

But writers are not assigned their genres by God. Nor do they really choose them by conscious and considered acts of will. They move into them, even into literature, by a kind of ecological process. All through my adolescence I wrote novel after novel, pitched at the center of the literary tradition as I mistily saw it: you know, out of Hemingway by Faulkner and Joyce, with a good 19th-century underpinning. That was my adolescent reading history, at any rate. I sent them to publisher after publisher, but although they got me a couple of scholarships, and some of my shorter pieces even won me the odd amateur prize, they were all finally rejected.

Then I wrote an SF novel. Actually, it was rather borderline SF. (I had to go through four published SF novels before, in the fifth, I got brave enough to put in a spaceship!) And it was accepted, published, reviewed…!

Now there's a developmental aspect here that must be taken into account. I'm sure the SF novel I wrote at 19 was, indeed, a *little* better than the literary novels I wrote at 16, 17, and 18—though "literary" here is only a polemical distinction. None of them were good books. Still, one does a lot of growing up, fast, in those years, and some of that goes onto the page. But even in my teens, what I was being told by literary editors, some of whom from time to time got rather excited about me, was that the final reason the novels weren't being published was that they were *too* literary—and weren't commercial. Even at 17, I knew some of this was an attempt to make a kid feel a little less crushed by rejection. Nevertheless, with all that taken into account, there's still a bottom-line situation here: Literary publishing wasn't very accepting—they didn't accept me through a *whole* lot of tries—while SF publishing was: They snapped me up on my first submission. And what they accepted was me, with all my socially-laid-down constraints, my limited talent, and my individual concerns, as manifested in what I wrote. And even during my first couple of years in the field, the genre tended to say to me: "You can do what you want."

Now that's not, "Anyone can do anything he or she wants." Rather, that's "The kind of things *you* seem to want to do are more or less within acceptable bounds."

If you look over my first four SF novels, all of which were written during my first three years in the SF field, as I've said you won't find spaceships. What you'll find is characters quoting poetry at each other. There's more than a passing interest in the female characters. Small sections are in play form. Other sections are in stream of consciousness. (The books that followed were, if anything, more technically conservative.) Bits of the story are told from multiple points of view. Once, in my sixth SF novel, written when I was 23, I was told that the printer simply couldn't handle one of the sections; it had to wait for computer typesetting and the most recent edition, in 1983, for the text to be printed as I wrote it back in 1965.

Now none of this is terribly profound as far as experimentation is concerned. The point is only that the SF publishing situation could accept it; my SF editor could say to me, "That's kind of interesting. I wonder what the readers will make of it." And for what it's worth, the books are still in print. And this is a very different situation from the one in which a literary editor in 1960 at Harcourt Brace, who liked an early novel of mine enough to recommend me for a scholarship to the Bread Loaf Writers' Conference, said to me about similar devices in the book I'd submitted: "Well, if we *do* publish it, those are the first things that will have to go in the editing." Then she looked at me, rather sadly, and said: "Chip, you tell a good story. But, right now, there's a housewife somewhere in Nebraska, and we can't publish a first novel here unless there's *something* in it that she can relate to. And the fact is, there's *nothing* in your book that she wants to know anything about at all. And that's probably why we *won't* publish it." And after two more readings and an editorial conference, they didn't.

The housewife in Nebraska has, of course, a male counterpart. In commercial terms, he's only about a third as important as she is. The basic model for the novel reader has traditionally been female since the time of Richardson. But his good opinion is considered far more prestigious. He's a high school English teacher in Montana who hikes for a hobby on weekends and has some military service behind him. He despises the housewife—though reputedly she wants to have an affair with him. Needless to say, there wasn't much in my adolescent "literary" novels for him either. But between them, that Nebraska housewife and that Montana English teacher tyrannized mid-century American fiction.

If you look at the first novels published by literary houses between 1950 and 1965, there's not one that doesn't have something in it for this ubiquitous non-couple.

Good-bye, Columbus, *The Floating Opera*...? Salinger, Heller, Pynchon? That doesn't mean that there weren't other things in their books as well. Some of those were not there for that obsessive pair, and some would quite offend them, were they noticed. The point is, however, that the things that were there for them come quite honestly from those writers. They were not there because Barth or Roth or Updike decided out of controlled, calculated, and manipulative intentions to put them there. These writers moved into the literary field in which they were most comfortable by the same ecological forces that moved me into mine. Writers are not born into the world the day they write their first salable work. There's a history of reading, a history of attempts made and attempts rejected that maneuvers a writer, however random it all seems at the time, into the position at which he or she is accepted; and that's also a position at which she or he *can* be accepted. That individual variation we started off with? The situation I sketched above is the over-determined one by which generic demands are fitted to individual writerly talents. But that individual variation means the fit is *never* perfect; there's still going to be conflict.

I don't know about literary publishing today, but in SF I've always had the wheedling suspicion that when an editor says to a writer, "Your work is too far out for us to handle," there's usually a silent message that goes along with it: "And it's too clumsily written, ill-thought-out, and badly executed to be worth it, because it won't interest those readers with the higher stylistic standards that go along with broader topic interests." I felt this way back at 17 and 18 when my early "literary" novels were being rejected; I suppose I still feel it.

Now to assume that this is how the entire real and social world of art production—or, more accurately, art *re*production—works is, I suppose, finally a personal strategy to make rejection an occasion for initiating a personal attempt at improving what you do, a strategy for keeping rejection from being simply and hopelessly paralyzing. It's very hard to be any sort of artist without some belief to the effect that if the surface is crystalline *enough*, if the aesthetic logic is both vigorous and rigorous *enough*, someone somewhere will *have* to say "Yes" to it. On the other hand, we all know how frightening/baffling/boring the new can be to people who feel that they are guardians of a tradition, any tradition; so that to stand behind such a view too firmly as anything else *but* a personal strategy may be suicidally naïve.

Rejection and acceptance are both complex processes; and the complex truth is that writing must, itself, be complex enough to remain stable in the face of both. Current poststructuralist jargon would probably talk about this complex stability in terms something like: "The struggle between reification and deconstruction that any text worth the name initiates among its endless play of possible meanings. . . ." The older phrase—much less popular right through here—is: "The dialectical nature of art. . . ."

Looking Back at the Autumnal City

by Samuel R. Delany

[published in the *Barnes & Noble Newsletter* on-line, June 2001]

Twenty-seven years ago, *Dhalgren* began life as a paperback original science fiction novel. After nineteen paperback printings, two hardcovers, and a university press edition, this month Vintage Books will bring it out in a trade paperback.

As author, I've been asked to write about what's made the book endure—in a world where current volumes hit the bookstore shelves like flash-paper squares, frequently leaving, a month later, not even an ash trace. A true explanation, I think, must hold open room for a large element of luck—and the parts that are more than luck, the writer is the last to know. Still, from the considerable mail *Dhalgren* netted during its first decade, I recall what readers wrote me. Letter to letter, the repeated theme was: "You're writing about people I actually know, people I just don't see written about in most novels"—often followed by a "Thank you." What I was doing, of course, was writing about people *I* knew.

Not four full months after Pearl Harbor, I was born in New York's largest black neighborhood: boisterous, colorful, crowded Harlem. The 'forties saw World War II close and, by the 'fifties, the Korean War open; and the crowding in the city's ghetto neighborhoods began to displace the color, all efficiency, and—soon—most remnants of civil community. In the summer of 1953, my family moved from Harlem's center to a set of co-op apartments, Morningside Gardens, integrated, liberal, and part of the brave new vision of post-war affluence, just above Columbia University. At the time, we were unaware we were the first wave of what would become a mass exodus, leaving Harlem, along with other black neighborhoods in the city—the South Bronx, Bedford Stuyvesant—broken, devastated, subject to fires, even greater vandalism, and all but deserted.

Twenty years later, when I came to write *Dhalgren*, no matter what catastrophic solar or lunar portents floodlit them now and again, these deserted avenues, those boarded-up and burned-out buildings were my models for the streets and buildings of Bellona, where my long-haired, leather-vested characters walked, ran, or sometimes staggered. As well, the empty halls of the Labrys Apartments were modeled on the echoing hallways of Morningside, which, in their fluorescent lit emptiness, seemed nowhere near as far from the void streets a block or two to the east as they were supposed to be.

If Harlem's devastation had been only a New York City problem, *Dhalgren* might have sold far fewer copies. By the mid-'seventies, however, when the book first appeared, practically every major city in the country—Cincinnati, Los Angeles, Atlanta, Philadelphia...—had developed its own blighted, burned-out inner city, frequently occupying as much as a fourth of the urban area, so that even people who did not live there had still looked at those streets, had driven through them, had skirted them on foot in the evenings, and had experienced a little wonder, if not some awe, as to what they meant for the American dream—or, as it seemed, more and more, for the American dream-world.

I can only assume that my early readers recognized those images—the streets of burned-out Bellona—and drew the correspondences with those streets so close to them in their own cities, though whether it was with relief or anxiety, I wouldn't dare to say. For most people, even the ones with the socio-economic explanations as it what was happening, those streets represented a mystery. In *Dhlagren* they are a mystery too—not the same one, of course. But the story veers toward, and swoops away from, that mystery in a manner that, over its first dozen years in print, readers found interesting enough to carry the book through a million sales.

When *Dhalgren* had been out only a single year, one astute young woman wrote me from Indianapolis: "I just realized, in Bellona—your city that's supposed to be in the center of the country—the exteriors are all New York and the interiors are all San Francisco." I can't argue. Despite the final rewrite in London, San Francisco and New York were the cities I lived in mostly through the initial drafts.

Finally, however, the reasons a book remains in memory are the mystery underyling the simple statement in so many of those letters: "I really liked it..." However mysteries transform into clarity, or insights translate into mystery, if they hold the book in the reader's mind, the writer can only be grateful.

—New York City
April 16, 2001

Sources

In San Francisco during the 1970s, after nearly a year of work on the manuscript of what would become *Dhalgren*, an encounter with John Ashbery's (July 28, 1927, Rochester, New York– September 3, 2017, Hudson, New York) poem "The Instruction Manual" (first collected in *Some Trees*, Yale University Press: New Haven, 1962) resulted in a major restructuring of *Dhalgren*'s material. Delany also cites as influential the Richard Howard essay on Ashbery in Howard's study *Alone with America* (1969)—as well as Michel Foucault's *Madness and Civilization* (Vintage Books: New York, 1973).

Another influence on the novel was G. Spencer-Brown's *Laws of Form*, discussed by Ken James in the next section (**Critical Reactions**), in his essay "Subverted Equations." Delany has also cited Frank Kermode's study *The Sense of an Ending* (Oxford University Press, 1968: see Steiner, "Remarks Toward a Reading of *Dhalgren*," note 17): In *Dhalgren* Delany's critic/poet Earnest Newboy has written a book-length study called *A Sense of Commencement*.

Atheneum 177 $12.95
RICHARD HOWARD
ALONE
SOME TREES
JOHN ASHBERY

The Instruction Manual

by John Ashbery

As I sit looking out of a window of the building
I wish I did not have to write the instruction manual on the uses of a new metal.
I look down into the street and see people, each walking with an inner peace,
And envy them—they are so far away from me!
Not one of them has to worry about getting out this manual on schedule.
And, as my way is, I begin to dream, resting my elbows on the desk and leaning out of the window a little,
Of dim Guadalajara! City of rose-colored flowers!
City I wanted most to see, and most did not see, in Mexico!
But I fancy I see, under the press of having to write the instruction manual,
Your public square, city, with its elaborate little bandstand!
The band is playing *Scheherazade* by Rimsky-Korsakov.
Around stand the flowers girls, handing out rose- and lemon-colored flowers,
Each attractive in her rose-and-blue striped dress (Oh! Such shades of rose and blue),
And nearby is the little white booth where women in green serve you green and yellow fruit.
The couples are parading; everyone is in a holiday mood.
First, leading the parade, is a dapper fellow
Clothed in deep blue. On his head sits a white hat
And he wears a mustache, which had been trimmed for the occasion.
His dear one, his wife, is young and pretty; her shawl is rose, pink, and white.
Her slippers are patent leather, in the American fashion,
And she carries a fan, for she is modest, and does not want the crowd to see her face too often.
But everybody is so busy with his wife or loved one

I doubt they would notice the mustachioed man's wife.
Here come the boys! They are skipping and throwing little things on the sidewalk
Which is made of gray tile. One of them, a little older, has a toothpick in his teeth.
He is silenter than the rest, and affects not to notice the pretty young girls in white.
But his friends notice them, and shout their jeers at the laughing girls.
Yet soon all this will cease, with the deepening of their years,
And love bring each to the parade grounds for another reason.
But I have lost sight of the young fellow with the toothpick.
Wait—there he is—on the other side of the bandstand
Secluded from his friends, in earnest talk with a young girl
Of fourteen or fifteen. I try to hear what they are saying
But it seems they are just mumbling something—shy words of love, probably.
She is slightly taller than he, and looks quietly down into his sincere eyes.
She is wearing white. The breeze ruffles her long fine black hair against her olive cheek.
Obviously she is in love. The boy, the young boy with the toothpick, he is in love too;
His eyes show it. Turning from this couple,
I see there is an intermission in the concert.
The paraders are resting and sipping drinks through straws
(The drinks are dispensed from a large glass crock by a lady in dark blue),
And the musicians mingle among them, in their creamy white uniforms, and talk
About the weather, perhaps, or how their kids are doing at school.

Let us take this opportunity to tiptoe into one of the side streets.
Here you may see one of those white houses with green trim
That are so popular here. Look—I told you!
It is cool and dim inside, but the patio is sunny.
An old woman in gray sits there, fanning herself with a palm leaf fan.
She welcomes us to her patio, and offers us a cooling drink.
"My son is in Mexico City," she says. "He would welcome you too
If he were here. But his job is with a bank there.

Look, here is a photograph of him."
And a dark-skinned lad with pearly teeth grins out at us from the worn leather frame.
We thank her for her hospitality, for it is getting late
And we must catch a view of the city, before we leave, from a good high place.
The church tower will do—the faded pink one, there against the fierce blue of the sky. Slowly we enter.
The caretaker, an old man dressed in brown and gray, asks us how long we have been in the city, and how we like it here.
His daughter is scrubbing the steps—she nods to us as we pass into the tower.
Soon we have reached the top, and the whole network of the city extends before us.
There is the rich quarter, with its houses of pink and white, and its crumbling, leafy terraces.
There is the poorer quarter, its homes a deep blue.
There is the market, where men are selling hats and swatting flies
And there is the public library, painted several shades of pale green and beige.
Look! There is the square we just came from, with the promenaders.
There are fewer of them, now that the heat of the day has increased,
But the young boy and girl still lurk in the shadows of the bandstand.
And there is the home of the little old lady—
She is still sitting in the patio, fanning herself.
How limited, but how complete withal, has been our experience of Guadalajara!
We have seen young love, married love, and the love of an aged mother for her son.
We have heard the music, tasted the drinks, and looked at colored houses.
What more is there to do, except stay? And that we cannot do.
And as a last breeze freshens the top of the weathered old tower, I turn my gaze
Back to the instruction manual which has made me dream of Guadalajara.

Critical Reactions

The first piece here, by the young novelist Jean Marc Gawron, initially appeared as the introduction to the novel when, in 1977, *Dhalgren* was reprinted by the Gregg Press in a hardcover library edition. The piece was also included in the James Sallis 1996 volume *Ash of Stars*. The Gregg Press version played metafictively with the fact that it appeared in the beginning of an actual edition of the book. The Mississippi Press edited out much of that playfulness for *Ash of Stars*. This is the Gregg Press version.

Mary K. Brey's synoptic overview of *Dhalgren*, "Rites of Reversal: Double Consciousness in Delany's *Dhalgren*," first appeared in the *Black American Literature Forum* (Vol 18, No. 2, Summer 1984).

The subsequent two pieces, by Fox and James, first appeared in *Ash of Stars: On the Writing of Samuel R. Delany*, edited by James Sallis (University Press of Mississippi, Jackson, 1996).

The final piece in this section, Steven Shaviro's "Amnesia," appeared as an online review in the 1990s that synopsizes much of *Dhalgren*'s story.

dhalgren

samuel r. delany

Foreword by William Gibson

"*Dhalgren*'s the secret masterpiece, the city-book-labyrinth that has swallowed astonished readers alive for almost 30 years. Its beauty and force still seem to be growing."
—Jonathan Lethem

Amnesia

by Steven Shaviro

The protagonist of Samuel Delany's 1974 novel *Dhalgren* remembers everything, except for his own name. His experiences are rich and varied; only a name is missing, a self to refer them to. In the course of the novel's 879 pages,[40] he is variously called Kid, the Kid, and Kidd. But there's really no right way to name him. His identity is dispersed, in space and in time. For instance, he says he is 27 years old; but he looks a lot younger, and a count from the year of his birth makes him out to be much older. All these versions coexist; none by itself is the correct one. There's no common measure for the events recounted in the book, no focal point at which they might converge. "It is not that I have no past," Kidd muses at one point. "Rather, it continually fragments on the terrible and vivid ephemera of now." Time is shattered, as in a kaleidoscope. Without a center to ground the flux, it's impossible to distinguish past from present, or memory from premonition, or actuality from dream. There's always an odd sense of déjà vu. Each new scene Kidd comes across seems vaguely familiar, as if he had encountered it before. He even finds a notebook in which portions of his story are written before they have happened. The novel's last, incomplete phrase—"I have come to"—almost loops back to its opening line—"to wound the autumnal city." But if you try to read the book as a closed circle, the stutter of the repeated word "to" will throw you off course. There's a glitch in the process of repetition. The details are subtly different each time. Things return, but they are changed by the very

40. In its initial Bantam Books edition, NYC: 1975. Among the things Professor Shaviro does not mention in his synopsis is that the Kid was fathered by a "Georgia cracker," who worked for the Air Force, and his mother was a Native American. This puts the Kid in a racially ambiguous relation to both the black and white characters who people the novel. His eccentric education includes a scholarship to Columbia University in New York, where he took no degree, and a vagrant history that has at least once taken him across the country's southern border and back, before a stretch in an unnamed mental hospital.

fact of returning. Just as time is skewed, and no longer linear, so space is no longer homogeneous. The city of Bellona has been altered in a strange cataclysm. The familiar laws of physics don't entirely hold. You can't quite be sure of distance and direction. Fires break out at random, and burn inconsumably. Buildings twist and collapse. The dense fog almost never clears; smoke and debris are everywhere. The city is largely depopulated. The few remaining inhabitants scavenge in the rubble. They make a living out of waste and ruin. There are always more abandoned supermarkets to plunder, always more empty apartments in which to squat. The destruction is never-ending, but it is also never total. Even after the apocalypse, life goes on. The activity is as frantic as it is pointless. Neurotic white people hold dinner parties and pretend to go to work, striving to maintain a facade of bourgeois normalcy. Multiracial gangs roam the streets, disputing empty turf. Cliques and factions rapidly form, and just as rapidly dissolve. Earnest social workers make their rounds. A psychiatrist keeps office hours. There's a daily newspaper, a bar with drag shows, and a church with regular services. But none of these activities has any point to it; none can be done for a profit. The principle of scarcity doesn't apply. Either what you want is there for the taking, or else it can't be found at all. In both cases, money has no use. The city's economy produces no tangible goods. Its one medium of exchange is gossip. Everyone knows about everyone else's business. The tiniest details undergo intense scrutiny. Why does Kidd wear a sandal on one foot, but leave the other foot bare? Why are those fingernails chewed down to the root so sexy? Who slept with whom last night, and in what odd configurations? Who got beaten up by whom? How is it that the fog for once parted, and an immense, bloated sun glared for hours in the sky? Such events defy interpretation. They are wholly gratuitous signs. They cannot be ascribed to any one particular cause. They don't mean anything in themselves, but they provide endless matter for speculation. They are seen as portents, and they give rise to stories. Power flows from them, as they circulate around town. Kidd becomes a prestigious figure in Bellona, through no particular merit of his own. Really, he just drifts passively through it all. But as the gossip flows, he finds himself acclaimed as a poet, credited with enormous sexual magnetism, recognized as the leader of a gang. His amnesia is his one great asset. For it frees him from the burden of goals and expectations. What good is a proper name, when you're stranded at the exhausted end of time? All enterprise is futile. Tomorrow will be no different from today. Time cannot be used productively; it can only be wasted. *Dhalgren* is a huge, beautiful paean to wasting time. There's nothing left to do, except fuck, fight, and party.

An "Introduction"

by Jean Mark Gawron

[from the Gregg Press Library Edition of *Dhalgren*, Gregg Press, A Division of G.K. Hall, Boston, 1977.]

On the brown desk in the brown-paneled study in which I am sitting, there is a hexagonal container composed of six trapezoidal compartments surrounding a seventh hexagonal. Each compartment is covered by a padded flap embossed with a word or words in gold letters. The words on the six outer flaps are *clips, rubber bands, stamps, coins, matches,* and *keys*. Under *clips* there are two lengths of plastic left over from a package of nylons, a price tag for $9.44, a curtain hook, a mysterious blue pill, a safety pin, and two screws; under *rubber bands*, washers, a suspender clip, a molly nut, and a tie pin; under *stamps*, two cuff links and a tie clip; under *coins*, screws, a button, and, at last, a paper clip; under *matches*, a discarded electric shaver head, some nails, a hat pin, and a rubber band; under *keys*, several blocks of staples and a fistful of paper clips.

The central compartment bears the trademark of the drug company that manufactured this container for promotional purposes. It is empty, but there is a funny groove and a hole in the plastic, apparently left from a time when the container served as an ashtray.

One aspect of this container that may immediately strike readers of *Dhalgren*, even before they lift the flap to find its purpose, is its playful juggling of expectation, the manner in which it creates a growing sense of pattern which, ultimately, is never realized. The patterns, of course, are there to be found, but we began by looking for them in the wrong place. A second time round the hexagon will change the game drastically, and will reveal more about what is outside the container than what is inside.

Another reader, cognizant of *Dhalgren*'s intense concern with language, might observe what a neat linguistic illustration the container makes, demonstrating what is known as the inmixing of the signified, the way meaning smudges, metonymically distributing throughout the surrounding structure, and changing its very nature. One might, of course, expand to a dodecagon, adding compartments for buttons, pills, electric shaver heads and so on. But the completion of such a container is a hopeless cause. The compartments are close together and easily accessible to one another. There must always be more things than compartments, or we would have to turn matters around and begin assigning compartments to things. In order for it to function, the actual organization of the container will have to be far more flexible than its labeling.

In any case, whatever speculations readers make regarding the nature of the above container, they will doubtless be influenced by the label heading this text, "Introduction," and by the label on the outside of this volume, *Dhalgren*. Such expectation is essential if containers are to exist at all, and cements knowledge together. The next time I hunt for a paper clip, I will immediately know which compartment *not* to look in.

But, in an introduction to a work that is really about the mechanics of expectation, let me shy from the expected topic a little longer and address myself to the curious objects which sometimes are and sometimes are not found *in* the container: clips, rubber bands, stamps, coins, matches, and keys. A little reflection will show that they are all mechanisms, of one kind or another, for making specific correspondences in the world, for imposing order. Stamps calibrate a certain payment with a certain service. Coins sharpen the contours of value so that they will exactly match—after myriad arcane transformations—those of production. Rubber bands and paper clips keep the right sorts of things together; keys keep the right sorts of people and the right sorts of things together. Matches package fire, a prime commodity, into discrete quanta. Each of these tiny artifacts may be called an instrument of order.

But the paper clip found while hunting a cigarette invariably recalls the time ransacking the den turned up only loose credit card invoices. These objects are subject to the same mechanics of muddle as everything else, perhaps more so because of the precision demanded of them. The fact that they dispense order makes their muddle the more memorable; that muddle may even launch us on an examination of the nature of order. Note that the container we began by considering is an instrument for ordering the instruments of order. The fact that such a container exists at all shows how quickly the instruments of order become the emblems of disorder.

In *Dhalgren*, in what is really a very similar process, the emblems of disorder are made instruments of order. The chaotic landscape of Bellona, with its leather queens, quasibikers, ex-pimps, hustlers, drifters, and deserters, all embroiled in the occasional Apocalypse, is the scene of a powerful ordering force that shapes the minds and actions of its inhabitants. As Tak tells Jack, the latest of many newcomers he introduces to Bellona: "It's a strange place, maybe stranger than any you've ever been. But it still has its rules. You just have to find them out" (p. 87). The emblems of disorder are as subject to the forces of organization as any emblems, and may become, as leather freak Tak does with this assertion, an instrument of order.

The container for this process, the novel itself, sometimes ordering, sometimes assigning emblems, is the instrument for ordering such emblems. Ultimately, like our real-world container, it proves subject to the same forces it wields.

Order, of course, is a function of the grid we put to it, of expecting to see certain things in certain boxes. Being entirely a creature of thought, it is fair game for the dialectical games we have been playing. On the social plane, as well as on the "absolute" plain of the technical, the very specification of the emblems of disorder is a powerful ordering act. Because the Pope excommunicated Michael Cerularius in 1054, the Orthodox Schism was created and the Church redefined. Because we have specified randomness, computers call up random numbers by rigorous laws. We develop sets of expectation for order and disorder alike, and there is no procedure for determining either set the more complex.

Let us begin, then, with expectation, the binding force of the grid. When we expect, we work within a field of relative probabilities; some things seem more likely than others. As we open to *Dhalgren*'s first page, we do not begin with an empty field. We have, at the very least, the trained fictional expectations of those who have read novels before, perhaps of those who have read science fiction novels. We have the title, perhaps some hearsay knowledge of the work, perhaps a familiarity with Delany's previous books; in the paperback edition we have the cover and the cover matter (both are elegant and misleading); in this edition we have this introduction.

Traditionally, the basic thrust of the novel has not been towards order. What is desirable is the improbable, the incongruous, the unexpected, because that gives the most information in the shortest space. But at the same time it is necessary to establish a rich field of events in which expectation can flourish, so that the *conditions* for surprise are there.

From the first word, *Dhalgren* plays off against that initial set of expectations we bring to any reading. It begins mid-paragraph, mid-sentence, marked off by no indentation, and no upper-case letter: "to wound the autumnal city." Many will instantly suspect an experimental work, and a reading of the next two paragraphs will seem to uphold that suspicion. To some, such a beginning will instantly suggest circularity; a quick flip to the last page will again result in confirmation. It is curious that all these expectations are structural. In place of the usual fictive signals of setting, voice, or situation, we have certain structural signs that bid us be wary of the purely fictive. Throughout the novel to follow, signals that *seem* fictive, and seem to be further elaborations on the fictive world, will prove to be structural, elaborating only on the fiction. This does not reduce Bellona to a series of empty compartments. In fact we are given an enormous amount of information about the city, and that particular kind of information, the textural, the language of color and smell and feel, we will learn to trust.

The second paragraph of *Dhalgren* is also one line long and moves towards grammatical completeness: "So howled out for the world to give him a name." We have a sentence fragment with a third person dative which will not be given true rhetorical direction until we fix its missing subject. "I," "he," or "she" howled? Or even "you"? The bulk of the novel that follows tends to make us supply the masculine third person, but before backreading we have only the dative pronoun for our orientation, a suspended "him," both nameless and sourceless, a being-there with little more than tense and grammatical position.

The third paragraph, beginning with the intriguing line, "All you know I know"—adding a suspended second and first person to our already suspended third (first, second, and third, a discord)—follows with a series of scattered sensory impressions. The sense of a single, dominating identity emerges. The "you" resolves into the general you of informal prose, the "I" into the thinking I of récit.

We are further reassured in the fourth paragraph when, on the pick-up note of "a full minute" we move into more or less standard, heavily foregrounded prose. We are definitely in the third person now. A man and woman meet, make love, talk. He does not know his name. Lulled, we may begin to forget our early warnings.

That the protagonist does not know his name is a fact we may look at as our first textual surprise (if we have skipped reading the cover flap of the paperback edition), at least in the sense that it gives us more information than the conventional fact it replaces. (To know that our hero's name is Marcel tells us less, fictively speaking, than to know he has no name at all.) The motivating force of the novel, and of information in general, is that a surprising datum correspondingly narrows the field of expectation with its informative impact, thus increasing the chance for further surprises.

Our next surprise is a straight-out foray into magic heavily laced with myth. The woman of this first sequence goes hamadryad and turns into a tree. The mysterious yet relatively mundane tone of her encounter with our protagonist is shattered, and we are now prepared to weight the incidents that follow with all the significance that accrues to details in a myth. The shadows of madman and god have fallen across our nameless drifter. He enters a city in the aftermath of a disaster as nameless as he is, hazy, aflame, largely abandoned.

We have begun by now to develop a whole matrix of what and what not to expect: this book is about a nameless drifter who enters a strange city seeking his name. After a number of events of great import (enough to fill all the pages we have in hand), perhaps he finds it.

In fact these expectations are met; and in fact most (if not all) of the expectations raised in *Dhalgren* are met, as long as they are put in the form: more information about X. Yet somewhere along the line, for some readers, at least for many of *Dhalgren*'s reviewers, something in the game goes wrong. The general analysis goes something like: there are too many disordering events. The field of expectation is thrown open so far that there can be no more surprises. The game stops.

It is worth pausing a moment in our consideration of expectation to take note of some of the real-world expectations *Dhalgren* has confounded. For a novel so obviously ambitious and difficult, one carrying about it the "taint" of the experimental, for a science fiction paperback published with little fanfare, which opened to a storm of critical displeasure, *Dhalgren* has done astoundingly well in the marketplace, selling upwards of half a million copies in its first two years of existence, still far short of the hallowed land of the best seller, but enough to fall comfortably within the ranks of the top ten bestselling science fiction novels of all time. Why?

And here we have blundered near one of those mysteries which completely transcends our container, like the drug company trademark.

Because, obviously, people liked it. As to why they liked it, those reasons were doubtless as multifaceted and various as the novel is rich. As to why so many critics should speak so vituperatively against the book (and, in all fairness, there were a number of favorable critical reactions as well), that is equally a mystery. If we were, however, to hazard a guess, it might be: because they knew what they were looking for. Most of *Dhalgren*'s bad press has come from within the science fiction world (and again, there *were* highly favorable reactions), both fan and professional; and much of its audience, to judge by its unusual numbers, has been drawn from outside that world. It may simply be a question of certain fixed expectations not being met.

Let us return to the game with which we began this essay. Someone only interested in finding clips under clips and stamps under *stamps* could only be frustrated once they reached the sixth flap. They would know in advance that, underneath, there were not keys. Even if the slim hope of finding a key were rewarded, the response would have to be: "so what's wrong with the other five?" Our hypothetical spoilsport takes all signals as signals about the container. He sees it as utterly cut off from the world around it, and believes that if the labels are not "true" labels, then they are superfluous.

We alluded above to the central flap, which bears the trademark of the drug company that made the container. Obviously the nature of the relation between the word on the flap and what is inside (always problematic) has radically changed. The drug company trademark is the emblem of a vast and essentially unfixable world beyond the bounds of our immediate evidence. Much as the trademark "explained" the box itself, so the world "explains" the trademark. This explanatory outside world, completely beyond the bounds of any experience we may apprehend, is a concept every bit as abstract as Berkeley's God, who integrates the scattered illusions of individual perception as the underlying consciousness of the world. The world, as an explanation for things in general, has in its turn demanded explanations of the most intricate sort from philosophy. The central compartment, then, is the compartment of explanation; it is empty. Its position in the container is far more important than anything that may be found inside it. Syntax outweighs semantics. Our clearest emblem of this sort of naming in *Dhalgren* is the title, but we shall postpone consideration of that until the very end of this essay. For the moment let us simply note that, in a reading of *Dhalgren* as in our reading of the container, the positions of things in the network may be far more important than what they are.

There is, of course, another point to the parable. All our considerations of the container have taught us about what we have come to expect of containers. Likewise, *Dhalgren* teaches us about what we expect of novels.

Dhalgren is, first of all, a self-referent work. Traditionally, self-referent works have essayed some sort of commentary on their own form. André Gide's *The Counterfeiters*, in which Edouard is writing a novel entitled *The Counterfeiters*, ends with a journal just as *Dhalgren* does—ends, in fact, with three journals, Edouard's, Gide's and Lafcadio's (Lafcadio being a character from another novel entirely). Gide's is an author's journal which openly discusses problems of fiction. So does *Dhalgren*'s journal, but its imbedding in the text is of a completely different nature from that of Gide's journal, and, if we are to heed our own warning about position and syntax, we must examine that imbedding for new properties.

To begin with, the authorship of the notebook is ambiguous. Shortly after our drifter's arrival in Bellona, a notebook, many of its pages already written in, is found and given to him. In some ways this notebook resembles Edouard's novel more than Gide's journal, for it is the most openly self-referent of the texts in *Dhalgren* (the others being the drifter's poetry, which we never see, and *The Bellona Times*); the opening of the novel is transplanted into this notebook in the first passage we read from it: "to wound the autumnal city." (p. 32) (But the notebook soon diverges from the text as we know it.) It is tempting, in a novel by the same man who wrought the author's journal of *The Einstein Intersection*, to read this notebook as the author's, somehow dropped, through the magic of Bellona, into the text of the novel itself, to read the passage just alluded to as a first draft. This notion may persist with us for six chapters; by the seventh, when the notebook has moved into the foreground and become the text, it becomes apparent that the relation between notebook and novel is far more complex (and we shall later examine that relation). Yet it is certainly suggested, regardless who wrote it, that the notebook reflects many of the concerns of the novel at hand:

> Poetry, fiction, drama—I am interested in the arts of incident only so far as fiction touches life; oh no, not in any vulgar, autobiographical sense, rather at the level of the most crystalline correspondence. (p. 360)

And because this is a statement not only about the novel we are reading, but also in it, we may conclude that one of *Dhalgren*'s subjects is the relation of fiction to reality.

Yet *Dhalgren* is more than a self-referent work. It is a self-conscious work as well; the fictive structuring forces may, from time to time, be perceived as such by the characters:

> "Then be glad you're not a character scrawled in the margins of somebody else's lost notebook." (p. 5)
>
> My life here more and more resembles a book whose opening chapters, whose title even, suggests mysteries to be resolved only at closing. But as one reads along, one becomes more and more suspicious that the author has lost the thread of his argument, that the questions will never be resolved, or, more upsetting, that the positions of the characters will have so changed by the book's end, that the answers to the initial questions will have become trivial. (pp. 755–56)

This last is a straightforward capsuling of *Dhalgren*; one reason some readers may have been unhappy with the book is that, for them, those initial questions never became trivial, either because they never read far enough for the necessary shift of perspective to take effect, or simply because they ignored that shift, preferring to focus on matters which grew smaller and smaller in the Bellonean glass, their positions in the network radically changed.

In this self-conscious mode, we may read the "you's" at the beginning and ending of the novel as, respectively, author and character:

> I want to know but I can't see are you up there. (p. 801)
>
> All you know I know. (p. 1)

And the “I’s” are, respectively, character and author. There is the suggestion of another confrontation between the two in the Emboriky department store much later, or earlier, when the protagonist (by then named Kid) looks into a mirror and sees a complete stranger (p. 338). Further on, we read in the journal:

> “Consider: If an author, passing a mirror, were to see one day not himself but some character of his invention, though he might be surprised, might even question his sanity, he would still have something by which to relate. But suppose, passing on the inside, the character should glance at his mirror and see, not himself, but the author, a complete stranger, staring in at him, to whom he has no relation at all, what is this poor creature left…?” (p. 360)

“All you know I know,” then, as a vertical statement, may only move downwards, from author to character; the character is constrained to a pitiful, “I want to know.” The task of the novel is to effect this epistemological transfer from author to character. He begins a drifter with no purpose and no name, his face too young for his years, his years, in any case, frozen like those of a character in a novel: “Well, if you were born in nineteen forty-eight, you’ve got to be older than twenty-seven” (p. 5). The text we read gives him movement, purpose, name, informs him as it informs us.

Dhalgren is a coming to consciousness, an exploration of the constitution of knowledge. “I have come to,” (p. 801) the novel ends—“coming to” signalling consciousness regained—“to wound the autumnal city.” (p. 1) It is this act of consciousness, the constitution of the text we read, that effects Bellona’s apocalyptic limbo.

And what of Bellona? Before coming to grips with the structural problems of *Dhalgren*, we must encounter its texture. Thus far we have spoken only of the novel’s dispositions, its beginning and ending, its edges. What of the inside, the city coextensive with its book, this city of words, Bellona?

It is easy to see how *Dhalgren* could have been made a far more conventional science fiction novel (and we shall presently argue that it is science fiction). With only a few alterations here and there, a panel of lights, a constellation out of whack, a paragraph placed in the mouth of a passing physicist, Bellona could have been made the center of some bizarre dimensional warp. With perhaps a few more changes, it could have been set in a depopulated future, its visitors flocking from a more conventional part of the landscape. Instead it is left to coruscate weirdly in our own 1970s America, in the perilous immanent present, where it becomes deniable (no such thing is likely to happen) and immanently dated. One reason, of course, is inherent in *Dhalgren*'s self-consciousness. The "cause" of Bellona's predicament is that it is in a novel, and novels, ultimately, mine their material from the eras in which they are written (even a historical novel is bound to the latest histories). They are cut off from the "real" present the way Bellona is cut off from the world. As our "real" world ages, Bellona becomes more and more impossible, if only because of that "nineteen forty-eight" line cited above, which locates the characters, and Bellona, within a lifetime of that date. This positioning in the real world does not invalidate *Dhalgren* as science fiction (which, after all, is dated all the time and still remains science fiction), but does lend it a different sort of fictional suspension from that of most science fiction, or that of most fiction, period.

Each miracle in such a Bellona demands a corresponding miracle in our outside world. The modern day megalithic republic is a vast organism which would inevitably mobilize powerful defensive mechanisms should some part manifest as great a disorder as Bellona's. These mechanisms are briefly alluded to in *Dhalgren* (there was at one time television coverage; there were at one point National Guardsmen), but are quickly allowed to fade away. This is plainly miraculous. A real life Bellona would be proscribed, investigated, destroyed. It would never be ignored. Bellona's miraculous inevidence to the outside is no more unbelievable than much of its inside, but it is significant that the fictional suspension must cover our real world entirely, that *Dhalgren* is a science fiction novel literally set now. The net result is to shade every event in Bellona with doubt. As long as there is some chance of error in the report, some hint of refraction in the seeing, some whiff of swamp gas, some hint of translucence, then what we call the real world is still the real world. After two moons have shown up one night in Bellona's cloudy sky we read, in the *Bellona Times*:

> "...any 'agreement,' 'certainty,' or 'definiteness' about these moons are cast into serious doubt—unless we are prepared to make even more preposterous speculations about the rest of the cosmos?" (p. 118)

Thus Bellona remains in the most delicate of fictive suspensions, a bubble, already fragile because it is fiction, then set to quivering with doubt. We have already suggested a model with similar properties; this is the "world" to which we were led through the central compartment of our container, at once explanatory and emblematic of the inexplicable. Just as the unfixed, abstract "world" of everyday speech is a fiction which may, in fact, be incoherent by the usual laws, so is Bellona, to its inhabitants, intractable to any logical laws, a fiction on which they suspend judgement, a "world" in itself. The only difference is that Bellona is something they immediately experience. For Calkins, writing in *The Bellona Times* above, the moorings of the immediate city have had to be loosened so that "the rest of the cosmos," the world outside Bellona, may remain fixed. For Calkins Bellona is a fiction of that cosmos. For us, who must, as we have argued above, regard that cosmos dubiously, it is a fiction of a fiction. And if that cosmos is, literally, a "world," a fiction of the fictional entities outside Bellona, then Bellona is a fiction twice removed, removed entirely through our efforts to keep other fictions intact.

Dhalgren is a novel that deals with the relationship of fiction to reality —one of Chinese boxes. Truth, as Calkins realizes, is a function of a given system. We call certain things false because we want others to remain true. It will become apparent in our exploration of *Dhalgren* that all the phenomena of Bellona cannot be encompassed in a single system, that there must be different fictive levels, fictions within fictions without end, a construction reminiscent of Gide's two mirrors effecting their mise-en- abyme, but with the added complication that our real world, and not just the novel, also consists of such mirrors.

In a rare breach of his usual reticence concerning his work, Delany has written:

> "Anyone who finds it helpful may approach *Dhalgren*... as (and in) an attempt to explore and respond to the deep structure (to use a deceptively topical phrase)

> of the language of human signs. It tries to focus on the deep structure of that language by dramatic stripping of these signs' surface coherence."

We must not, of course, be too trusting of this declaration. In the pages to follow, the poet Ernest Newboy eloquently outlines the enigmatic nature of the artist's relation to his or her work. The easy equations authors give us for their books often bear only the most fragmentary relations to the long process of creation or the finished product itself. "One does not finish a work of art, one abandons it," Valéry tells us. There is a world of anxiety connected with this abandonment. Nevertheless, this suggestion, however suspect its source, provides an interesting prospect from which to launch another consideration of Bellona.

Deep structure, then, may provisionally define the relationship of Bellona's signs to those of the real world, and explain why that relation is not a linear one. Deep structures in linguistics provide a new grid on which to map sentences, hopefully the same grid which generates them. The classic examples:

John is easy to please.

John is eager to please.

Here we have two sentences whose surface structures are perfectly identical, which, because their meanings are so different, must go through entirely different mental processes to be interpreted. Representations of these processes are called kernel structures.

The sign relationships of Bellona, then, may be seen as transformations of sign relationships in our real world. Because these transformations operate within a different grid, their final configurations may first be perceived as chaotic, particularly when applied, as Delany has applied them here, to real world emblems of disorder. Just as the kernel structure of a simple sentence will be incomprehensible without the proper coaching, so will Bellona's signs seem confused if not read by its special laws. This is why Kid, in his first introduction to those laws, is beaten up outside Calkins' estate. Entering a city in which all the traditional boundaries of privilege and property are inevident, he has yet to learn that, nevertheless, such boundaries do exist; they have merely changed form radically.

Having said the words "deep structure," however, we are not obliged to assume that Delany has penetrated to the core of human experience.

Willard Van Orman Quine, in his essay, "Methodological Reflections of Current Linguistic Theory," makes the useful distinction between fitting and guiding grammars, pointing out that we may have two sets of rules, both accounting for every sentence in the language, only one of which is actually used by speakers to guide their speech. Quine goes on seriously to question whether there can be such a thing as a guiding grammar in the Chomskyan sense. We shall echo Quine's note of caution in our consideration of whatever deep structures *Dhalgren* may reveal, and acknowledge the grammar that exhibits them only as fitting. (Some may object here that the very term "deep structure" implies some preexistent truth which has been uncovered; this is undoubtedly so, but we shall take the deep structures as belonging, not to the sentence under consideration, but to the grammar we are employing to consider it; the "truth," then, is entirely grammatical.) Whether or not they actually reflect the generation of social surfaces, such kernel structures are bound to illuminate new relationships in the surfaces themselves. They may also highlight differences analogous to those between "easy to please" and "eager to please," or the similarities in the relations of sentence parts in active and passive voice—comparisons that may be far less apparent on the social plane, where sign and sense are by nature far less distinct.

The mechanisms for such transformations in Bellona are evidently tied up in that peculiar illusionary quality that we have already noted. With no fixed reality, there are no fixed entities arbitrarily defined as signs. All relations become associative as the laws of the signified become dominant; things are freed to mix in the endless alchemy of metonymy and name. Let us examine some of these names, and their associations, within the informing field of Bellona.

The city has somewhere near a thousand inhabitants who, by and large, have taken up lodging in whatever abandoned homes they find convenient. There is a largely black band of outcasts and lowlifes called the Scorpions, led jointly by a black woman named Dragon Lady and a white ex-pimp named Nightmare. When Kid joins, Nightmare willingly concedes him his position and moves to Dragon Lady's Nest. The traditional black ghetto area, Jackson, still houses a relatively large population of blacks, and the roughest section, Cumberland Park, is the home of both Dragon Lady's nest and a large group of blacks who have rallied round George, Bellona's resident folk-hero/demi-god. In the city's spacious park, under the leadership of an earnest organizer named John, a number of more wholesome, sixties-vintage freebooters have banded into a commune which forever embarks on long, never-to-be-finished, work projects. The social center of Bellona is Teddy's, a leather bar through which every visitor to Bellona must at some time pass. Teddy's is owned by an Eastern Aristocrat manqué named Roger Calkins, who continues to publish the city newspaper (authoring, as we have noted, some its articles) and lives on a sprawling estate up on Brisbain Avenue.

Calkins is the nearest thing Bellona has to a central government, but he has relatively little direct influence on the lives of its inhabitants. He remains behind the scenes except for a single dialogue with Kid in the last chapter which, even then, is conducted from behind the screen of a confessional. By means of his newspaper, his bar, and his parties, he is, to some extent, able to concentrate the attention of Bellona where he wishes (and this seems at least partly the reason for his retiring presence, for he seems not to wish to draw that attention to himself). His role is somewhat that of a lighting man, a not inconsiderable power in this city of illusion; he is Bellona's social artist.

Both Kid the poet and Calkins the politician wonder, at different times, whether one must be a good man to pursue their respective paths with any real success. The question is, of course, unanswerable, and though it would be unanswerable in any world, its suggestion of a correspondence between Kid's and Calkins's roles is particularly resonant in the compressed world of Bellona. Here, with all social constraints and conscriptions dissolved (there are no immediate pressures making people do things, no state to serve), politics and art are equally a set of conventions and a game. The politics of any artistic endeavor and the aesthetics of any political act are signs of the same order. Indeed, this is probably the single aspect of the Bellonean condition that most deeply distresses Kid. His political roles of Scorpion and hero become obstacles to his work as an artist. At Calkins' party, and particularly during his interview with Bill, we glimpse the enormous distortion his other roles wreak on Kid the artist:

> "Do your friends in the nest like your book?"
>
> "I don't think most of the guys read too much."
>
> "Hey, man!" Nightmare called out. "I ain't even in his fuckin' nest and I read every fuckin' one!" Which

> caused someone else to call: "Yeah, they're great! The kid writes great," and someone else: "Sure, ain't you got this party for him?" (p. 639)

Clearly, there is no way that anyone in Bellona can read his book of poems purely as "poetry," even, considering the vast associative matrix through which art may escape being itself, if they could be written that way.

We may occasionally view the drawing on the cave wall as a unified exercise in art, religion, and politics, but in fact art as such does not yet exist. To add all three as we know them gives us a quantity quite different from what we began considering, a drawing associated with a specific complex of responses in the cave dwellers who view it. It would be difficult to sift out from that complex any one response that we could safely call aesthetic, religious, or political. The parallel here is that Bellona, because of its smallness, because of its distortive nature, tends to blur and sometimes to eliminate the distinctions between the political, religious, and aesthetic spheres. All we have said noting correspondences between Kid and Calkins might just as easily apply to Kid and George; all three—Kid, George, and Calkins—have large entourages, mass produced artifacts lending presence to their public persona (printed poems, posters, and newspapers), and an impact that definitely crosses over from the social plane on which they are most comfortable; but to exhaust all the resonances of this particular trinity is to re-examine *Dhalgren* from an entirely different perspective, one beyond the bounds of this introduction. Let us simply note that the fields of influence of Kid, of George, and of Calkins interpenetrate extensively, that each in some way does his bit to extend or sustain the influences of the others (Calkins' paper rockets George to stardom; George makes Kid the hero when he and Kid save five children from a fire; Kid gives June Richards, George's rape victim, one of George's posters and keeps that all-important interaction alive). In sum, were we given a glimpse of Kid's poems we, as readers of a real work of prose in a real world, would render more or less "purely aesthetic judgements," whatever that phrase may really mean. But that peculiarly mixed system of responses of the native Bellonean—in which Kid must to some extent have participated when he wrote the poems—would be inaccessible to us.

It is not that the Bellonean's response is non-aesthetic. It is rather that aesthetic responses themselves may be more complicated than we have until now supposed. Perhaps the only thing peculiar to such responses is that they can at once be called many things—moral, political, religious, philosophical, scientific, and playful. The inhabitants of Bellona exhibit each of these various responses. The aesthetic may in fact be some function of differentiation itself, of the interplay of a whole complex of internal responses, an endlessly rearranged collage that mirrors (constitutes?) our own endlessly shifting internal state. And what of our cave dweller, with no theogony, no schooling, no politics, who cannot share in all the above responses? Does she, staring fixedly at the cave wall, experience stirrings we might call aesthetic? We shall assume here that the word is a generous one. Whatever unknown map of the world she carries about inside her, traced with shapes we can never name and boundaries we cross daily without thought must—at the instant the drawing forever alters her conception of bison and drawings—be reformed and recolored. Her response is as inaccessible to us as a real Bellona, and so, ultimately, is her bison.

We have argued that the aesthetic response requires some extensive, perhaps even holistic, reference to a conceptual map of the real world. That lands us once again in the central compartment of our container, which is where Kid's poetry ultimately must fall—with the nameless and misplaced, the abstract and explaining, the unattainable "world." We may see its antecedents, its referents, even hear it moving towards utterance, but we may not see it as such. We shall presently extend this notion of inaccessibility, but for the moment let us continue with our brief overview of Bellona, armed with the knowledge that certain of its compressions may make vast differences.

Another notable such transformation may be observed in the social role enjoyed by the Scorpions, the closest thing Bellona has to a police force. As Bunny, Teddy's resident male go-go dancer comments:

> "You Scorpions do more to keep law and order in the city than any one else. Only the good and pure in heart dare to go out on the street after dark. But that's the way, I suppose, the law has always worked. The good people are the ones who live their lives so that they don't have

> anything to do with whatever law there is anyway. The bad ones are the ones unfortunate enough to become involved. I rather like the way it works here, because, since you *are* the law, the law is far more violent, makes much more noise and isn't everywhere at once: so it's easier for us good people to avoid." (p. 322)

Here, stripping the surface channels of power from the social edifice has created the context for a statement about power's underlying patterns: power is something that accrues to social entities merely because of their position in the network. Of course this particular portioning of power has completely redesigned the role in question. Bellona has no laws, apart from those discoverable by hard experience (such as Kid's when he is beaten up outside Calkins's wall). Yet the Scorpions, privileged by their numbers, their coherence, and their potential of violence, are clearly granted the same powers granted the police. The park commune pays "taxes" in care packages filled with food. Calkins hires Scorpions for protection.

All this, again, is done by convention rather than constraint. Thus the relations between certain signs prove recognizable, although the signs themselves have changed: the relations between Calkins (the state) and the Scorpions (the police) is one of mutual mistrust and ignorance. The *Times* frequently misreports Scorpion escapades. The Scorpions have, until the occasion of Kid's publication party, never been inside the Calkins estate. This matches much of what we know, historically, of the capricious relations between the state and its armed enforcement agencies. What such correspondences show is merely what the invention of a science of semiology presupposes, that we "read" the relations between signs rather than their references; but the fact that such relations are shaped within the fluid society of Bellona, where traditional mechanisms of constraint are inoperative, suggests they are the results of "deeper" forces. This reading is, of course, supported by Delany's suggestion regarding deep structures, and it is a highly persuasive one. But to avoid the appearance of seeking ultimate truths in a novel so highly ambivalent about the relation between the true and the real (its epigraph, "You have confused the true and the real"), we shall note that the surfaces of Bellona do not necessarily claim any fixed, privileged relation with those deeper forces. In other words, a different set of outcasts might have assumed new configurations, in which a different set of contouring relations would be familiar. This is in line with what we have supposed about Bellona's being only a fitting grammar.

What seems to emerge now is that under Bellona's transformations and compressions, the same social spaces, no matter how radically changed in shape, exercise about the same amount of power. (Kid's power, of course, proceeds not from his status of artist, but from that of enforcer, and as artist he struggles to remain aloof from it: "I do not tell how I gain or maintain it [power]. I only record the ginger stroll through the vaguely fetid garden of its rewards." [p. 679])

The single glaring exception to the constancy of power is on the racial plane, where the high percentage of blacks left in Bellona has given them majority rule. Nevertheless, because Bellona does still sit in the real world, blacks as a group in Bellona continue to act like blacks, a people severed by history from the lines of power. Asked why Nightmare, a white man, and then Kid, a half-Indian, were chosen leaders of the primarily black Scorpions, Glass (black) replies:

> "...I think more or less everybody has got it in their head that after one of these runs or other, the shit is gonna come down. Hard. When it does you gonna see niggers fade in the night like nobody's business. But the chief scorpion, maybe, ain't gonna be able to fade quite so fast." (p. 768)

We earlier promised to argue that *Dhalgren* was a science fiction novel. Hopefully, that argument has been taking shape throughout the course of this essay. We have been making of Bellona a society which, though some parts of it may be inaccessible, still bears correspondences enough with our own to allow an understanding of its peculiar why's and how's. The particular informative suspensions employed here are native to science fiction. To present an oversimple model: in the mundane novel we are given events with the understanding that we know the rules they follow; the novelist then shows that, given these rules, here is what must really happen. In a certain kind of science fiction novel, we are given events in order to induce or deduce the rules; the novelist shows that, given these events, these rules must apply. There is frequently the further implication that these rules are in turn the consequences or metaphorical extensions of real-world events now in progress, but this is generally a vertical process. The capsule account of this type of science fiction novel is, simply: we are given a peculiar society, and shown why and how it works. In practice, of course, the distinction between rules and events is not as clear-cut as we have made it. Mundane novelists are perfectly capable of stringing events so as to imply a rule that, although imbedded in a perfectly familiar situation, is not at all evident; we may, for the sake of argument, claim that the events are based on more familiar rules, and that the inevident rule is only an heuristic reduction of what "really" happens, but it is clear that the boundary line is already growing fuzzy. This should cause us no great distress since it is the general fate of boundary lines between literary genres; they may serve one specific purpose but, turned to another, they quickly fall apart. Ours was drawn in hopes of showing that the rhetorical thrust of *Dhalgren* parallels that of a whole class of science fiction novels.

Science fiction is a literature of edges. Often knowledge of the why's and how's of a science fictional world is gained by experiencing the edges of a society, by tracing its contours through its outcasts or its elite, those who have the most at stake because of its fundamental assumptions. Bellona is composed almost entirely of outcasts and aristocrats structured round the ghost of the old society; it is practically a pattern case.

The fact that Bellona is practically all contour seems just one more aspect of its illusory nature; yet there are still survivors of the old social center in the city, and these Belloneans are perhaps the most deeply wrapped in illusion of them all. These are the remnants of Bellona's once-powerful middle class like the Richards, acting out a fantasy-life bourgeois existence amidst the ruins of the city. June Richards, the family's only daughter, has been tied in with the center of the apocalypse because of her rape by a "hulking, sadistic, buck nigger" (p. 248), which may have been one of the triggering events of Bellona's peculiar retribution. It is also the event which, thanks to the publicity given it in *The Bellona Times*, has elevated George to demi-godhood. June's parents, however, although they are shown June's front page picture in flagrante, fail to recognize George's blond partner. Obviously to do so would be to bring Apocalypse within their thin apartment walls, shattering their rigorously constructed retreat. The fragility of that retreat emerges with almost agonizing clarity in one of the novel's major high comic scenes, Kid's first dinner with the family. Mr. and Mrs. Richards blithely discuss June's plans for college, although she is really "daddy's little girl," and not really the college sort, although, outside, Bellona's mist churns round mayhem and anarchy. Mrs. Richards gushes over Kid's poetry and Mr. Richards, in response, maunders on about a friend of his who has written an engineering instruction manual (an allusion to John Ashbery's early poem, "The Instruction Manual"?). Witty, pathetic, exhaustive, the scene is a ghastly study in social forms drained of all content (Bellona again: all edges). It reads like a sitcom by Proust.

What is left of the middle class in Bellona is diseased or dying. In a second dinner party with the Richards, we are treated to a generous sampling—three couples whose male halves Arthur seems to have met through "his work." Participants in this affair later make appearances, armed and dangerous, at the Emboriky, a department store from which a number of white snipers conduct an informal war on all those (mostly black) who approach, and at a religious meeting at George's where, stripped of their "surface coherence," they discuss shooting niggers. Mr. and Mrs. Richards host a strange evening in which all the usual pleasantries of place and occupation have become taboo, while, two floors down, emblematic of the disease that has struck down his city and his social class, the body of their teen-age son rots in his old bedroom.

To find the living personality of Bellona, one must leave the partial vacuum of the social center and move outwards. What emerges, of course, is the collection of outcasts we have been examining all along—thieves, pimps, hustlers, punks, drifters, deserters, the human flotsam of Bellona. "What is the simplest way to say to someone like Kamp or Denny or Lanya," Kid wonders at one point, "that all their days have rendered ludicrous their judgement of the night?" (p. 514). Like the city itself, the days and nights of Bellona have been turned inside out. Those who rule Bellona's misty days are the very same creatures of night who once made Denny's, Kamp's, and Lanya's afterhours so fearsome. They have filled Bellona's sky with cosmological wonders and proven all judgements, social and scientific, inadequate. And in the circular text of *Dhalgren*, in a world where all the traditional landmarks, down to the basic fixing of night and day, have been toppled, it is impossible to read either of these phenomena as controlling the other.

The basic pattern of Bellona is curiously reminiscent of that ascribed by the young R.D. Laing in *The Divided Self* to the schizophrenic personality. The pre-schizophrenic, faced by continuous double binds, retreats behind a series of shells which may then suffer the inevitable consequences, turning paradox to paralogism and freeing the self. These masks the pre-schizophrenic regards as divorced from the self, as demands made by the other and thus surrendered to it. But in time more and more of the self is invested in these masks, leaving the interior hollow, marked only by an elaborate boundary, a self whose inside is no different from its outside. The schizophrenic may either treat everything as external, making of themselves a machine, or a catatonic, or everything as internal, becoming that supremely sensitive organism, the paranoid.

Kid's description of his own bout with madness leans towards the paranoid, but it is curious how his picture also calls up Bellona, where, as we have seen, once invisible forces may become screamingly evident:

> "...the real mind is invisible; you're less aware of it while you think than you are of your eye while you see... until something goes wrong with it. Then you become aware of it, with all its dislocated pieces and its rackety functioning, the same way you become aware of your eye when you get a cinder in it. Because it hurts... Sure, it distorts things. But the strange thing, the thing you can never explain to anyone, except another nut, or, if you're lucky, a doctor who has an unusual amount of sense—stranger than the hallucinations, or the voices, or the anxiety—is the way you begin to experience the edges of the mind itself." (p. 48)

In the city of edges, it would be monstrous paranoia to claim every illusion as your own, and pure catatonia to deny them all. Bellona forces recognition of its contours, and makes its presence, its process, keenly felt. Like Laing's schizophrenic, a society under stress invests more and more of its energy in its edges, then denies them more vehemently than ever.

Bellona is the image of those edges freed from their empty center; it is an optative madness, a form for illusion, a consciousness.

The "real" Bellona is invisible to the world ("the electric nation") just as the "real" schizophrenic self is. It has, by redesigning "knowledge and perception to pass it by" (p. 14), eluded all real-world consequences. But in so doing it has freed certain forces of anxiety and terror; it has become a city of "inner discordances and retinal distortion" (p. 14). The result is a dreamlike apocalypse, always in progress but never progressing, a strange amalgam of fears found only in the mind, a projection of social terrors, fire, earthquake, lightning, assassination, the rape of a white woman by a black man, all events that, in our modern myth cycle, may bring on the crumbling of the social order.

Meditating on the death of the Richards' teenage son, who is "accidentally" pushed down an elevator shaft by his sister June, Kid wonders at one point if it was murder. Bobby had, not long before that, threatened to tell their parents about the poster (of George) Kid had brought. But then a far more horrifying possibility strikes Kid. Suppose it was an accident; suppose it just happened:

> "...that means it's the city. That means it's the landscape: the bricks, and the girders, and the faulty wiring and the shot elevator machinery, all conspiring together to make these myths true. And that's crazy." (p. 249)

We are left with the grim possibility that in Bellona it really does bring down death and destruction for a black man to have sex with a white woman. In Bellona it really is wrong.

Whatever the myth may be in this case, the outcast of Bellona has no trouble distinguishing the forces behind it. Kid writes (and in the passage following "they" are those at the social center, the well-adjusted):

> ...they are sure that any social structures that arise, grow out of patterns innate to The Sex Act—whatever that is; while we have seen, again and again, that the psychology, structures, and accoutrements that define any sex act are always internalized from social structures that

> already exist, that have been created, that can be changed. All right: let me ask the terrible question: could it be that all those perfectly straight, content-with-their-sexual-orientation-in-the-world, exclusive-heterosexuals really are (in some ill-defined, psychological way that will ultimately garner a better world) more healthy than (gulp...!) us? Let me answer: No way!... any madness is preferable to that. And madness is not preferable! (p. 720)

The myth of George, that any sex between a black man and a white woman is rape, and the myth that homosexuals are sick really belong to the same cycle; they are both fictions founded on the assumption that there are "normal" sexual patterns anterior to the social patterns that cast them. That the city should function to make myths such as these true is, as Kid tells us, madness.

Thus the city's madness is evident on a number of different planes, while Kid's madness, his forgotten days, his fractured internal monologues, his queasiness at certain passages in the notebook, occupies much of the novel's foreground. Ultimately the two reflect one another indistinguishably, neither signifying the other, joined at the juncture of mirror and mirrored into a single whole. It is this specific lack of definition which makes knowledge of his internal state so difficult for Kid. If Bellona, with its capricious cosmology, its fantasy apocalypse, its gray sky, is some vast solipsistic projection, then it is true, as Kid thinks at one point that: "I am traveling my own optic nerve" (p. 84). But he leaps to the complementary hypothesis in the very next sentence: "Limping in a city without source, searching a day without shadow, am I deluded by the inconstant emblem?"

Have the names of things changed so that he can no longer make sense of them? The names and emblems of Bellona, as we have seen, have changed, just as its street signs do from day to day. The reason given us for this, extending at once over Kid and all the other things without name in the city, other Scorpions whose appellations are as new as his, the gigantic sun which one day covers one quarter of the sky, is: "...certain images lose their freedom and resonance if, when we regard them with a straight face, we do so through the diffraction of a name" (p. 491). Names, even as they mythify and exalt, draw inviolable limits; and, extended, they may become immobilizing constraints. Can anything fix George's position in the Bellonean mythos more completely than the extension of his name to cover the second moon that rises over Bellona? And though that moon quickly surrenders its place in Bellona's night, the nature of the name, though it again refers only to a mortal man, has been irrevocably transformed.

We are of course given our closest look at Bellona's inconstant emblems in connection with the name Kid; the nameless drifter who enters the city is variously called kid, the Kid, and Kidd (the first "calling" made by Tak, the guardian of the gate who seems to greet all of Bellona's newcomers), but acceptance of some form of the name is universal. It is pointedly the special gift of Bellona itself: "So howled out for the world to give him a name" (p. 1). The gift, however, is not completely validated until he has committed himself to the city. On page 156, after he has eaten of his first food there, after he emerges from his first bath—after, in other words, ritual gestures of Eucharist and Baptism—Kid is for the first time referred to as Kidd by the narrator, who has until then kept entirely to "he." Kid's name, then, sits uneasily within the web of the conspiring city's myths, associated both with rites of naming and of sacrifice. At first, within the warped field of the Richards' home, it is written Kidd, but as soon as he moves into the more authentic Bellonean world of the Scorpions, it reverts to its original (but now capitalized) form. Kid's novelistic name is, indeed, Kid—Kidd, with two d's, represents a corruption of that name that only adheres to him while he is with the Richards, i.e., while his vision of his own priorities is doubled, distorted, and rendered a stuttering parody of that same vision, once it is freed from the Richards' set of anapocalyptic "blindnesses."

Kid is a specifically Bellonean name, both moniker and common noun (like those of many of the Scorpions), at once associated with false appearances (his seeming youth), and with deeper truth (through its ritual antecedents). It is both truth and fiction, more and less than a name. As Kid puts it: "To find who I am I've had to give up my name and who knows what part of my life" (p. 727). Kid, then, may not be a name, but it may be who he is.

But the inconstant emblems of Bellona are only capable of capturing essences within the web of Bellona's other emblems. Bit by bit, the whole network of associations has become unique. Kid tells us:

> In any house here, movement from room to room is a journey from a place where twin moons have cast double shadows of the windowsill upon the floor to a place where once, because the sun had grown so immense, no shadow was cast at all. We speak another language here. (p. 754)

There is hint of Eden in this state of inconstant reference and continual naming; yet Bellona is unquestionably a landscape over which apocalypse has burst forth. How, then, are we to tell the post-apocalyptic from the pre-lapsarian? Bellona has its share of plenitude, food, companionship, shelter, spiritual comfort; but it also has its share of want, of sickness and violence. Every surfeit of light sheeting the sky as if by celestial fiat also has its obliterating mist, its dissolving night. Which way does Bellona's arrow point, towards or away from entropy, towards constitution and creation, the mooring down of things, the closure of signifier and signified, or towards apocalypse, the complete rupture of sense, the all-consuming fire?

We have called *Dhalgren* a coming to consciousness. Implicit in that, because of the novel's circularity, is a leaving-of-consciousness. Apocalypse and Genesis, in Bellona, are coextensive terms with different meanings, like Russell's morning and evening star, like George before a second moon rose, and George after. Bellona is the act of consciousness through which we perceive it, and consciousness is fluid, an endless exercise in Adamic magic, like our readerly constitution of the text before us, the naming of the fiction. Yet *omnis determinatio est negatio*, to resurrect a motto of Spinoza's. Consciousness is an equally fluid deconstruction. Each designation of order strikes out another emblem of chaos over previous designations, assuring the continuous coincidence of naming and named. To constitute the miracle of order is to reconstitute equally miraculous disorder (and Bellona belongs among these "cities of reconstituted disorder" [p. 646])—not merely in the act of drawing boundaries between them, but in necessarily obliterating others, in creating a great field claimed by both, the field where Bellona is located, in the emptiness of the mid-American plain, an utter plenitude, a barren form, a being and a nothingness. We evoke here the first two terms of

Hegel's famous dialectical triad in *The Logic*, so that we may turn instantly to the third, becoming, which is the truth of Bellona. Bellona is inconstant boundaries; and the man of many backgrounds who makes our only interface with it—whose consciousness constructs it for us—is equally unfixable, is half-Indian, half-white, half mad, half-named bisexual, one-shoed, ambidextrous, willful, labile, poet, and hero. He is a model of dialectical progression, and his very loss of memory, his emptiness of content, is a model of its adherence to form. Kid is the consciousness the text fills, and the emptiness with which it begins is only made the more emphatic by the novel's violent, mid-sentence opening. Ultimately it must end the same way, all the same questions unanswered, brought up short against the same violent emptiness, unpunctuated, its boundary incomplete. Neither knowledge nor consciousness can be completed any more than the container with which we began this exploration can, because each must deconstruct itself in order to continue; the container must open and close to function.

We have from time to time made reference to *Dhalgren*'s solipsistic undertones, prompted by the novel's persistent reference to illusion and distortion. In fact, illusion and distortion prop up some of the strongest empiricist arguments for sense data and against idealism, in its simplest form of *esse est percipe*. If anything, *Dhalgren* shows traces of a later, more fashionable, phenomenological sensibility:

> On the dismal air I sketch my own restraint, waking, reflexively, instant to instant. The sensed center, the moment of definition, the point under such pressure it extrudes a future and a past I apprehend only as a chill, extends the overlay of injury with some retentive, tenuous disease, the refuse of a brick-and-mortar-grinding violence. (p. 266)

The "sensed center" here is of course consciousness, interpenetration is between the awareness and the thing in its phenomenological aspect. But it is important to note that this passage, and others like it scattered throughout, written in a difficult, splintered diction in the first person, are those which most closely approach the feel of madness. In *The Phenomenology*, once he has proven that all categories derive from consciousness (Geist), and that things and their attributes can only be constituted by a consciousness, Hegel goes on to assert the mutual dependence of thing and consciousness, thus identifying the true with the real, and consciousness with self-consciousness. It is this very identification, of the edges of the world with the edges of the mind, that Kid has equated with madness in the passage already cited (p. 48). In *Dhalgren*, the world of pure thought, where the true and the real blend indistinguishably, is a nightmare.

Knowledge is the mind's mooring to reality. It is specifically uncertainties regarding what he knows that most distress Kid, because these are the uncertainties that may leave him trapped in the nightmare world of the purely mental. When a giant sun blots out Bellona's sky, Kid is panic-stricken until he knows that his friends also see it. Truth, as we have noted, is a function of what other things one wishes to keep true. To affirm the giant sun does not entail denying his friends, and thus, for the moment, Kid's system of knowledge is safe. He grows calm, then ecstatic. The edges of the world have been pushed back out; the boundary of the self has held.

But for how long? In Bellona, the act of observation has broken down, "the miracle of order has run out" (p. 96). At times what Kid knows is inaccessible to him simply because words fail him, because the language itself has changed, and he does not know "what sticum tacks words and tongue" (p. 514).

We shall need a brief digression to fix this curious slippage of word and tongue. It has been a fairly common assumption among non-skeptics since Kant that in order to know something you must at least be able to say it. This assumption is implicit in both Kant's and Hegel's use of categories to constitute knowledge. Following the canon of the positivists, Wittgenstein eschews metaphysics entirely and concentrates on what can be said, assuming that what can be known will then be taken care of (but then changing his mind).

It is Wittgenstein's argument against a private language that will be of use in investigating the slippage towards the unsayable in Bellona. Wittgenstein first asks whether it would be possible for someone to have a name E for a specific sensation for which there is no word. It would of course be possible, but there is no sense in which E is part of a private language. E is understood in exactly the way other words are, by its connection with an entire associative network of words and ideas, beginning with the word "sensation." The problem of constructing such a private language would be where to begin. If we did in fact create a word without a matrix of words in which to sit, in what sense could we be said to know what it means? For Wittgenstein knowledge is a linguistic function bound up with meaning.

It is not clear from a reading of *Dhalgren* exactly what Samuel Delany understands by that curious verb "to know;" but it is clear that, in Bellona, he constructs a certain class of experiences which, known or unknown, is linguistically inaccessible, not because it lies beyond or between the words, but because it is directly beneath them. Three times in the course of the novel we read sentences launched with: "Speech is in excess..." each followed by a different concluding term, three examples where the words are simply too large for what they need to say:

> Silent on the circuit of the year, speech is in excess of what I want to say, or believe. (p. 266)
>
> Speech... is always in excess of poetry as print... is in excess of words. (pp. 266, 268)
>
> Speech is always in excess of poetry as print is always inadequate for speech. (p. 709)

The "circuit" of the first occurrence suggests that is what we are dealing with here, a conjecture supported by the novel's circularity and other loops we shall presently consider. Here, if we take "words" to suggest "speech," we complete the small rhetorical loop:

> Speech > Poetry > Print > Words (speech)

We see that the "excess" of words is not simply some quantitative measure of reference, some inadequacy of resolution. It is a property of the network itself, which positions its elements so as to achieve maximum interdependence, so that translation tends, in general, to decrease that interdependence to imply more (and bury the original) in a positive feedback loop.

In the shifting world of Bellona, referents may utterly transform and remain bound to, under enormous tension, the same word. A room is still a room even though two moons and a gigantic sun have shone through its window. How can these enormous translations be made? Here is something "known," in the peculiar Bellonean sense of the word, but unsayable. Indeed it is the very phenomenon that Wittgenstein has described which freezes the tongue and halts the stream of utterance. The shift of one word cannot be described except by what has now become the inadequacy of the others towards the singleton. And how are words to express their own inadequacy? The singleton, like the sensation E, has been displaced from the network.

But the problem is one implicit in language from the beginning and not simply native to the Bellonean cosmos. We have an instinctive and completely false confidence that language makes a seamless armor over all of reality, that each word clicks in perfectly with its partner words and its counterpart thing. But language is always in a process of slow translation; its referents are always in rapid transition, and there is no built-in symmetry, either in the world or in language, to prevent the inevitable distortion. We have already alluded to Kid's unanswered question, "What is the simplest way to say to someone like Kamp or Denny or Lanya that all their days have rendered ludicrous their judgement of the night?" (p. 514). It is a question that makes special sense in Bellona, since it has been immediately preceded by the rising and setting of Bellona's giant sun. The classic judgement of night: night is the absence of day. But what is the presence of day? Day and night are asymmetric; night falls, but the sun rises. What if day rose huge and opaque, like a vast sun, into the sky? Or what if night shone from a single heavenly body, a second orb placed beside the moon? Such imposed symmetries proceed from the island of ideal thought which is madness, where word and thing fit so well together that nothing is visible round the edges. Sanity necessarily entails that much be left inaccessible behind the word, lost in the shadow of its excess.

Bellona is a city in a book. That much we have taken for granted; and we have gone on to see it function like one, its myths typical fictional reductions (the coupling of a black man and a white woman brings destruction), its apocalypse a composite anxiety projection. But it is also a city of words.

The flow of its names and its people models that of any language space in continuous translation. Bellona's maddening mixture of the arbitrary and the formal mirrors the arbitrariness and the formality of language, at once marvelous in the multiplicity of its determination and the absolute haphazardness of what is determined. *Brass Orchids*, Kid's book of poems, is a Bellonean case in point. The title is a pun on brass in the sense of nerve or chutzpah, and the etymology of orchid, the Greek for testicles or balls. "Brass Orchids" is also the legend on a rack of ornamental weapons in the city's strange warehouse of artifacts; and "orchid" is the name of the steel weapon, given him upon arrival, that Kid wears strapped to his wrist. When we gaze, with Kid, upon the rack, the title of his book becomes a perfect triple pun and the language of Bellona a fraction more ramified.

The arbitrariness and formality of the Bellonean order are further underlined by other artifacts in the warehouse. There also can be found the optical chains, the holographic projectors, and the red eyecaps of Bellona, the last presumably for achieving the effect of a stare of red glass which Kid occasionally notes among Bellona's denizens. But how these quarter-sized circles of Ping-Pong ball plastic could possibly work is left unexplained, as is the purpose of this warehouse in the Bellonean matrix. That it is the Mateland Systems Engineering Warehouse, the same firm which employs Arthur Richards (who, we remember, goes somewhere from nine to five) does raise certain chilling specters of a middle class conspiracy, but these specters are like the red eyecaps, gestures towards explanation empty of content. Like the central compartment, this is the place in the network where we expect an explanation; and just as the eyecaps fall far short of explaining the Bellonean stare, so the gigantic spools of optical chain, the cartons of orchids, the holographic projectors labeled by bestial aspect, fail to explain chain, weapon, or aspect, or the privileged social position any of these artifacts have taken. Here in the warehouse they are signs as enigmatic as the drug company trademark would be to a Martian archeologist. The warehouse is not a source, merely one of numerous crossover points in the matrix, as arbitrary as the arbitrary sign itself.

Yet those signs which give us our realest vision of Bellona, Kid's poems, remain inaccessible to us. Each time Kid opens to a page of *Brass Orchids*, there is a sudden perceptual shift, and it is as if that page of print turned mirror: we are reflected directly back onto Kid. We go so far as to see the poems entry into the machinery of impression, but the poems themselves we are denied.

In our closest approach, we move from impression (the narrative), to first draft, to second, but stop short of the completed poem. First, impression:

> Charcoal, like the bodies of beetles, heaped below the glittering wall on the far corner. The sharpness of the incinerated upholstery cut the street's gritty stink. Through a cellar window, broken, a gray eel of smoke slithered the sidewalk to vaporize in the gutter. Through another, intact, flickerings.... (p. 79)

Seven pages later, Kid sits down to write and we read:

> "Charcoal... like the bodies of burnt beetles, heaped below the glittering black wall of the house on the far corner." He bit at his lip and wrote on: "The wet sharpness of incinerated upholstery cut the general gritty stink of the street. From the rayed hole in the cellar window a grey eel of smoke wound across the sidewalk, dispersed before," at which point he crossed out the last two words and substituted, "vaporized at the gutter. Through another window," and crossed out window, "still intact, something flickered..." stopped and began to write all over again:
>
> "Charcoal, like the bodies of beetles...." (pp. 83–84)

We are treated to another entire draft and the first line of a third, but then, abruptly, we pull away: "He folded the torn paper in four and put it back in the notebook when he had finished the next revision." That next revision we are never allowed to see. It is as if, in becoming a completed poem, the text had ceased being part of this city of words and, though made of words itself, moved out somewhere beyond it.

In the crudest possible terms: Bellona is not just a city of words. It is a city of prose.

Kid discussed the difference between his poems and his other verbal efforts (to wit the journal, to which we are given access) in a passage labeled "the falsification of this journal":

> ...When something really involving, violent, or important happens, it occupies too much of my time, my physical energy, and my thought for me to be able to write about. I can think of four things that happened in the nest I would like to have described when they occurred, but they so completed themselves in the happening that even to refer to them seems superfluous.
>
> What is down, then, is a chronicle of incidents with a potential for wholeness they did not have when they occurred; a false picture, again, because they show neither the general spread of my life's fabric, nor the most significant pattern points.
>
> To show the one is too boring and the other too difficult. That is probably why (as I use up more and more paper trying to return the feeling I had when I thought I was writing poems) I am not a poet... anymore? The poems perhaps hint it to someone else, but for me they are dry as the last leaves dropping from the burned trees on Brisbane. They are moments when I had the intensity to see, and the energy to build, some careful analog that completed the seeing. (pp. 734, 735)

The poems, then, are part of the experience they portray. We are instantly supplied with one reason for the poems' departure from the text: they are parts of completed experiences. As such they belong to that set of experiences that "so completed themselves in the happening that even to refer to them seems superfluous." They are verbal constructs closing off a portion of reality, real rather than true, divorced from the fiction at hand.

It is notable that Kid tells us several times in the course of the journal that it is a failure; if he is trying solely to recapture his poetry then the reason is obvious. But his most keenly felt failures seem always to occur in some effort to fix words themselves. He is obsessed with the problem of speech and the vast quantity which escapes the written word:

> George's speech can't even be written down for the common reader. Throckmorton (at the party) speaks only in inane combinations of serial phrases that become

> satires on themselves as soon as they are recorded but that, during utterance, make miracles of communication. I suppose I'm just getting frustrated by what written words can't do. (pp. 680–681)

Or to return to the translation that began our rhetorical loop above, simply in moving from thought to words, he notes: "This is not what I am thinking: this is merely (he thought) what thinking feels like" (p. 514). It is in the attempt to bend words back on words, always a work of radical translation, in which Kid ultimately fails, particularly the attempt, in the journal, to fix his poetry. Those places in the network where words will most often yield paradoxes like our loop, are places where they point to themselves. Most, if not all, of the paradoxes of modern logic are self-referent statements of the form:

> *This sentence is false.*

Kid's description of his poems as completing the experience they portray makes them self-referent entities. They are also self-referent in that, as verbal objects of high energy, poems are always partially about words themselves. Prose, even in a self-referent context like *Dhalgren*'s, can only be about its subject, even if that subject is fiction's relation to reality.

"This is not what I am thinking; this is merely (he thought) what thinking feels like." Specifically this sentence refers to those first person paragraphs of splintered diction which circle round the edge of madness. Yet the same could be said of *Dhalgren*, if it is truly to be read as a work about fiction's relation to reality. It is not so much about what that relation is—the truth or reality of this link between the true and the real—but what it feels like; and let us say that "what it feels like" signals a gap between the text and its subject that may never be completely closed, but that the text may suffuse the network around that gap sufficiently to capture its shape and "feeling." Prose is opaque verbiage and can never capture its relation to the real without, as Kid tells us, its own bulk changing that relation. Poetry, with its aural effects, its energy, is able to become transparent, attaching itself to experience without obscuring it, and as both itself and part of that experience, it is implicit in the relation between the two, a pure rhetorical stance revealed in all its crystalline beauty.

In the last chapter of *Dhalgren* we move from ordinary third person narrative, what, by fictive convention, is reality, to a journal, what, by the same fictive convention of privilege, is truth. Because the novel is circular, we then ideally proceed back to the beginning, making the transition back from truth, the gesture itself, that of flipping all the pages, removing us momentarily to the world of experience, the world above the page, "reality." The text of that transition reads, "I have come to… to wound the autumnal city." We have already taken this as a signal of the coming to consciousness that the novel enacts, the finding of a true self. There is another reading, which is simply that the to's at beginning and end are the same, a repetition, a stutter, an overlap. This overlap is the image of the gap discussed above, the interior of the transition from fiction to reality, that fragment of "truth," of "resemblance," which must exist for anything to model anything else, that single impurity which resides in both the truth and the fiction. If we view *Dhalgren* as a Moebius Strip, one side of which we begin by labeling reality, the other fiction, until we discover that the two run indistinguishably together, then the to's make up the narrow tabs where the ends of the paper join, the flaw by which we know there is a transition, although its location is forever indeterminable.

In order to appreciate the indeterminacy of this transition we shall have to examine more closely that concluding journal chapter, on which the greatest formal weight of the novel rests, where the key to *Dhalgren*'s ruling triad of city, mind, and language may be found.

The central problems of Chapter VII do not become apparent until we try and wrestle its many fragments into some chronological order. To begin with, there is simply not enough information to establish a unique chronological order for the chapter. Many strings of events—such as the comings and goings of various nest members, Fireball, Black Widow, California, and various vignettes of nest life—run on parallel tracks. For example, we know because of a glass of water that Kid considers in the fragments describing three conversations in which Lanya took part (beginning p. 721), that it comes before the concluding apocalyptic sequences, in which Kid asks Tak about the strange bubbles observed in the glass. We also know, from mentions made in the text, that it comes after both the mugging fragment (p. 697) and the visit to Calkins at his monastic retreat (p. 736). But there seems no way to date these fragments against one another.

Far more troubling difficulties, however, crop up in connection with the fragments we can arrange. We can follow the entry marginal to the last entry (p. 787) back to where it picks up on page 661, now as a major entry. These two fragments chronicle Kid's stay at Madame Brown's and his return to poetry. We may assume that the stay at Madame Brown's, being marginal to it, occurs after the last apocalyptic entry (the editorial intrusion on page 662 instructs us to make this assumption). But then, when it takes up as a major entry, the rubric marginal to it involves the children Kid saved in the fire at the end of Chapter VI. This means the apocalypse occurs some time before the end of Chapter VI. We have come to a smaller loop within the large loop of the novel.

Or again, the entry marginal to the penultimate entry describes the abandoned women's commune to which Denny's girlfriend belonged, complete with an abandoned sculpture of a lion. Upon his arrival in Bellona Kid meets a group of women, one of whom is said to have completed a sculpture of a lion. This places the bulk of the novel between apocalypse and the insert on page 785, which, since it happens after apocalypse, being marginal to it, happens before the bulk of the novel, and so on.

Clearly, the notebook is a jigsaw which may be reconstructed in a number of ways, but with many pieces missing, and those present tending to work either side up.

It is interesting that Kid's memory, once one examines the notebook, is such as to be at all times in harmony with a linear chronology; this keeps his sensibility entirely readerly, the reader being unable to experience circularity. Shortly after his arrival in Bellona Kid begins to forget the surrounding circumstances, so that by the novel's close he is unable to perceive any paradox. We are thus spared any troubling debate, full of ambiguities of tense, subject, and voice (ambiguities signaled at in the novel's opening), on which event, arrival or departure, happened first.

There may be a glimpse of the actual mechanisms by which Kid joins diverging chronologies in the entry in which he remembers two of his three names and an initial. We have already shown how the matter of the children and their rescue is a chronological sore point. They may fall into the readerly blind spot between departure and arrival. When the children are brought up in this scene, Kid is at first unable to remember them, then: "Inside it felt like two disjoined surfaces had slipped flush; the relief was unbearable" (p. 780). At the same moment, various commune members and Scorpions dance within a taut network of their own optical chain; the resonance here is with Kid's arrival, the moment he receives his own chain: "...what he apprehended was insubstantial as a disjunction of the soul" p. 7). The temporal loops of *Dhalgren* are not concentric or even tangent; those of the notebook may rejoin the narrative in any of a number of places. The final image, focused by the optical chains, is of an intricate network controlling illusion. It is immediately after these two disjoined surfaces slip flush that Kid begins to remember his name, setting him onto a new chronological track which buckles at apocalypse.

One might attempt a simple cyclical reading of *Dhalgren*. For some reason time is circular in Bellona; and many of the journal entries were written before Kid arrived in Bellona (we see them shortly after the notebook is found) because, before arriving, he naturally left. But this fails to explain the discrepancies between early versions of journal sentences Kid reads in passing in the notebook, and their later incorporations into Chapter VII. As an example:

> *...first off. It doesn't reflect my daily life. Most of what happens hour by hour is quiet and still. We sit most of the time* (p. 84)
>
> ...first off, it doesn't reflect my daily life. Most of what happens hour by hour here is quiet and dull. We sit most of the time... (p. 734)

The alterations here of orthography, punctuation, words, and type are all undeniable, but so minor as to seem almost pointless. The fact that the first version is set in italics, of course, allows us to read it as a reading, or a misreading by Kid, in this case, and take the second, notebook version as definitive. This would be fine except that other deviations, like that between two of the speech is in excess lines already quoted, seem too large for this explanation. There are also other curious distortions, not simply between notebook and notebook, but between notebook and text, that would remain problematic. For example, Kid's arrival and departure on Bellona's bridge bear a striking symmetry to one another, a man meeting women, a woman meeting men, each group with an artist, each newcomer given a weapon, the very dialogue of each scene almost line for line mirroring the other. One is in the notebook, one in the text, and the relationship between the two seems that kind only found in the transition from reality to fiction; on our Moebius Strip, we have located two points directly across from one another, on "opposite" sides.

The question of which is real is here undecideable, but the occurrence of reference, of one incident being about the other, and the distortive nature of that occurrence seem undeniable. It is not only in the relation between texts that distortion occurs in Bellona. There is, in *Dhalgren*, a whole system of imagery about false doubles or "stuttering;" the names Kid, kid, and Kidd, the to's beginning and ending the book (which are and are not the same), the names Tak, Mak, and Jack, the gesture of fist against chin transplanted from June to Rose to Stevie (the last stutter indicated by our "editor" on p. 662), and the altered texts and scenes discussed above. All of these have to do with some kind of "fictionalizing" of real experience, even if, occasionally, the direction of the fictionalizing is unclear—fictionalizing represented in its microscopic form by transplanted gesture, in its vast all-consuming form by the lives of the Richards family.

Every fiction distorts; and those distortions are unretrievable because all we have to refer to are other fictions. The circularity of *Dhalgren* is the circularity of the search for truth, which depends entirely on a network of interdependent descriptions for its sense, on the decision we must make, just as the Richards have, of which are expendable and which are not.

Delany, by reinserting text into text, by all his crossing loops, here makes self-conscious the fiction-making process. His objectives do not differ that greatly from those of Gertrude Stein in much of her fiction, and particularly in her essays. Stein, with her repetitive, syntax-fracturing prose, constructs a number of sentential micro-loops; her many-jointed sentences reach back, by endlessly rebeginning, to the verbal processes behind the writing itself. With the various parts of the sentence mapped, as it were, onto themselves, what may show through is the nature of the links between them, the mental twist at each syntactic pause. Ideally, unattainably, the act of sentence generation would be fully experienced.

In his admirable critical effort *The American Shore* (to be published in 1978 by Dragon Press), Delany elaborates on a distinction originated by Roland Barthes, that between readerly and writerly functions, which will be useful here.

Stein's loops are writerly loops. She is interested in the act of setting words to paper and its relation to speech. Delany's loops are readerly; he is interested in the act of reading and its relation to perception. Hence, his intensively foregrounded prose, on the microscopic level, is one absorbed with perception, with the constitution of sensations. The concerns of both Delany and Stein intersect where speech and perception do, on the level of thought.

By its many repetitions of texts in various states, including the simplest (for the reader) state of pure narrative, *Dhalgren* minutely maps the passage from reality to fiction. Within a framework of distortion we have three (again the trinity) Bellonas: the Bellona of experience (narrative or notebook, undecideable), of report (*The Bellona Times*), and of fiction (narrative or notebook). Since all three are mutually dependent there is no end to the proliferation of fiction within fiction that makes up *Dhalgren*.

In such a flux, with all the moorings of reference loosened, there is no place to draw the final line between the ordering of perception and the structuring of the narrative. At the limits of self-distortion, the aesthetic and the perceptual become hopelessly entangled; representation and thing become one. Report becomes perception, if it is no longer fiction, and perception report, if it is stripped of the status of truth. Yet in ordering a fiction as readers we perform tasks of figure recognition and arrangement analogous to those in the simplest act of perception. *Dhalgren*'s fictional illusions, its momentary resolutions that quickly slide out of focus like the Mateland Warehouse, are in this sense no different from its giant suns and double moons, or the optical tricks of an Escher (who crops up as one of the artifacts of Bellona, one of his volumes of drawings stored in Denny's miniature collection of artifacts).

Similarly, to make the obligatory mirroring reading, to constitute a sensation is to perpetrate a small fiction.

As a final illustration, let us take the name *Dhalgren* which, throughout the novel, is no more than a readerly expectation, but out of which, with the reader as accessory, Kid constructs a small fiction. The name *William Dhalgren* is, first, one among an arbitrary ranking of names, an unexplained list in the notebook. Later, *Dhalgren* is the one name in the list that Kid remembers after it has been lost (again, his perception completely readerly). Still later we are given the subtlest of nudges in the letter from Calkins which bears, at the bottom, the intriguing legend, RC:wd. We have by then met Bill who, as a reporter on the *Bellona Times*, seems to be Roger's righthand man. Thus when Kid, in the same scene where he spontaneously remembers part of his name, jumps to the totally unfounded conclusion that Bill is William *Dhalgren*, we are more than ready to cheerfully conclude that all questions of names and titles have been resolved.

Need we insist on it? The identity of Bill and William Dahlgren is never established.

The title of *Dhalgren* extends over no fixed thing in the world of Bellona, and connects only with a readerly expectation in ours: expectation, the quantity most commonly transferred from reality to fiction, its most powerful ordering force.

As readers not otherwise informed we must assume that Kid lacks the most important ingredient of our expectation, the knowledge that this is a novel called *Dhalgren*, but what he has instead is the constitution of the word itself, the experience that prepares its later elevation to a fiction. After hearing the word Grendal at orgasm, Kid later reports:

> "Grendal grendalgrendalgrendalgrendalgren..." still ran through my head. Suddenly I realized I hadn't been listening carefully enough; I'd stuck the brake in at the wrong place. The actual word I'd heard at orgasm and that, for the last few minutes, had been repeating in my head was "...*Dhalgren*..." I wiped myself with part of the second page of the Bellona Times, January 22, 1776. (p. 679)

Epiphany is followed, as in Raymond Chandler, by some stagey bit of humdrum. *Dhalgren*. Grendal. The allusion is chthonic, a journey into the underworld, a descent past the conscious and pre-conscious to the dangers of desire—of expectation—that lie beneath. *Dhalgren*: a word heard at orgasm, one of the tiny experiments in linguistic alchemy conducted eternally in our heads, out of which all reality is made.

—Jean Mark Gawron
New York

REFERENCES

1. Samuel R. Delany, "Of Sex, Objects, Systems, Sales, S-F, and Other Things," p. 27. In typescript.

2. Willard Van Orman Quine, "Methodological Reflections on Current Linguistic Theory" in *On Noam Chomsky: Critical Essays, Gilbert Harmon*, ed. (Garden City, New Jersey: Anchor Books, 1974).

Rites of Reversal: Double Consciousness in Delany's Dhalgren

by Mary Kay Bray[41]

[from *Black American Literature Forum*, Vol. 18, Number 2, Joe Weixlmann, editor, Terre Haute, Summer 1984]

One of the pleasures of reading *Dhalgren* comes from the fact that, as Delany says in his dedication, it is a "book about many things." This 1975 novel, Delany's masterwork to date, captures its readers' imaginations on so many levels that any one area might well be the subject of nearly limitless discussion. One approach which has not received much attention, however, is that which views Delany's blackness as a context for his works. Delany has never made an issue of race, nor has he written at any length specifically about racial issues except to the extent that his main characters tend to be outsiders, alienated in some way from their cultural frameworks. Still, he reminds readers that knowledge of a work's contexts is important. In his essay "Of Sex, Objects, Signs, Systems, Sales, SF, and Other Things," he discusses the necessity of an understanding of the then-recent discovery of the Earth's roundness to a reading of Shakespeare's *Tempest*: "a contemporary play-goer who did not 'believe' in the roundness of the earth, nor in the existence of out-lying tropical islands, and had no feeling for the new distinctions between fantasy/magic/reality/science that were being etched... would... be totally at sea." In the same essay he reminds readers of his own contexts: "I am black, I have spent time in a mental hospital, and much of my adult life has been passed on society's margins. My attraction to... [these contexts] as subject matter... is not so much the desire to write autobiography, but the far more parochial desire to set matters straight...."[42]

---

41. Mary Kay Bray is a Chair of the Department of Literature and Language at Wilmington College in Ohio. She received her Ph.D. from the University of Colorado, where she was the first person to write a dissertation on science fiction.

42. An unpublished manuscript circulated by the author, pp. 9–10, 23.

Delany's blackness has, in fact, received some discussion. Both Emerson Littlefield, in his discussion of Delany's use of a new, black mythology, and Jane B. Weedman, in her book on Delany, see the writer's blackness as an essential frame of reference.[43]

Since Delany does not make race a sole focus in his works, in what sense is his being not just an American science-fiction writer but a black science-fiction writer a context important to *Dhalgren*? Here Weedman sheds some light. She points to *Dhalgren*'s epigraph, "You have confused the true and the real," as pertinent to the conflict suggested in the novel between the prevailing idealism of the American dream and "black American reality...." This conflict comes from what she calls Delany's "double consciousness," which she defines as a "psychological dichotomy which results when an individual lives in a culture, such as the black community, yet must be aware for his survival of the workings and expectations of a dominate (sic) culture...."[44]

Although Weedman does not refer to it, her concept of double consciousness echoes the classical formulation of the term, from W.E.B. Du Bois' *The Souls of Black Folk* (1903):

> ...the Negro is a sort of seventh son, born with a veil, and gifted with second-sight in this American world—a world which yields him no true self-consciousness, but only lets him see himself through the revelation of the other world. It is a peculiar sensation, this double consciousness, this sense of always looking at one's self through the eyes of others.... One ever feels his twoness....[45]

---

43. Emerson Littlefield, "The Mythologies of Race and Science in Samuel R. Delany's *The Einstein Intersection* and *Nova*," *Extrapolation*, 23 (1982), 235–42; Jane B. Weedman, *Samuel R. Delany* (Mercer Island, WA: Starmont House, 1982).

44. *Samuel R. Delany*, pp. 61, 12.

45. Rpt. In *Three Negro Classics*, ed. John Hope Franklin (New York: Avon, 1965), pp. 214–215.

Delany himself attributes to his works his awareness, as a black, of two cultural worlds—"I had a chance to compare different cultures in a way that still influences what I do and what I write."[46] It is this cultural double consciousness which is manifest in *Dhalgren.*

In particular, this double awareness manifests itself in *Dhalgren* not as a specific presentation of black experience—characters and events in the novel represent a variety of races and experiences—but as irony. *Dhalgren*'s readers are brought to an ironic cultural double perception of "the true and the real," akin to the "twoness" felt by Du Bois as, repeatedly, archetypes of American thought assumed to be "true" undergo ironic reversals in the "real" experience wrought by the novel. Delany provides a key to his use of irony in discussing how to break away from what he calls "old" ways of perceiving:

> If you have a gut response to a story, you are not responding to something new; you... are really responding to... a story you were told when you were six or seven, which has been so overlaid, you don't recognize what it really is. But your subconscious recognizes it. If you're going to work with those old things, I think you do better to work with them with a sense of irony.... You also have to know what those old stories are and what they mean in order to actually say something new....[47]

It is through just this "sense of irony" that *Dhalgren* creates its "new," double perception of American experience.

The novel contains ample clues to the fact that its focus is distinctly American. First, its setting is exclusively American. No other Delany novel has been set solely in the United States, and no other main character of his has remained in the same place from start to finish. Further, *Dhalgren*'s particular setting, Bellona, seems to be located right at the center of the country. It is equally far from the east and west coasts and

---

46. Interview with Samuel R. Delany in Charles Platt, *Dream Makers: The Uncommon People Who Write Science Fiction* (New York: Berkley Books, 1980), p. 73.

47. Ibid., pp. 72–73.

from the country's northern and southern borders.[48] We are never told more definitely where Bellona is, for the city seems to function primarily as a symbolic center of American consciousness and behavior. That Bellona is presented as "internal landscape" (p. 440), a "city of inner discordances and retinal distortions" (p. 14)—in fact, as a city within a mind—combines *Dhalgren*'s focus on American experience with a particular emphasis on American perception. Another telling indication of such a focus in *Dhalgren* is the character of Kid himself. Here is a main character who is significantly half Native American and half white—a kind of personified doubleness—and who lives out patterns familiar in American literary and historical experience. He is brought up in a small, upstate New York town where he is exposed to sex and death, those American preoccupations noted by Leslie Fiedler in *Love and Death in the American Novel*. His youthful travels in foreign lands are a kind of search through various "frontiers"; yet when he enters Bellona he is still an innocent, an innocent on an overt quest for identity. Viewed from this perspective, Kid is an American dreamer who winds up at a symbolic center of American dreams. Only in *Dhalgren*, such dreams do not have archetypally American results.

By means of its ironies, *Dhalgren* brings readers to a simultaneous awareness both of traditional American myths and preoccupations and of their failure to be viable, at least for some. Among the myths and preoccupations reversed or undercut during Kid's stay in Bellona are ones which have characterized American letters. In particular, ironies in *Dhalgren* emanate from the pattern of quest and initiation suggested above, from a variety of plays upon the concept of American individualism, and from a thirst for moral absolutes set against an intensely relative background.

That *Dhalgren* contains a theme of quest and initiation is nothing new to American writing. Even a partial list of American works concerned with this theme, such as *Huckleberry Finn*, *Billy Budd*, *The Red Badge of Courage*, *The Great Gatsby*, *Go Down, Moses*, and more recently *Catch-22*, reads like a roll call of American masterpieces. All of these works

---

48. Samuel R. Delany, *Dhalgren* (New York: Vintage, 2001), p. 13. This and subsequent in-text page references are to the Vintage edition of *Dhalgren*, containing the author's corrections to the original printing.

contain an innocent main character who undergoes a basically linear series of experiences which lead him to a mature realization that frees him to act rather than be acted upon. Although one critic argues otherwise,[49] the quest pattern is as clearly apparent in *Dhalgren* as in any of these mainstream works. In Delany's rendering, however, the resolutions of the hero's journey are ironic.

Kid, when he arrives at Bellona amnesic and nameless, is more extreme an innocent than most other American literary figures of his type. Once in Bellona he undergoes a series of different experiences which parallel those in traditional tales of quest and initiation. Bellona contains four different types of social order, and Kid receives some sort of initiation into them all: a woodland "utopia," middleclass civilized life, Calkins' world of wealth and power, and the scorpions' lawless street society. During this time Kid also experiences the realities of becoming an artist and of being loved, and he apparently "finds himself" when he settles in as leader of the scorpions.

Numerous other incidents and images related to Kid's quest symbolize forms of initiation. *Dhalgren* opens with Kid's being sent by a mysterious female "guide" into a cave where he finds and drapes himself with the chain of prisms, mirrors, and lenses which he sees in the light of knight-errantry, an archetypal reminder of quest and initiation—"Three gifts, he thought: armor, weapon, title (like the prisms, lenses, mirrors on the chain itself)" (p. 18). Too, a pattern of sexual encounters begins just before Kid enters Bellona and continues thereafter, with significant activity taking place at the outset of each new stage of participation in Bellonan life. Patterned in this way *Dhalgren* becomes a kind of rite of passage which precedes each new form of experience. Other initiatory incidents have to do with blood and bathing. Twice Kid must wash himself clean of blood—first when the scorpions beat him and again after he has retrieved Bobby Richards' body from the elevator shaft. Such incidents are almost stock symbols of baptism into new life, symbols of purification and rebirth Indeed, all of Kid's baths, preceded by baptisms in blood or not, are described in such thorough detail that they assume ritual proportions.

---

49. See Douglas Barbour's *Worlds Out of Words: The SF Novels of Samuel R. Delany* (Frome, Somerset: Bran's Head Books, 1979), p.92.

One begins to see Kid as a *perpetual* initiate, and it is precisely in this circular cycle that one begins to see Delany's rendering of the traditional pattern as ironic. Quest and initiation do not have the results that they have in the "old stories."

Even the pattern of the various names Kid receives, culminating in his partial recovery of his supposedly real name, sheds ironic light on his quest. Kid goes through three forms of the name originally given him by Tak—"The Kid," "Kidd," and "Kid." All of them, of course, connote innocence. The first two also suggest that he is an outsider, still on a search, who does not fit into his surroundings (as neither Billy the Kid nor Captain Kidd fit theirs). The last, however, the name that comes to him through Denny when he finds a home with the scorpions, does not suggest a mature, realized identity, but only youthfulness, newness, and, again, innocence. As implied through the Daphne-figure who starts him on his quest and then turns into a tree, he retains his original state rather than growing from experience. Further, he achieves his goal of finding his identity only partially and ambiguously. His name may be *Dhalgren* or it may be Michael Henry something—another doubleness embedded in the novel and each uncertain possibility comes to him set in an ironically conventional context. It is after undergoing still another sexual rite of initiation in the gangbang of Risa that Kid half remembers the name *Dhalgren* (p. 679). And again, it is when Kid enters a Dionysian dance in the park—a dance which, as image, suggests a mandala, an Eastern symbol of wholeness—that he has his incomplete recollection of being Michael Henry (p. 779). These contradictory revelations are confusing rather than enlightening, and, in a further heightening of their irony, may not even matter: "...one becomes more and more suspicious... that the position of the characters will have so changed by the book's end that the answers to the initial questions will have become trivial" (pp. 755–56).

Such ironic trivialization of Kid's initial concerns is intensified when he is contrasted to his literary predecessors, Huck Finn, Ike McCaslin, Nick Carraway, et al., who begin their quests more or less unconsciously but end their rites of passage in full control, as conscious, self-directing individuals. Kid, however, begins his quest through Bellona with the conscious goal of finding out who he is and ends his experiences drifting with the tide of events, not consciously an identified individual and not consciously choosing his actions. He leaves the city not because he wants to go but because a catastrophe strikes and its momentum carries him to Bellona's edge. Even the structure of the final chapter "Anathemata," a non-linear palimpsest of chaos, reflects the directionlessness of his life.

In fact, the structuring of the initiation theme in *Dhalgren* as a whole is ironic. From first to last Kid repeats his journey of initiation so that *Dhalgren*'s thematic sequence becomes a circular one—it moves from innocence to initiation to innocence to initiation to innocence in an endless chain much like the closed loop with which Kid girds himself in the book's opening pages, the chain which, when broken, signifies nothing. Kid's non-linear journey becomes an ironic parody of the literary archetype; readers are brought to a double awareness both of the traditional pattern in American thought and of its failure to function in the actual American experience which Bellona embodies.

Another concept idealized in American consciousness and treated with irony in *Dhalgren* is that of romantic individualism. Delany plays with several familiar American variations on this theme, from the rugged individualism associated with the frontier experience through the notion of the self-made man who lives out the dream of success to the idea of the outlaw as hero. Again, readers are both given the traditional assumptions and simultaneously reminded that they do not work.

The mythical American frontier, for instance, is a place of beginnings, a place where the individual, free from the customs and restrictions of society and set in a context of infinite possibilities, is able to shape a meaningful existence for himself, to grow up by means of his own individual choices. Certainly *Dhalgren* contains ample reminders of this traditional mold. Bellona offers in its park a landscape which can be viewed as a type of frontier, a landscape which, though John and Milly try to civilize it, remains wild in many ways. It is a basically unstable setting, difficult to navigate because its paths seem to take a limitless number of directions (p. 318). While Kid is in the park, he is first exposed to all of the possibilities from among which he can choose the course of his life. Here is the setting in which he first meets Lanya, first acquires the spiral notebook that is to be his means of becoming a poet, and first sees or hears of the different Bellonan social orders. *Dhalgren* even provides an appropriate symbolism for the stone lions which guard the park. These lions may "pick up their paws, apocopate, and go to town" (p. 731). Lions, phonetically apocopated, are lies, and one cannot help thinking of that aspect of the frontier myth which sees society negatively, as the realm of the artificial, and the frontier positively, as the realm of the natural. Indeed, Kid responds to society's artificialities in the stock manner. Ultimately he rejects both the middleclass, reality-denying "labyrinth" of the Richards' Labrys apartments—significantly fronted by a "young, dead tree" (p. 122)—and the jaded, highly sophisticated upper-class civilization to which he is exposed through Roger Calkins' minions.

Dhalgren's presentation, then, of the individualism emerging from the frontier experience might appear to be the conventional one. The groundwork for Kid's experiences in Bellona is laid in a setting of infinite possibilities from which he seems to gain much of value. Yet Kid turns out to be one individual upon whom the frontier experience has no real effect. He breaks with Lanya and life in the park in what is at best only a semi-conscious state, a five-day blackout from which he can recall only one day's worth of events. Shortly thereafter he abandons his poetry as well—"I don't think I'm gonna write any more poems" (p. 357). During this time he takes up with the scorpions, but since his decision to do so comes after he has done so (p. 368), he cannot be said to have purposefully chosen his new life. Even the idea that his experience has made Kid a better person than he once was, evidenced in his ability to judge and reject the artificialities of society, is undercut by his alliance with the scorpions, who are, literally, nothing more than a gang of marauders. Far from fulfilling the mythical pattern of conscious choice based upon individual maturity gained through the frontier experience, Kid's behavior amounts to directionlessness and desertion. In fact, his early desertions of Lanya and his poetry, although he returns to both for a time, only serve to prefigure what, in one possible reading of *Dhalgren*'s "ending," is his ultimate desertion of his whole experience in Bellona.

Concomitant with this ironic undercutting of the American ideal of frontier individualism is Delany's further reversal of the romantic archetype in his rendition of the self-made man living out the American dream of success. This view of material prosperity and renown, possible for the self-reliant individual who through skill, ingenuity, and hard work finally makes his fortune, is the other side of the myth of the frontier. If on one hand the implied rewards of life in the new land are moral and emotional, on the other hand they are most certainly concrete and socially advantageous. Delany's metafictional remarks on science fiction, which come to us through Tak, also pertain rather directly to the uniquely American success myth which emphasizes self-reliant action directed purposefully toward a goal: "First: A single man can change the course of a whole world.... Second: The only measure of intelligence or genius is its linear and practical application.... Three: The Universe is an essentially hospitable place...." (p. 372).

Kid "follows all the conventions" (p. 372). He goes to work for the Richards out of a sense that he needs to get a job and make money. Having contracted to deliver his services for a fair price, he persists in his efforts even when his employers and conditions of employment become increasingly bizarre. When Arthur Richards makes only partial payment for the work he has done, Kid feels cheated. Likewise, Kid fits the conventional mold in his desire for fame as a reward for his being a poet. He wants all the accoutrements of success: "His eyes dropped in a well of *Time* magazine covers ('Poet Refuses Pulitzer Prize'), the audience's faces as he stood on Minor Latham's stage where he had consented to give a rare reading. He hauled himself back before the fantasies' intensity hit pain" (p. 170). To this extent, Kid is a typically American dreamer who applies his skill in search of financial and social rewards.

Unfortunately, in *Dhalgren* all this linear and practical application of Kid's "genius" does not have the expected outcomes. The money he gets from Arthur Richards, despite his anger at being cheated, finally doesn't matter. He gives it back. In fact, money in general is valueless in Bellona except when it is used to play elaborate games, as when Lanya tries out prostitution or Kid experiments with mugging. Too, when fame comes for his book of poems, Kid is no longer even sure that he wrote *Brass Orchids* and, ironically, cannot recall the meaning that it once had for him (p. 633). These reversals are congruent with Tak's response to Kid's request for further explanation of the way in which he has Bellona "figured out" according to the science-fiction paradigm given above. Now the conventional model is gone:

> "I don't understand anything about it. I'm a God-damn engineer. I take a plug; I put it in one socket; and it works. I put it into another one; and it doesn't. I go into an office building and one elevator works, and only the lights on the top floor. That's impossible, by anything I know

> about. I go down a street: buildings are burning. I go down the same street the next day. They're still burning. Two weeks later, I go down the same street and nothing looks like it's been burned at all. Maybe time is just running backward here. Or sideways. But that's impossible too." (pp. 376–77)

Once again, *Dhalgren* sets up a pattern common to the expectations of American experience only to undermine its traditional significance.

A third means by which American romantic individualism is ironically reprised in *Dhalgren* is through the myth of the exceptional outlaw. Because American culture has been fascinated by tales of individuals who make their own laws in dramatic ways, figures like Billy the Kid (with whom Kid's first name associates him), Jesse James, Butch Cassidy, Bonnie and Clyde, and so on have become legends in American thought. American literature, too, abounds with heroic outsiders like Thoreau, Huck Finn, Tom Joad, and a great many more who break laws and defy the system in response to some "higher" code of their own. Here is rugged individualism run rampant, and it clearly holds a kind of attraction. Once again *Dhalgren* places Kid in the traditional context. He becomes leader of the scorpions, Bellona's resident "outlaws," who in their energy and restlessness, their unpredictable and violent behavior, may be seen as a force for growth and change in Bellonan life. Like other outlaws, they break the stasis that has overcome society, as illustrated in particular by their first raid on the Emboriky department store where they disrupt and permanently alter the small society of people living there (pp. 332–44). Thus Kid is not only in a situation in which he is free to become himself outside the constraints of any settled social order; apparently he can also influence the forms society takes. Further mythical overtones surround the scorpions and their activity, for much as notorious outlaws have become larger than life in American consciousness, the scorpions have literally become larger than life in Bellonan consciousness by means of the images they project for themselves with their holographic light-shields. They also, and Kid among them, adhere to an unspoken code of behavior—as an outsider discovers when he violates that code (pp. 700–04). The idea of such a code among outlaws is at least as old as the myth of the outlaw itself.

Nonetheless, the view of the American outlaw in *Dhalgren* ends up an ironic one. The scorpions appear to be lawless and free to mold their own destinies, but actually they are restricted by their own directionlessness. They have no plan of action, no goals; most of their time is spent watching "the dull sky slipping" (p. 734). Kid, as their leader, neither grows into selfhood nor visibly affects the forms of society. He realizes that although "people think of us as energetic, active, violent. At any time… a third of us are asleep and half have not been out of the nest for two, three, four days…" (p. 760). Further, as a force for change set in an already confusing and mutable context, the scorpions have no real sting. They frighten most other inhabitants of Bellona, but they are largely ineffectual. The Richards simply try to move out of their reach at the Labra apartments, and Calkins' group, on the night the scorpions attend his big party, uses them as a source of entertainment. The American outlaw, to gain mythical stature, must do something purposeful and spectacular; the scorpions do neither. Their dull lives undercut any mythical view. In its ironic denial of the substance of the outlaw-hero myth, as in its similar denials of other aspects of American romantic individualism, *Dhalgren* creates again a double perception of American assumptions. Viewed from this double perspective, what American consciousness presumes to be true is not necessarily what really happens.

Another major, typically American, preoccupation in *Dhalgren* is the hunger for absolutes which emerges in Kid's quest. American society has been characterized by a kind of cultural Manichaeism; things are either right or wrong, good or evil, and this concern has dominated much American fiction.[50] Ahab is metamorphosized into evil incarnate by choosing to believe that Moby Dick is evil: Hester Prynne redeems herself through absolute expiation of sin, and even Silas Lapham, with his business morality, repudiates his fortune for the sake of moral unrightness. In Kid, *Dhalgren* too contains such absolutism. As Ahab wishes to pierce the "paste-board mask" in *Moby-Dick*, Kid wishes "to reach up and peel off all that sky" (p. 378). We are further reminded of Ahab's absolutism when Kid sees "pale leviathans" in the skies outside the Labrys

50. See Richard Chase's *The American Novel and Its Tradition* (New York: Anchor Books, 1957), p. 11.

apartments (p. 220). In fact, Kid's whole quest for identity, love, sanity, and artistry is a quest for absolute truth. Being "Kid" is identity enough for the context of Bellona; yet Kid pursues his true name. Being loved by Lanya and Denny is love enough; yet Kid is haunted by reminders of the woman who turned into a tree. Being assured by Madame Brown that he copes adequately with his surroundings is sanity enough; yet Kid continues to fear that he is crazy. Being the author of *Brass Orchids* is artistry enough; yet Kid fears that somehow his poems are not "good" poems and that good poetry cannot be written by a "bad" person (pp. 352–53). Kid's search for absolutes culminates in his interview with Calkins at the monastery. Although it is Calkins he has wanted to see, Kid keeps turning the conversation back to the mysterious Father who heads the monastery, and asks three times, "Is the Father a good man?" (pp. 744–46). Calkins' reply pinpoints the issue: "You're afraid that for want of one good man the city shall be struck down?" (p. 745).

The trouble is that the only thing absolute about Bellona is its relativity. Bellona is, as one critic puts it, a moral labyrinth, "itself the projection of the hero's moral confusion."[51] The landscape in which Kid's moral search is set is a subjective, mutable one in which any such absolutism is simply irrelevant. Kid has picked the most ironic location possible in which not to be satisfied with relative answers. Predictably, his search is futile. Kid's reaction to not receiving the answers he seeks heightens the irony related to his search for them in the first place. The difference between Kid and Ahab or Hester Prynne is that the latter characters confront the dilemmas with which they are faced and make moral decisions which determine their subsequent actions, whereas Kid simply records moral crises such as his interview with Calkins in his notebook and goes on drifting from one situation to another, his choices apparently not affected one way or the other. He comes to embody neither evil, like Ahab, nor redemption, like Hester Prynne; his quest for truth finally leaves him unchanged, and herein lies the irony in *Dhalgren*'s treatment of moral absolutism—traditional expectations are raised, then thwarted. Again readers are left aware both of archetypal American patterns and of their unworkability in actual practice.

---

51. George Edgar Slusser, *The Delany Intersection: Samuel R. Delany Considered as a Writer of Semi-Precious Words* (San Bernardino: Borgo Press, 1977), p. 62.

In addition to these major thematic ironies, *Dhalgren* is filled with other significant ironies, such as the inversion of character stereotypes in the black man-white woman rape plot, in which George is the knowledgeable, sensitive individual and June is driven by her lusts, perhaps even to murdering her brother. By means of such inversions, readers are not allowed to come away from *Dhalgren* without an ironic double awareness of American experience, an awareness through which they are brought outside their standard perceptions, outside the old stories they may have assumed to be "true" to a new perception of the "real" which cohabits American life. This new perception surely contains that "twoness" of which Du Bois speaks. One might add that such double consciousness pertains equally well to other non-dominant groups in American culture: For all such groups, dominant cultural assumptions are ironically unworkable. Bellona's name, that of a minor Roman war goddess, suggests the conflict between the true and the real, but it would be a mistake to view *Dhalgren*'s presentation of this "war" in American awareness as a didactic one. Delany is not a didactic writer, and *Dhalgren* is not a didactic work. Rather, it is a holistic one.

Bellona, as a symbolic center of American consciousness, embodies in its interactions with Kid the whole of American experience, and for that reason, "Very few suspect the existence of this city. It is as if not only the media but the laws of perception themselves have redesigned knowledge and perception to pass it" (p. 14). It takes a certain doubleness of perception to be able to see Bellona, for it is a place in which a person can become an initiate and still not learn, in which he can build a new life and still not have a home, in which he can seek a moral basis for life and then forget his moral concern in going about his life. In Bellona, these dualities accumulate, so that at times the city's streets seem to "underpin all the capitals of the world" while at other times the whole place seems "a pointless and ugly mistake" (p. 354). Through such ironies, *Dhalgren* confronts and embraces the doubleness of American life.

Operating very much in accord with MacLeish's injunction that "a poem should not mean/but be,"[52] Delany does not use this ironic mode or elicit its contingent double consciousness in his readers in order to instruct

---

52. In *Ars Poetica*.

them in some message about American life. In fact, he has cautioned readers about trying to pin *Dhalgren* down to a particular meaning.[53] Rather, he gently leads his audience back to the experience he has created, and back, and back again. For however we view *Dhalgren*'s structure, whether as a circle, a Moebius strip, a series of perceptions and perspectives like those provided by Kid's optic chain,[54] or even as a subjective account of events recorded by a dyslexic epileptic,[55] the fact is that this is a structure which does not point outward to any external message but continually returns its focus to itself, to the experience it embodies. Denny's book of M.C. Escher prints is a key here, since Escher's experiments in perspective often combine inside and outside so that images flow endlessly back into themselves. It is through this sort of topology that *Dhalgren* captures that American experience which is hard to see unless one can see double. All events—both mythical and, ironically, anti-mythical—return to themselves: The reader does not journey through them to some conclusion and new beginning as is the case with much of the apocalyptic literature echoed by the disaster in Bellona; he or she simply is brought into and left with experience itself. In this sense, *Dhalgren* "exposes" rather than teaches, does not "mean," but is.

This nonjudgmental quality of *Dhalgren* is one of its many strengths. The novel's ironies serve to widen its readers' field of vision by bringing them into contact with the complicated reality of there being more than just archetypal possibilities in American experience. But *Dhalgren* makes no pretense of weighing that experience in terms of positive and negative, right and wrong any more than Ishmael, for instance, chooses between Ahab and Starbuck. "I can't judge," Newboy says, "because I am still in it. Frankly I will not be able to judge once out of it" (p. 354). Even Kamp, the American astronaut who searches while in Bellona for the clear and simple truth of stars and is thwarted by the ambiguous veil of fog which shrouds the city, sees that America is "such a big country now.... I guess

---

53. "Of Sex, Objects, Signs, Systems, Sales, SF, and Other Things," p. 27.

54. Barbour, pp. 108–12.

55. Wedman, p. 63–65.

it's hard for anyone to know..." (p. 707). America is like Bellona, a "great maze—forever adjustable, therefore unlearnable—" (p. 383). What Delany, as a black writer, does in *Dhalgren* is to superimpose the "real" upon the "true" in such a way that readers are brought to that double consciousness concomitant with a complete view of American life. The country cannot be taught by *Dhalgren* or any other book, and it cannot be learned by readers of books, but its essence can be shaped in loops of words containing both its myths and ironic denials of those myths. The experience of America is one of the experiences created by *Dhalgren*. What the reader does with that experience is up to him or her.

This You-Shaped Hole of Insight and Fire
Meditations on Delany's Dhalgren

by Robert Elliot Fox

Dhalgren can best be characterized by the words that Kid, the novel's protagonist, uses to characterize his own book of poems: "a complicitous illusion in lingual catalysis, a crystalline and conscientious alkahest" (707). This is the sort of language one would expect to find in contemporary criticism, not in a work of fiction, except that, since the advent of the postmodern, the borders between these ostensibly different sorts of texts, the creative and the critical, have been jumbled, if not abolished. Moreover, the choice of terms is interesting: one drawn from alchemy (alkahest, the sought-after universal solvent), the other drawn from chemistry (catalysis, the action of a catalyst, a substance that modifies a chemical reaction). One suggests "magic," the other "science," but chemistry grew out of alchemy, so the two are not fully dichotomous. Moreover, alchemy should be understood as a spiritual process, wherein the alchemist himself is the subject of transformation, from that which is "base" to that which is "golden," refined. We might say that whatever its materiality, there still is something magical about language; that this also is true of art; that our language may change as we change, and that we may also be changed by language (art).

Again, "magic" is the province of fantasy, "science" that of (classic) SF. Delany has written both, and *Dhalgren* participates in both.

At the start of chapter 2 of Book I, we are told that the past of the narrator/protagonist "fragments on the terrible and vivid ephemera of now" (10). The first line of the novel contains the word "wound" (used, like "fragments," as a verb), while the adjectives "shattered," "dead," and "broken" are found in the first three lines of the third chapter. If this is not the wasteland, it is, surely, an Ozymandian realm in which the pride of late capitalist society has been (at least within this particular "circle") shaken, if not yet fully humbled.[56] "Civility, for Europeans, has always been a life lived in cities. Outside the polis, as Aristotle said, there were only beasts and heroes."[57] Delany has reversed this scenario: the city of Bellona, at least, has lost all civility, and it is precisely within this city that we find the "beasts and heroes," or, at any rate, their anemic/anomic contemporary reflections.

"Very few suspect the existence of this city," we are told (14). Yet Bellona is (or was) a major mid-western metropolis,[58] with a population of nearly two million now reduced to about a thousand. It can't really be a secret, yet, curiously, despite whatever catastrophe has occurred, the only "explorers" (temporary immigrants, actually) seem to be countercultural recruits (with some exceptions like the astronaut, Captain Kamp) drawn to Bellona the way aspiring hippies were drawn to San Francisco during the Summer of Love in 1967[59] (which was just two years before Delany began writing *Dhalgren*, and which I take to be one of the novel's prime catalysts; indeed, the first draft of the novel was written in San Francisco. Significantly, Kid's companions are described as the "slightly demonic heirs" of the "flowerchildren" [754]). Why would the National Guard, the news media, the Red Cross abandon Bellona to its unaccountable fate?

---

56. Mrs. Richards' comment that "Management must be having all sorts of difficulty while we're going through this crisis" (225) takes on a whole different level of meaning if we read "management" as implying "the established order" and not just the operators of one largely abandoned apartment building. This is not Mrs. Richards' own implication, but to the extent that Bellona represents, not just some paranormal event(s), but a crisis at the core of our whole system, the implication is the text's.

57. Anthony Pagden, "The Translation of America," *Times Literary Supplement* (December 13, 1991), 11.

58. An assumption based on the statement in the novel that New York and San Francisco are "a ways to go, either direction" (12).

59. *Heavenly Breakfast*, in fact, documents what Delany calls "The Winter of Love" on New York's Lower East Side, in the winter and spring of 1967/68. A literal winter, yes, but also a "winter of discontent," suggesting not simply a contrast to the neo-Edenism of West Coast psychedelectation, but also implying that the Summer of Love itself had a cold underside, which *Dhalgren* surely reflects more than it does any hoped-for state of bliss.

Bellona is like a cyst in the American body politic, present but encapsulated. *Dhalgren* was written, after all, during a period when this country's general population (seemingly a blind, rather than a silent, majority) was being surprised by sudden eruptions of an unpleasant reality which, for the most part, it had not bothered to acknowledge. When the previously "invisible" ghettoes of America exploded in violence, for example, it might have been said of the urban areas in question that "few suspected their existence," because the country had bought the illusion that the cities were steel-and-glass monuments to success and was unwilling to explore what lay in the long, deep shadows.[60]

There are three quotations from Geoffrey O'Brien's *Dream Time: Chapters from the Sixties* that provide illuminating resonances with regard to *Dhalgren*: (1) "Tribes are emerging from the midst of a terminally mechanized civilization; our parents have mysteriously given birth to their own ancestors." (2) "Democracy had evolved into the most sophisticated con game in human history.... Freedom was permitted as long as it didn't change anything." (3) "To improvise is to invent heaven."[61]

According to G.S. Kirk, "Chaos in archaic Greek means 'gap' rather than 'disorder'..." The earth and the sky had to be forced asunder before the world of man could come into being; chaos was the gap between the two realms.[62] There is clearly a "gap" between Bellona and the "real" world, and, to get from one to the other, you literally have to cross a bridge.

Bellona is the labyrinth in which you stalk your self.

In classical mythology, Bellona, sister of Mars, is the goddess of war. (Bellona is mentioned at least once in James Joyce's *Finnegans Wake*

---

60. Delany has stated that "American readers—at least most urban American readers—recognize [descriptions in *Dhalgren*), through the allegorical scrim, as all too realistic portraits of vast areas of our great American cities: burned-out, under-populated, all but abandoned. The specificity of those descriptions weights the reading (of the novel's significance) away from the universal and toward the local" (Interview with Samuel R. Delany, *Diacritics* [Fall 1986], 36).

61. New York: Viking, 1988, 96, 129, 36.

62. *The Nature of the Greek Myths* (Penguin, 1974), 46.

[78.31]. This book's circular structure, its last, incomplete sentence leading back to its first, likewise incomplete one, provides the model for *Dhalgren*'s own tale-in-its-mouth structure.) Indeed, elsewhere in his work, Delany speaks of a city on the planet Mars called Bellona (it is mentioned frequently in Triton, for example). Delany has claimed that the Bellona portrayed in *Dhalgren* is the "original" city after which the Martian city of Bellona is named.[63]

The exhaustion yet inescapability of myth seems to be one of Delany's main themes in *Dhalgren*. Sandra Miesel has written that Delany "treats myth as 'metacommunication.'"[64] As Kid thinks to himself about his own work: "These things I'm writing, they're not descriptions of anything, they're complex names" (177). If one thinks of names, not in the sense of "*Dhalgren*" or "Kid" (although they themselves are complex), but rather as subject, semblance, or essence—"hermetic syllables" (219)—Kid's comment is applicable to Delany's work and the nature of mythopoesis in general.

Kid's pilgrimage reflects the depletion of the hero myth. (Think of the still apparent need for heroes in our own society, and the feet-of-clay character of many of those whom we turn into heroes.) Kid crosses the threshold (here, a bridge) into an/other realm and comes back across that same threshold after many pages, having gained no new awareness that will help to redeem the wasteland, having, indeed, not even discovered who he is. Moreover, the other realm is itself a wasteland, where mystery offers no revelations, and where confusion and mundanity appear to be the rule.[65]

---

63. Conversation with the author, February 13, 1975.

64. "Samuel R. Delany's Use of Myth in *Nova*," *Extrapolation* (May, 1971), 86.

65. In Brian Aldiss' *Frankenstein Unbound* (1973), two moons appear without warning in the sky, but Aldiss not only has given a possible explanation of this phenomenon (the breakdown of space/time which is crucial to the plot), he has also given the apparition a symbolic meaning, since it comes at the moment when the monster and his "bride" appear together for the first time. Similar apparitions in *Dhalgren* allow of no such clear reading; they remain inscrutable.

Time is supposed to be "out of joint" in Bellona, too, but this seems truer in the Shakespearian than in the science-fictional sense, apart from Kid's occasional temporal disorientation and the possibility that time may be looping to allow what has happened already to happen again, as the circular structure of the novel suggests. On the other hand, Roger Calkins' freewheeling dating of his newspaper (which

Delany is concerned, not with the duplication, but rather the replication of myth: with echoes, repetition, things folding back upon themselves. In *The Einstein Intersection*, those beings who take the place of the human race appear doomed to act out parodies of human mythology; in *Dhalgren*, Kid, along with some of the other characters, might well ask (with Bob Dylan) "what price you have to pay to get out of going through all these things twice." Which is why, as the "plague journal" notes, "In this city, where nothing happens, it is worth your sanity to refuse anything new" (665).

Dhalgren needs to be contextualized by reference to Delany's pornographic novel *Tides of Lust* (1973) and his autobiographical works *Heavenly Breakfast* (1979) and *The Motion of Light in Water* (1988).[66] In the case of *Tides*, we are provided with a far more extreme portrayal of sexual themes, while *Breakfast* and *Motion* re/collect personal experiences that in part inspired/incited the fictive "circle" that *Dhalgren* inscribes.

One of the characters in Delany's "essay" *Heavenly Breakfast* is named Grendahl. And some of the section titles of *Tides* read like they could have been employed in *Dhalgren*: "Riders of the Scorpion," "Alchemica," "Labyrinths." Delany's preface to his second porno novel *Hogg* is entitled "The Scorpion Garden."[67]

---

lends a punning resonance to last word in the name, *The Bellona Times*), has to do with historical "play," with a postmodernish pastiche of allusions, freedom *from*, rather than freedom *of*, information, at least as far as chronology is concerned.

"Roger Calkins," by the way, was the name of a young man who apparently disappeared around 1950. Ads seeking his whereabouts were printed frequently in alternative newspapers like the *East Village Other* and the Berkeley *Barb* during the late sixties. While working on *Dhalgren*, Delany realized that the sought-after Calkins probably would be approaching forty. Fiction could "solve" his disappearance. Thus Calkins "turns up" in Bellona, not as a burnt-out case, but as an entrepreneur with his own newspaper—one with a monopoly on the news in the absence of media competition, but nonetheless "alternative" in its approach to what passes for reality in Bellona.

66. It is worth noting that Delany has called autobiography "only another kind of fiction" (*Diacritics* interview, 44).

67. This preface, dated 1973, was published in *The Straits of Messina* (Seattle: Serconia Press, 1989). When *Hogg* finally appeared two decades later (Boulder and Normal: Fiction Collective Two and Black Ice Books, 1994), the preface was omitted.

Why "scorpions"? Is Delany thinking of Kenneth Anger's film *Scorpio Rising* (1961), a homoerotic motorpsycho nightmare?

Anyway, the scorpions already have their counterpart in the pteracycle gang in Delany's story "We, In Some Strange Power's Employ, Move On a Rigorous Line." (In the case of *Dhalgren*, it is more on the order of, "We, in some very strange circumstances, move in complex loops.")

The "end" of the novel is identical to the last words in the notebook Kid finds (261). The "beginning" of the novel is identical to the first words of the notebook (32). The first and last pages have been torn out, so the "story" begins in medias res and ends inconclusively. *Dhalgren*, to the extent that the notebook contains the same story/information, thereby contains itself, making the novel the literary equivalent of a Klein bottle, the inside of which is also the outside. There is, then, literally nothing outside of the text(s).

Pages 801, 1: "Waiting here, away from the terrifying weaponry, out of the halls of vapor and light, beyond holland and into the hills, I have come to // to wound the autumnal city."

"Holland" is Middle English, from the Dutch *holtlant*, meaning "woodland." There is a Holland Lake in Bellona, which is where the monastery is located. But since the lower case "h" in "holland" in this instance is not a typographer's error,[68] the word is employed here in its etymological sense.

Note the use of alliteration:

> Waiting/away/weaponry/wound; here/halls/holland/hills;
> halls/light/holland/hills/autumnal,

as well as this repetition:

> *and*/holland/*and.*

"I have come to // to": The repetition is a kind of stutter, in keeping, perhaps, with the broken grammar of some of the book's last sentences (e.g., "Just in the like that, if you can't remember any more if" [801]).

---

68. There indeed have been numerous typesetting errors in *Dhalgren*, and Delany has been endeavoring to track and correct these from printing to printing.

There is at least one earlier example of this, when Kid is trying to describe his book of poems: "I'm trying to-to…" (640).

The "end" of the novel is really a pause before the recorso, therefore functioning like a comma: I have come to, to…

Moreover, to "come to" is to "come around," (re)gain consciousness, get "started" again.

Remember that Kid is a former mental patient, a partial amnesiac. He has to (re)discover what has already happened, what already is. Literally, as an artist (poet), and figuratively, as a damaged individual, Kid cannot simply write himself, he has to rewrite himself, which is one reason why it all comes around again. (The emphasis on revision in *Dhalgren*, especially with regard to Kid's poems, reinforces this notion.)

"Autumnal" may refer to the season, but it is also freighted with various connotations of decline, decay, etc. It is seemingly the twilight of Bellona, but is Bellona itself not symptomatic of the twilight of the city in general?[69] "Wound" presents more of a problem. If the city is "autumnal," in its last days, is it not already wounded? And in what way can Kid wound Bellona? Indeed, the very idea of wounding the city is a reversal of the traditional pattern of the quest, which is salvational, in the sense of reinvigorating that which is ailing or dying. Wounding Bellona only makes sense if Bellona is a threat to the outside world from which Kid comes, but insofar as it is a threat, it is so only to those aspects of ordinary reality to which Kid would be unlikely to give allegiance—aspects which, in fact, may have had something to do with his own breakdown. Karen L. Shuldner[70] supplies a very suggestive reading of the meaning of "wound" when she refers to it as "an emotional plateau from which the book is scarcely allowed to descend" and when she reminds us that "The wound was long the symbol of both art and sexual love for Delany[.]"[71] Art and sex, after all, have been at the core of Delany's concerns since his first novel, *The Jewels of Aptor* (1962).

---

69. Delany has explicitly stated, "I had a lot of cities in mind while I was writing *Dhalgren*—in a sense the city there is Every City, Any City." *Alive and Writing: Interviews with American Authors of the 1980s*, ed. Larry McCaffery and Sinda Gregory (Urbana: University of Illinois, 1987), 104.

70. Pen name for Camilla/Mog Decarnin.

71. "On *Dhalgren* and *Triton*," *Riverside Quarterly* 7.1 (March 1980), 6.

Kid's left foot is bare; he writes with his left hand; the left-hand pages of the found notebook are blank. On the level of political symbolism, is Delany suggesting that the right is an already completed (overdetermined) category, while the left has not yet been fully scripted? Or does this have something to do with right brain and left brain? Or ambidexterity?[72]

But then Kid writes his poems on the left-hand pages, filling the book and creating a complex of juxtapositions.

There is a confusion of narrative voices, first and third person. The third-person voice is apparently that of the novel, while the first-person voice is that of the journal, which Kid finds, but which he has also apparently already written.

If Kid is both narrator ("I") and protagonist ("he"), at what point does the latter become the former (while still remaining "in" the story)? And if Kid is the narrator and he is still partially amnesiac, he cannot be an omniscient narrator, nor can he be a reliable one. Recycling/recircling, "plot"-wise, brings, perhaps, greater awareness of detail, but it does not seem to unveil more essential "facts." The histories of Kid and of Bellona remain, to some degree, a mystery.

Kid wears a boot on his right foot and keeps his left foot bare. Mouse, in Delany's novel *Nova* (1968), also wears a boot on one foot and keeps the other bare. (And like *Dhalgren*, *Nova* ends in mid-sentence.) A few of Kid's other precursors are Hawk, juvenile delinquent poet in Delany's story "Time Considered as a Helix of Semi-Precious Stones," and Vol Nonik, poet and member of a gang of malis (malcontents) in Delany's *Fall of the Towers* trilogy.

What about Kid's mythological analogues? One would be Jason, a famous itinerant who was to be recognized by the fact that he wore only one sandal. There is also Dionysus. As Sir James Frazer informs us, "Another animal whose form Dionysus assumed was the goat. One of his names was 'Kid'."[73] Reinforcing this is the possibility that Kid is a cousin

72. Delany has stated that some of the things that Kid experiences are based on a dyslexic's experience of the world. "Some things are also taken from my being somewhat ambidextrous—which often goes along with my particular sort of dyslexia." *Alive and Writing*, 98.

73. *The New Golden Bough*, ed. Theodore H. Gaster (New York, 1964), 421.

of sorts to George, John Barth's goatboy/messiah. George has a gimp; Kid, who wears only one boot, appears to hobble. Furthermore, George's discovery of Lady Creamhair's timepiece, which he wears around his neck (*Giles Goatboy* 77), parallels Kid's discovery of the loops of chain bearing the prisms, mirrors and lenses (*Dhalgren* 7ff.).

It is perfectly in keeping with the allusive, multiplicitous nature of the narrative in *Dhalgren* that the actual identity of the main character remains unknown. In fact, Kid himself never does learn who he is, though this would seem to have been a major element in his quest.[74] Kid is a kind of palimpsest of mythic and mundane identities, a sort of composite hero/antihero with selective amnesia. It is also significant that he is a former (incompletely cured?) mental patient.

Is *Dhalgren* properly classified as "science fiction"? The holographic projectors which the scorpions use are the only example of technology that we can't immediately recognize in our own world. The catastrophe that has struck Bellona is never explained or even specifically identified, nor are any explanations ever given for the odd phenomena of the two moons, the gigantically swollen sun, etc. (These things are reminiscent of the weird happenings, dismissed or ignored by science, that Charles Fort [1874–1932] collected.) Even the presence in the novel of a man who has been to the moon and back is something that is no longer speculative, since Neil Armstrong first set foot on the moon in 1969 and *Dhalgren* was published in 1975. (The actual writing of the novel occupied Delany from January 1969 through September 1973.) One might argue that apart from some examples of the seemingly gratuitous unknown, *Dhalgren* is very close to being a mainstream novel, if that mainstream can be said to include books like John Barth's *Giles Goatboy* or Nabokov's *Ada*. In fact, Delany's undertaking in *Dhalgren* is partly informed by his reading of three novels, two of which could be classified as "literature": Nobel laureate Miguel Angel Asturias' *Mulata*, Elias Canetti's *Auto-de-fé*, and J.G. Ballard's *The Burning World*, books which he did not particularly like but whose employment of fantasy or "magical realism" nonetheless intrigued him.

---

74. In *Finnegans Wake*, there is a character named Kurt Iuld van Dyke, whose identity has yet to be discovered, and whose initials, fortuitously, spell KID (*FW* 100–31).

On the other hand: Tak says, of the circumstances in which Bellona finds itself, "'I suspect the whole thing is science fiction'," (372). He bases this judgement on what he terms the "Three Conventions of science fiction":

"First: A single man can change the course of a whole world: Look at Calkins, look at George, look at you! Second: The only measure of intelligence or genius is its linear and practical application: In a landscape like this, what other kind do we even allow to visit? Three: The Universe is an essentially hospitable place… Here in Bellona—… you can have anything you want…" (372)

Delany, when asked, "Isn't *Dhalgren* a dream outside of historical time…?," replied, "It's very much a dream."[75] Science fiction dream, "mundane"[76] dream—these specific categorizations are probably only of interest to those hung up on definitional niceties. For the writer, and perhaps also for the reader, in science fiction (and, I would argue, in that fictional tradition which includes works like *Don Quixote*, *Tristram Shandy*, and *One Hundred Years of Solitude*), you can have anything you want, you can have it any way you want it, so that dream and waking reality, science fact and science fiction, imagination and reportage become no longer distinct, become (even) (perhaps) interchangeable.

The novel is divided into seven parts, or books, the last of which is entitled "The Anathēmata: a plague journal." There is a lengthy poem by British writer David Jones entitled *The Anathēmata*, which W.H. Auden, a poet Delany knew and admires,[77] considered "very probably the finest long poem written in English in this century."[78] David Blamires, author of a critical study of Jones, calls *The Anathēmata* "a poetic counterpart of

---

75. *Diacritics* interview, 36.

76. "Mundane" fiction is Delany's term for what ordinarily would be characterized as mainstream fiction.

77. The epigraph to the trilogy *The Fall of the Towers* is taken from Auden's Horae Canonicae. Also, see Delany's account of Auden in *The Motion of Light in Water*.

78. Sister Bernetta Quinn, O.S.F., "David Jones," *Contemporary Literature* (Spring 1973), 267.

Finnegans Wake."[79] Like the *Wake*, like *Dhalgren*, the poem is circular and encompasses much. In his Preface to the work, Jones quotes Nennius, from *Historia Brittonum*: "I have made a heap of all that I could find." This, Jones claimed, is essentially his own method. He intended his title to mean "as much as it can be made to mean...: the blessed things that have taken on what is cursed and the profane things that are somehow redeemed..."[80]

Pages 70–73: Joaquin Faust[81] claims not to "mean anything" by his use of the word "nigger," an epithet which is bandied about frequently in the novel, by various characters, including Kid.[82] Faust's argument is that his use of "nigger" is generic and in keeping with the common practice where he comes from. (Which is the West: Faust represents the European mythologem par excellence. Delany deals with this subject more fully [and obsessively!] in *Tides of Lust* [*Equinox*, Delany's original title] Here, the Hispanic first name invokes the identity of the first wave of conquerors of the New World, whose descendants, however, are viewed in the United States as minorities. We are reminded that multiculturalism has always been a reality in the Americas, and that this reality also has always harbored a congeries of prejudices, which have not been the exclusive "privilege" of the "white" man.) But Faust's occasional use of the term "colored" reveals that "nigger," for him, is indeed contemptuous; it is a word used to characterize "dangerous" or "undeserving" blacks, whereas "colored people" are those blacks he views as "respectable," with the inevitable concomitant that they are expected to defer to white hegemony.

Race and racism are not tangential; they are near the novel's center, especially when they overlap with the psychosexual, with patterns of

---

79. Quinn, 268.

80. *The Anathēmata* (New York: Chilmark Press, n.d.), 9, 28–29.

81. Joaquin Faust is based on a real person, known as Bo Maverick, who sold the Berkeley *Barb* in the Haight-Ashbury district of San Francisco during the period when Delany lived there.

82. See my remarks on racist discourse in *Tides of Lust* in "The Politics of Desire in Delany's *Triton* and *Tides of Lust*," *Black American Literature Forum* 18.2 (Summer 1984), 49–56.

desire. Think, for example, of the superstar status of George Harrison, celebrated rapist, posters of whom exploit the very mythos of black male potency which, under different circumstances, would have gotten him lynched. In Bellona, however, a literally phallocentric (phallofocal?) picture of Harrison becomes a different kind of "wanted" poster than one marking him as a target of vigilantes or bounty hunters: the poster itself is a prized item, a "bestseller," and Harrison is a kind of idol. It says something about the nature of Bellona's culture that walls display George Harrison, "soul on ice,"[83] rather than George Harrison, Beatle. The poster of Harrison is, in fact, a visual equivalent of the sexual braggadocio (phallogocentrism) found in a good deal of contemporary rap music.

Although it may not always strike the reader, a sizeable portion of Bellona's population is black. (Kid's own racial origin is "ambiguous" [753].) So it would appear that the "fright flight" that so drastically reduced the population of the city was also a "white flight" of the sort that has turned many of our urban areas into minority enclaves.

The orchid, the weapon Kid inherits when he enters Bellona and which he passes on as he departs: Was this the inspiration for the weapon Freddie Kreuger uses in the *Nightmare on Elm Street* films?

Whether or not Delany influenced Hollywood, it is clear that he has been influenced by Hollywood's corpus of sci-fi and horror films, and by the Gothic in general. Consider the periodic vision that Kid has of people (and in one instance, a dog) whose eyes are blood-red orbs. Like much else in the novel, this suggestion of terror (vampires? demons?) is undeveloped and unexplained. Such scattered images raise expectations in the reader that are thwarted as the book refuses to pursue "predictable" or familiar avenues. The unreal, in effect, is rendered incidental. It is not the purpose of the novel to give us explanations for everything; its actual thrust concerns the responses of (ordinary?) people to the odd, the unprecedented, indeed, the inexplicable.

The loops of chain with attached prisms, mirrors and lenses to which Kid is led at the "beginning" of the book and which he wears until the "end" provide an analogue for the structure of the novel itself. The book

---

83. See Eldridge Cleaver's disquisition on his rapist impulses in *Soul on Ice* (New York: Dell, 1968).

(the experience) is a "you-shaped [w]hole," in that it is, finally, what you make of it; the chains loop around a person's body, making a "you"-shape. The book itself is a loop, whose "end" is its "beginning."

Lenses make things bigger and can also reduce: compare the swollen sun on the one hand and, on the other, the almost microscopically-focused details imbedded in the narrative (characteristic of Delany's writing more generally). Prisms break down, refract; much of the text is likewise refracted. Mirrors reflect, and may also distort. It is not simply that the book begins again by having the last word lead back to the first word; in fact, the things that happen at the beginning happen again at the end in reverse order: Kid crosses the bridge one way, he crosses back the other way; he is handed a weapon coming in, he gives someone else this weapon going out, etc. Is the Oriental woman Kid meets going out [798] the same one he meets coming in [2]? Answering such a question with confidence is difficult because "the same," here, does not necessarily mean "precisely equal to." Amiri Baraka has a potently apt phrase to describe the dynamics of continuity/spontaneity in black music, "the changing same," that seems highly applicable to Delany's own practice in *Dhalgren*. Or to borrow a parallel formulation from Henry Louis Gates, Jr., another formidable commentator on the aesthetics of black culture, what we are confronted with in *Dhalgren* is, in many instances, "repetition with a difference."

Subverted Equations: G. Spencer Brown's Laws of Form and Samuel R. Delany's Analytics of Attention

by Kenneth R. James

I.

> Statements tolerable at the beginning of arguments are not acceptable as ends.
>
> —K. Leslie Steiner, *Tales of Nevèrÿon*[84]

On page 2 of Samuel R. Delany's *Dhalgren*, we encounter a sentence which, if we are familiar with modernist fiction, carries a curious resonance. The sentence—"The moon flung gold coins at her breasts"— recalls a similar sentence from the first chapter of *Ulysses*: "On his wise shoulders through the checkerwork of leaves the sun flung spangles, dancing coins."[85] Notice that the former sentence does not merely allude to the latter, but, like a mirror,

---

84. All page references to the Return to Nevèrÿon series are to the Wesleyan University Press/University Press of New England editions:

- *Tales of Nevèrÿon* (Hanover: University Press of New England, 1993), abbreviated TN;
- *Neveryóna* (Hanover: University Press of New England, 1993), abbreviated N;
- *Flight from Nevèrÿon* (Hanover: University Press of New England, 1994), abbreviated FN;
- *Return to Nevèrÿon* (Hanover: University Press of New England, 1994), abbreviated RN.

All references to *Dhalgren* (abbreviated D) are to the Vintage edition, published in New York in 2001.

Here I must give my heartfelt thanks to Samuel R. Delany himself, who very generously provided me with copies of his more difficult-to-find criticism and fiction throughout the writing of this essay.

85. James Joyce, *Ulysses* (New York: Random House, Vintage Books, 1986), 30.

inverts the value of its images: heavenly and mortal bodies traditionally taken as primary, central and luminous are replaced by bodies traditionally taken as secondary, marginal, and reflective.

And on page 649 of *Dhalgren*, we see that the concluding line of the penultimate chapter—the one-word question, "Where?"—matches the concluding line of the penultimate chapter of *Ulysses*. But whereas Ulysses answers with Molly Bloom's terminal, unmediated, stream-of-consciousness monologue, *Dhalgren* answers with a fragmented dialogue of marginal texts, running down each page in a double column, framed by the offstage activities of a pair of editors of dubious authority. This revaluation seems to mimic in its form what the first revaluation indicated in its content—a shift away from luminous singularity towards reflective multiplicity.

If these two examples suggest that a basic hierarchy of values in modernist literature is being inverted, their deprivileged position within the text enacts that revaluation. In *Ulysses*, allusions refer "back" to an original text or set of texts that ground the entire enterprise: the experience of the coherence of the text is open only to readers with privileged access to the intellectual/cultural armature lying "beneath" it. In *Dhalgren*, the experience of the coherence of the text is open to any reader attentive to the play of sign relations "across" the text—and since the concepts of reflection and revaluation are explicitly supplied by the text, the above two allusions merely offer supplemental resonances to readers with a certain kind of literary background.

Indeed, by beginning with a discussion of these allusions, I have constructed a fiction which exactly reverses my own experience—for I read Delany's novel first. Only later did I encounter the "original" passages in *Ulysses*—where they struck me as so many reflections of an earlier, more "primary" text. But this was a primary text that refused its own authority, always giving back an image of secondary reflection, even though for me it had provided the primary illumination. The subjective effect of this was that of a resonantial loop, fully present in neither text alone, but cycling endlessly between them.

In *Flight from Nevèrÿon*, the third book in his four-volume sword and sorcery series, Return to Nevèrÿon, Delany sets up the conditions of my own idiosyncratic experience by placing an account of a real-life event (Delany's early-morning stroll through the Port Authority bus terminal) after the fictive passage (in "The Tale of Fog and Granite") which it supposedly inspired. For the reader encountering these two passages in the order in which they are given, all the resonances are in the "wrong" direction. We experience what "should" be the primary content of the tale (Delany's original experience, or at least its image in his journal) as a secondary reflection, while we experience what should be a reflection (the tale) as the original content. This reversal throws the authority of both passages into doubt, since it is plain that only the order of their appearance in the text has determined whether they express a "proper" referential relation, or a "paradoxical" one.[86]

As in *Dhalgren*, our apprehension of the ambiguous relation between these two passages is enhanced by explicit discussion in the text itself of the notions of content, image, and reflection. But while in *Dhalgren* this discussion is relatively spare and oblique, in *Flight* (and indeed in the Return to Nevèrÿon series as a whole) it is overt, explicit, and pervasive. Just about every major character, at some point or another, discourses at length on the topic—and once we have sufficiently internalized the concepts themselves, we can see that they inform and pervade nearly every page of the series. And while it is not necessary to know the textual source of this trope to enjoy its intricate play across the texts, nevertheless the tantalizing promise of greater knowledge impels us to seek other texts—to search for origins.

As it turns out, we need not search for long. In his "Introduction" to *Alyx*—the Gregg Press collection of Joanna Russ's sword and sorcery series—Delany reveals that the source of the content/image/reflection trope is *Laws of Form*, a mathematical treatise by G. Spencer Brown. Delany appropriates this trope to clarify what he sees as an essential relation between the genres of sword and sorcery and science fiction; namely, that "sword and sorcery represents what can, most safely, still be imagined about the transition from a barter economy to a money economy," while "science fiction represents what can most safely be imagined about the transition from a money economy to a credit economy."[87] Delany argues that this relation can be better understood if

---

86. The same can be said of epigraphs at the beginning of critical essays.

87. Reprinted in *The Jewel-Hinged Jaw* (New York: Berkley Publishing Corporation, 1978), 197–8 (abbreviated JHJ).

we read barter, money and credit as a set of systems which relate to one another as, respectively, an original content, an image of that content, and a reflection of the image—and that a society shifting from one system to another will experience that transition as a reversal of social values associated with the earlier system. We find an image of this argument in the second story of the Return to Nevèrÿon series, "The Tale of Old Venn," where Delany expands the descriptive field of the content/image/reflection trope to include not just the relations between different modes of economic exchange, but also the relations between different orders of experience, representation, and narrative, and even between different metaphysical discourses.

But if we read the above passages from *Dhalgren* and *Flight from Nevèrÿon* as expressing something typical about Delany's whole approach to extratextual sources, then we might expect that the content/image/reflection trope itself—no matter how powerful a descriptive tool it might seem to be—has not simply been appropriated wholesale. We might expect that it too has in some way been revalued. And indeed, in those same passages such a revaluation does seem to be taking place, a revaluation specifically affecting the first term of the series—the notion of an original "content."

Now, it is probably safe to say that the sort of reader who would be familiar with *Ulysses* would not, in all likelihood, be familiar with *Laws of Form* (and the fact that it is safe to say this is not without significance). I shall therefore review some key ideas and structural points in Spencer Brown's text before discussing their reappearance and revaluation in Delany's series. In my conclusion I shall re-read *Laws of Form* in light of Delany's critique.

II.

> ...the determination of the complexity of a form depends, above all, on the choice of the simplest ground form, and in this choice lies a problem almost untouched by present-day topology.
>
> —René Thom, *Structural Stability and Morphogenesis*

First published in Great Britain in 1969, then in the United States in 1972, G. Spencer Brown's *Laws of Form* purported to offer a new calculus—a new mathematical system with unique notation, axioms, and operations. According to Spencer Brown, one could interpret this calculus as operating at a "deeper" or "more fundamental" realm of mathematics than that of Boolean algebra, the formal abstraction of algebras of logic and set theory.[88] With its appeal to metaphysical intuition, the book was immediately (albeit somewhat confusedly) hailed by such counterculture personalities as Alan Watts and John C. Lilly as a way of approaching mysticism through mathematics. At the same time, its formally rigorous argument (Spencer Brown had studied under Russell[89] and Wittgenstein) received a good deal of scholarly attention from mathematicians and computer scientists. And it sparked a raging debate in the pages of the highly technical *International Journal of General Systems* which carried on well into the '80s. This debate will have a direct bearing on our reading of Delany's reading of Spencer Brown, but to make any sense of it we need to know something of the mathematical discourse in which Spencer Brown's text is embedded.

An algebra generalizes an arithmetic by using variables to stand for distinct entities (such as numbers, sets and set elements, and logical propositions), and then manipulating these variables according to operations which hold true for all the entities under consideration. A Boolean algebra, in turn, generalizes the laws of both set-theoretical and logical algebras, by reducing—or elevating, depending on your theoretical

---

88. G. Spencer Brown, *Laws of Form* (New York: Bantam Books, 1973), xiv (abbreviated LF).

89. For the UK edition, Bertrand Russell wrote a brief introduction which called it "a calculus of great beauty."

bias—the shared properties of these algebras to a collection of purely formal laws which themselves have no representational content. For example, while propositions can be either "true" or "false," and elements can be either "members" or "not members" of a given set, Boolean expressions can be either "0" or "1"—a pair of values devoid of any particular content other than their binary relation.

What Spencer Brown wants to know is, what is the arithmetic of Boolean algebra? What are the distinct entities (not numbers, not sets and set elements, not propositions) that are subsumed under the Boolean variables? Notice that by even positing the existence of an arithmetic for a purely formal algebra—and by asserting furthermore that the entities of that arithmetic are in some way more "fundamental" than entities of other arithmetics Spencer Brown implicitly locates the legitimacy of Boolean algebra in its movement towards a kind of ideal abstraction, rather than in the fact that it is derived from more recognizably representational systems; in effect, he posits an ontological hierarchy in which the formal ideal is privileged over the informal real.

Spencer Brown begins his argument by declaring that the Boolean postulates "can be seen to represent two simple laws of indication which, whatever the nature of their self-evidence, at least recommend themselves to the findings of common sense" (LF xiv). To long-time Delany readers, this appeal to common sense should be ringing bells of alarm, but let us not get ahead of ourselves. Briefly, the two laws are based on the idea of drawing distinctions. One draws a distinction by "severing" or "cleaving" one space from another—as when one inscribes a circle on a plane, or blows a soap bubble in the air, or passes temporally from the state before one drew the circle or blew the bubble to the state after one drew or blew, and so on. Spencer Brown suggests that on a formal or ideal level, these three kinds of distinction are the same—and his two laws express that notion of sameness. Using the mark " ⌉ " to indicate the "marked state" or "cross," and the blank "   " to indicate the "unmarked state" or "void," Spencer Brown puts forth his two laws as follows:

1. The law of calling: The value of the call made again is the value of the call [in notation,

(1) ⌉ ⌉ = ⌉

the "form of condensation"]; and

2. The law of crossing: The value of a crossing made again is not the value of the crossing [in notation,

(2) ⌉⌉ =

the "form of cancellation"] (LF 1–5).

Now, equation (1) does not mean that two equals one, but rather that two equivalent distinctions are, in the realm of ideal forms, identical. To give a metaphorical example (and if it troubles the reader, all the better): From an ideal point of view it does not matter whether you have two apples or one apple—they are both, formally, the "same apple." Moreover, even if you have just one apple, if you indicate it with its name and then indicate it again, these two indications are formally indistinguishable. And equation (2) does not express the idea of the double negative, but rather the idea that distinguishing an already-distinguished space from itself places one back in the unmarked state. Or, metaphorically, if you walk into a house, or a city, or a text, and then turn around and walk back out again, your journey—formally—cancels itself out. With these two laws and their typographical forms, Spencer Brown is able to generate strings of equations like:

⌉⌉ ⌉⌉ ⌉ = ⌉⌉ ⌉ = ⌉

As this string suggests, and as Spencer Brown proves in "Theorem 1" of his arithmetic, any well-formed expression can (apparently) be reduced to either the marked state or the unmarked state, thus (apparently) preserving the binary relationship at the heart of Boolean algebra. Using variables to stand for collections of marks and blanks, Spencer Brown goes on to prove, step by mathematical step, that this "primary algebra" does indeed generate Boolean algebra. The proof is rigorous, powerful, and convincing. By the time one reaches its conclusion, one is convinced that not just the empty Boolean values "0" and "1," but all similar binary oppositions can be formally reduced to the "first distinction" between the mark and the void. But, as we shall see, it is precisely the apparent extensibility of the argument that Delany calls into question.

The notions of content, image, and reflection first appear in Chapter 8, in which Spencer Brown uses his notation to metaphorically illustrate the relation of an algebra to its arithmetic:

> Of any expression *e* call *e* the content, call $\overline{e}|$ the image, and call $\overline{\overline{e}|}|$ the reflexion. Since $\overline{\overline{e}|}| = e$, the act of reflexion is a return from an image to its content or from a content to its image… In the form of any calculus, we find the consequences in its content and the theorems in its image. (LF 42–3)

Which is simply to say that proving a theorem using algebraic variables is equivalent to—is the image of—demonstrating an arithmetical fact using the specific entities subsumed under those variables. Later, in his "Note" to Chapter 8, Spencer Brown elaborates:

> A demonstration, we remember, occurs inside the calculus, a proof outside. The boundary between them is thus a shared boundary, and what is approached, in either direction, according to whether we are demonstrating a consequence or proving a theorem. (LF 94)

In other words, a proof approaches certainty and a demonstration approaches exhaustiveness as each approaches the space of the other. But this idea clearly recalls—is in the image of—a passage in the Introduction, where Spencer Brown discusses the tendency of twentieth-century science to get tangled up in the problem of the presence of the perceiver:

> It becomes apparent that if certain facts about our common experience of perception, or what we might call the inside world, can be revealed by an extended study of what we call, in contrast, the outside world, then an equally extended study of the inside world will reveal, in turn, the facts first met with in the world outside: for what we approach, in either case, is the common boundary between them. (LF xix)

And at proof's end, Spencer Brown draws these two cloven spaces—the space of mathematical argument and the space of the physical universe together:

> We see now that the first distinction, the mark, and the observer are not only interchangeable, but, in the form, identical. (LF 76)

The power of these passages, taken together in this way, is undeniable and, yes, mystical. That they appear to be supported by an impeccably linear mathematical argument only adds to their power. But it must be noted that the order of the passages as I've presented them here is not the order in which they appear in the book. And only two of the passages appear within the mathematical argument itself. Yet the book's very structure seems to compel us to read these passages as though they are all informed, or pervaded, by the same linear argument—as though they can be shuffled into an order which suggests proof.

Laws of Form is divided into many textual frames. One must get through one Author's Note, two Prefaces, and an Introduction before arriving at the text "proper," which after just seventy-six pages gives way to a collection of Chapter Notes (half as long as the main text itself), two Appendices, and two Indexes. And, as we've just seen, these multiply-marginal texts are heavily dependent on one another for their own internal coherence. Another instance: the rules of proof governing the "central" mathematical argument are not formally justified until Appendix 2—and the significance of that justification is discussed not in the Appendix itself but in the preceding Chapter Notes. The overall effect of this interdependency is to give individual sections a greater apparent weight than they actually have—and to suggest that a rigorous proof of the ultimate reducibility of every conceivable distinction down to an original, ideal distinction has indeed been given. But that proof is nowhere to be found in the book. It resides instead within the cascade of resonances made possible by the book's intricately repetitive intratextual structure and activated by the reader's own tendency to find order in that repetition. It is, finally, not a proof at all, but rather a demonstration of a process—a specifically aesthetic process which depends precisely on the fact that to recross a textual space is not to cancel out the first crossing, that the value of a call made again is not the value of the call. And it is Spencer Brown's image of this process, as well as his structural method of generating it, which Delany appropriates and revalues in his own rigorously formal collection of marginal texts, the Return to Nevèrÿon series.

III.

> Imagine Plato's cave not simply overthrown by some philosophical movement but transformed in its entirety into a circumscribed area contained within another—an absolutely other—structure, an incommensurably, unpredictably more complicated machine. Imagine that mirrors would not be in the world, simply, included in the totality of all *onta* and their images, but that things "present," on the contrary, would be in them. Imagine that mirrors (shadows, reflections, phantasms, etc.) would no longer be *comprehended* within the structure of the ontology and myth of the cave… but would rather envelop it in its entirety, producing here and there a particular, extremely determinate effect.
>
> —Jacques Derrida, *Dissemination*

The first overt reference to *Laws of Form* in Delany's fiction can be found about two-thirds of the way through *Dhalgren*. In this passage, the character called Reverend Amy preaches to the denizens of Bellona, the mysteriously burned-out Midwestern city within which most of the action of the novel takes place. During her sermon—which the protagonist of the novel, Kid, only hears in snatches—we get our first glimmer of what Delany's position might be vis-a-vis Spencer Brown's. Reverend Amy begins: "'Who lives in this city?… Logicians love it here!… Here you can cleave space with a distinction, mark, or token, and not have it bleed all over you.'" (D 472) Later, when Reverend Amy is in mid-oration, Kid catches this fragment:

> "…of the crossing taken again is not the value of the crossing? Oh, my poor, inaccurate hands and eyes! Don't you know that once you have transgressed that boundary, every atom, the interior of every point of reality, has shifted its relation to every other you've left behind, shaken and jangled within the field of time, so that if you cross back, you return to a very different space than the one you left?" (D 480)

Like the allusions to *Ulysses* mentioned earlier, these references to *Laws of Form* are, again, merely supplemental: the efficacy and coherence of the passages do not depend on prior knowledge of Spencer Brown's work. And as I've already mentioned, this is equally true of Delany's use of the content/image/reflection trope in the Return to Nevèrÿon series. But there his elaboration of the critical position implied in the above passages is so rigorous and systematic that if we are familiar with *Laws of Form*, we find we can read the entire series as an extended critique of the metaphysical grounding of the mathematical discourse in which Spencer Brown's calculus is embedded.

Our first encounter with Spencer Brown in the Nevèrÿon series comes with the second tale of the series, "The Tale of Old Venn." This tale seems to serve the function that Delany elsewhere has suggested most "second tales" serve in science fiction and fantasy series—as an explanatory account of the images in the first.[90] Certainly one cannot re-cross the space of the preceding tale, "The Tale of Gorgik," without spontaneously applying lessons learned in "Venn"; but this is of course the fundamental experience of reading the series as a whole. At the same time, by providing the first explicit discussion of the theoretical possibilities of the content/image/reflection trope, the tale also gives us an interpretive tool that precedes, that prepares for, a later, intense image" (AS 229)—and indeed a whole encyclopedia of images. Moreover, the formal structure of the tale reappears in revalued form in subsequent tales—as, once again, the notion of content/image/reflection prepares us to recognize.

"Venn"—the very name recalls the Venn diagram, a visual method of representing the relations between sets, set elements, and universes of discourse. A brilliant, aged woman living in what appears to be a primitive observatory out on the margins of a port town in the Ulvayn Islands, Venn introduces many new ideas and inventions into Nevèrÿon's primitive universe of discourse, including celestial navigation, various kinds of writing, tools and machines, and certain mathematical proofs. Venn introduces most of these innovations rather offhandedly—in the

---

90. *The American Shore* (Elizabethtown, New York: Dragon Press, 1978), 229 (abbreviated AS).

case of this tale, as educational tools for the Ulvayn village children sent to Venn for daily lessons. During one such lesson, Venn presents a new idea to the three children present (two boys, Enin and Dell, and one girl, Norema), cryptically suggesting that there is something "funny" about this particular idea:

> "I know something. I know how to tell you *about* it, but I don't know how to tell you *what* it is. I can show you what it does, but I cannot show you the 'what' itself." (TN 86–7)

As her examples indicate, this epistemologically problematic something "is" the repeated appearance, in several very different realms, of the notion of content/image/reflection as an organizing descriptive principle. Venn first shows the children that writing, when viewed through the Rulvayn boys' "belly mirrors," reverses itself—and that when this mirror-image is viewed through a second "belly mirror," not only does the writing reverse itself again, but one can now discern writing on the reverse side of the paper, which had previously been hidden from view (TN 87–8). Next, Venn tells three short tales: the first, of her terrifying encounter with a sea monster; the second, of her first breathless recounting of this encounter on the following night; and the third, of her later retellings, revised after evaluating the responses of her first audience (TN 88–9). Obviously this example suggests a mise-en-abyme image of the writing of the whole Return to Nevèrÿon series—which Delany has explicitly described as a self-critical narrative enterprise (RN 271). But a dilemma emerges as soon as we cross over from the act of narrating to the act of reading: for how are we to read the relation of this, Venn's fourth retelling, to its antecedents, which it summarizes and presents as examples of what so far appears to be a tripartite process? More to the point, what does it mean to us if our own "original experience" is the hearing of this fourth tale? Where are we to locate the original "content" from which the other two terms in the model emerge?

After listening attentively to Venn's account, Enin and Dell leap to draw the connection between Venn's first example and her second, with the girl Norema reluctantly completing the interpretation:

> "What happened to you," Dell said, "was like the signs on the paper."
>
> "And what you told the first night," said Enin, "was like what we saw in the first mirror, with its meaning all backward."
>
> "And what you told again the next morning." Norema said, feeling rather like it was expected of her and terribly uncomfortable with the expectation, "was like what we saw in the second mirror. Something else entirely, with its own meaning."
>
> "As much as mirrors and monsters can be alike," mused Venn, whose sudden distraction seemed one with Norema's discomfort. (TN 91)

Venn's closing comment suggests that while one may readily see the similarities between two different things (as the boys did), one cannot reduce that similarity to identity—an implicit critique of Spencer Brown, who, we remember, claimed that one could formally reduce the human subject and the mark of distinction down to the same ideal first distinction. At the same time, in this passage the problem of reduction is rather ingeniously linked to problems of gender representation within the rhetoric of patriarchal discourse: for, as Norema uncomfortably realizes, a kind of strange rhetorical inevitability seems to have placed her as the third term in a series of individual speakers, and is now compelling her to "follow the boys" and complete the analogy. But if we carry this notion of a "series" of speakers further, then Venn, the last speaker in the above passage (and whose "distraction" Norema identifies—accurately? or reductively?—with her own "discomfort"), occupies both the fourth position in the series—which we've already identified as problematic—and the position preceding the first, since she told the original tale. And if we carry the idea to its logical conclusion, then we must include my own reading of the text, my presentation of that reading to you, and your reading of this reading as the fifth, sixth, and seventh position in the series respectively—with Delany and Spencer Brown occupying positions somewhere at the other end. But the point, of course, is that there is no "end"—there is no original "content" which provides the ontological ground for all the rest. The problem begins with the positing (both in the sense of postulating and in the sense of positioning) of a "first term." For once this (wholly arbitrary) postulation has been made, where one chooses to position that first term can have gigantic consequences for the ontological hierarchy that grows out of it—as well as for the individuals who find themselves subsumed within this hierarchy, as Norema dimly realizes.

We find a reflection of this argument in Venn and Norema's discussion of economic systems. Since in Nevèrÿon's primitive economy there is no such thing as credit, Norema and Venn must take the content/image/reflection concept, which up to this point has been used as an interpretive tool, and try to apply it speculatively or predictively to generate the third term in the economic series—thus inventing credit on the spot (TN 102–3). But despite this apparent confirmation of the power of her model, Venn swiftly realizes that to use the model in speculative fictions rather than descriptions is to change the model's status—to re-position it within the hierarchy of terms which it itself describes/generates. When Norema goes on to speculate that perhaps men and women are the image and reflection (or reflection and image) of a plan for an "ideal human being" (TN 104–5), Venn immediately and vehemently denies this possibility:

> "Look girl: where is your ideal plan? Floating in the clouds somewhere? I start with the real thing, like barter, words written on reed paper, an experience at sea, and discuss what happens to their value when series of reflections occur. You start with a value—an ideal human being—that is the result of so many real and imagined people's real and imagined actions, and then try to say the people are a result of this value..." (TN 105–6)

At this point Venn launches into a fascinating and minutely detailed account of her experiences in the neighboring Rulvyn tribe—a tale which we must here forego, as its complex interrogation of Freudian and Lacanian conceptions of sexual development and representation places it well outside the scope of this essay. When Venn is through, she challenges her listener to "think about my idea until you see what's wrong with yours—and indeed you may find out in the process things wrong with mine as well" (TN 117). Norema then begins a series of experiments, observations, and speculations to try to discern the real nature of Venn's inexpressible principle—an exploration ending with a sudden insight into the structure of human signs which, in its intensity, approaches the mystical. Norema suddenly realizes that while

> the world in which images occurred was opaque, complete, and closed… this was not true of the space of examples, samples, symbols, models, expressions, reasons, representations, and the rest… everything and anything could be an image of everything and anything. (TN 121)

What Norema has discerned here is the endlessness—and beginninglessness of the content/image/reflection principle. She has discerned the one property of the principle that Venn's very first example hints at, but which Delany does not explicitly reveal: namely, that when you gaze into a reflection of a reflection, what you get is not just a revelation of hidden perspectives, but an image of an endless hall of mirrors.

Although Norema at first considers her new conception "a glorious and useless thing to know" (TN 121), we may speculate over whether it is in fact so useless. After all, it dissolves the problem of ontological hierarchies suggested by the first model, rendering Venn's materialist interpretation and Norema's Platonic interpretation as simply two possibilities to be chosen at will by the interpreter—with neither model carrying any epistemological privilege over the other. More to the point, if we leap ahead to the opening chapter of *Neveryóna*, we find that later in life Norema has herself become a storyteller, whose narrative technique—involving leaving several choices of interpretation to the listener—rather resembles Delany's own. Clearly, Norema has appropriated something vital and powerful from this vision.

But appropriation cuts both ways, as we learn at the tale's conclusion, where, in a fit of xenophobia, a group of Ulvayn men put a visiting foreign ship to the torch. The significance of this event is not revealed until the end of the very last tale of the book, where we learn that the ship had been full of women from the Western Crevasse, a land where the gender hierarchy favors women. Carrying this image back to the story under consideration, we now perceive the ghastly irony in the fact that the men probably learned their torching method from one of Venn's other tales (TN 134). But despite this cautionary concluding note, we cannot help but notice that "The Tale of Old Venn" has been presented as a kind of proto-feminist, materialist "reflection" of a Platonic dialogue. We have already seen one passage in which boys are merely accessories to the insights of the women. There are many other examples throughout the book. But if Venn's critique of Norema's Platonic model starts precisely with a critique of her arbitrary hierarchizing of men and women, then how are we to interpret the gender hierarchy of this tale?

Let us jump ahead to "The Tale of Potters and Dragons." Armed with Venn's analytical model, we find complex patterns of images and reflections in both the content and form of the tale. It opens with a dialogue—or rather, with two parallel monologues, for the characters have not yet met—between two citizens of Kolhari, the bustling capital city of Nevèrÿon. The first character, a potter named Zwon, while preparing to send his young apprentice Bayle on a business trip to the southern Garth Peninsula, celebrates the power of money to bring people together and make "us all one" (TN 163)—reversing an earlier argument made by Venn that money, an image of the items for which it is exchanged, tends to "flatten" those items (which can include people) into empty commodities (TN 101–2). This dialectic mirrors the theoretical debate over the status of algebraic variables—which can, we remember, be read as either "reducing" distinct entities down to empty combinatory values, or "elevating" them to a higher, more ideal realm. The second citizen, a shrewd businesswoman tellingly named Madame Keyne, argues with her young secretary (the now grownup Norema, also being sent on a business trip to the Garth Peninsula) that "money draws to money" (TN 166)—recalling, though not reversing, Venn's earlier point that in a transition from barter to money, power tends to reorganize itself around those who have money (TN 93–4). At the end of the tale, we find a continuation of this dialogue—a genuine dialogue now, for Zwon and Madame Keyne have finally met. Only this time, the two have reversed their positions: Zwon now believes that money divides people by emphasizing the distinction between incomes over any other relationship that people might have, while Madame Keyne appears to be rid of her few misgivings about money, which, she tells Zwon, is "the greatest invention in the history of mankind" (TN 213). We can see, then, that this tale is framed by reflections: at its opening by two parallel monologues in which each speaker takes a position that mirrors positions found in an earlier tale, and at its close by a dialogue in which both participants have reversed their own positions.

But to discern just why these two characters have reversed themselves we must cross into the space of the embedded tale. In it we find that Bayle and Norema have in fact been sent on the same mission to petition Lord Aldamir, the mysteriously absentee southern governor, for an import franchise of a popular children's toy, the little rubber balls which bounce their sinister way all through the Nevèrÿon series. Having boarded the same southbound ship, Bayle and Norema meet a third passenger named Raven, who turns out to be from the matriarchal Western Crevasse. And while Raven is clearly something of a female chauvinist, she is not completely blind to the workings of oppression and appropriation. When, after much wrangling, she consents to tell Norema and the crew her country's creation legend, she warns Norema that the men "will try to take it away from us, as men take everything from women in this strange and terrible land" (TN 117). But her warning must be taken with a grain of salt, since it is rooted in her society's prior construction of a devalued maleness—as her story of genesis amply demonstrates.

Raven's doubly-embedded tale posits Paradise as a kind of radical separatist-feminist space where two women, Jevim and Eif'h, tend the garden with no man in sight. When Eif'h transgresses against her goddess-creator, the goddess mutilates her until she is "castrated"—she becomes a "broken woman," or " 'man" (another parallel: woman/'man, Raven/Venn) (TN 182). Like *Laws of Form*, this story valorizes the act of drawing distinctions (TN 179). But like "The Tale of Old Venn," it critiques the notion that real distinctions can be reduced to ideality—or rather, it morally forbids it: the transgression for which Eif'h is punished is precisely her attempt to conceive of an ideal distinction (TN 180–81)—an image of Norema's attempt in "The Tale of Old Venn." But in Raven's legend the transgression is explicitly identified with maleness (though, significantly, this "maleness" is bestowed after the fact; the story reverses the order of events of the Judeo-Christian myth in a way which highlights the constructed nature and retroactive logic of the cultural valuation of gender). Thus, this embedded tale does explicitly what we have seen "The Tale of Old Venn" do implicitly: it subverts its own critique of essentialism by gendering both sides of the debate in a way which presupposes an essentialist ontology. In other words, the tale deconstructs itself.

On the other hand, by the end of the frame-tale Raven's warning has come true. Once the franchise has been revealed as an elaborate sham, leaving Bayle most likely dead and Norema and Raven wandering the southern province, two messages are sent back to their employers which precisely reverse the true events. Zwon is told that Bayle, tempted by the lack of constraints on his actions in the south, has run off with the meager funds the potter had given him; while Madame Keyne is told that Norema had been immediately set upon by bandits—and that even though she'd been saved by the "good and loyal workmen on the dock," her injuries were fatal (TN 210–12). Significantly, these two stories actually confirm the "worst fears" of both employers, who "know" how common such stories are. Zwon muses:

> "Truly the south is a strange and terrible land, where every evil we here in civilized Kolhari can imagine of it comes reflected back to us with an accuracy as perfect as the image in the belly-mirrors that the young men of the Ulvayn from time to time wear on our docks." (TN 212–13)

Nevèrÿon's patriarchal discourse has appropriated the true story, reversed its value, and linked those new values to an implicit message about money: that men, in their autonomy, should be given more of it, and women, in their helplessness, should be kept away from it.

But this new message has not discouraged Madame Keyne, who, we learn, intends to make a killing by replacing Kolhari's ubiquitous three-legged cooking pots with new four-legged pots (TN 209). This can be read as an image of the transition from a three-termed interpretive model—which always rests on an original "ground"—to a four-termed (or many-termed) model—which always wobbles between at least two positions in an endless dialectical process. And just as Norema's appropriation of Venn's model and Raven's internalization of her society's metaphysics allow them both to resist—or at least recognize—Nevèrÿon's patriarchal discourse, so too does

Madame Keyne's invention allow her to resist the implicitly patriarchal message she has just received—by making a lot of money.

Leaving the last narrative frame of "The Tale of Potters and Dragons," we may believe that we have reached the outermost discursive "space" of the text. But when we reach the text's final Appendix, we find that we were mistaken. Like its formal precursors, the two Appendices to *Triton* (a novel peppered with epigraphs from Spencer Brown's text), this Appendix provides information which partially explains, as well as disrupts, everything that has come before. We learn here that all of the tales we've just read had originally been "inspired" by the recent translation (actually a fourth, comparative translation of three earlier translations—another image of Venn's tales) of an ancient text called the "Culhar' fragment," by the young mathematician K. Leslie Steiner. Just as Steiner's pen name recalls Spencer Brown's, her scholarly work is clearly an image of *Laws of Form*—with certain fundamental revaluations. First, Steiner posits that mathematical language, rather than being more primary than everyday language, is in fact preceded and pervaded by it: "'counting,' as it were, presupposes 'language,' and not the other way around" (TN 255). This exactly reverses Spencer Brown's position that Boolean algebra transcends the representational forms from which it arose. Second, Steiner's model of language itself—as a complex collection of "noncommutative substitution loops"—clearly recalls Norema's experience of the endless substitutability of semiotic associations: which endlessness, we recall, critiques Spencer Brown's notion of a primary "content" (TN 254–55). Thus Steiner's text both logically frames *Laws of Form* (by revealing the hidden discursive ground of its mathematical argument) while remaining marginal to it (as its fictive image), its ambiguous relation to that other text as both image and critique rendering both texts equally problematic. Furthermore, because Steiner's linguistic model does not generate a simple nomenclature, but rather a complex set of intersecting metonymic loops, any translation utilizing this model must involve selecting from among many terms present in a given "loop." This suggests a provisional fictive explanation for the apparent gendering of "The Tale of Old Venn," since we know from the Appendix (not written by Steiner, but by another fictive academic) that Steiner may incline towards a feminist translation: "since the sex of the narrator of a sexually unspecified text is always a fifty-fifty possibility, I simply take my choice, which is consistent with the rest of my work" (TN 258). On the other hand, since Delany would have us understand that the tales are his interpretation of Steiner's translation, this perceived gendering may reverse Steiner's "real" translation (all of which recalls the editorial "tampering" in the final chapter of *Dhalgren*). Thus, the "explanation" the Appendix provides does not close the issue, but opens it further—finally eliminating the possibility of locating an original, privileged interpretation.

Near the center of the series—towards the end of the second book, *Neveryóna*—we find an image of Steiner's (and, by extension, Venn's) problematic project, as well as an unexpectedly direct statement of the relation of the series as a whole to its mathematical antecedent. At the conclusion to Chapter Eleven, the southern earl Jue-Grutn presents the heroine Pryn with a short discourse on the origins of writing. Reviewing in turn a collection of tokens, an image of those tokens inked on reed fiber, and a reflection of those images branded on a dried strip of flesh, Jue-Grutn speculates that each writing sample can be interpreted as an aesthetic artifact, an objective description, or an ideological construction. But to discern their relation to one another within a hierarchical order of authority—and thus to discern what pattern of appropriation might have obtained between them—one must decide which sample is the original: "Which one of the three inspired, which one of the three contaminated, which one of the three first valorized the subsequent two in our cultural market of common conceptions?" (N 302). Jue-Grutn will ultimately conclude that one cannot know. But prior to this conclusion, while speculating about what it might mean if the original writing had been a disinterested description of an objective state of affairs, Jue-Grutn—right in the center of his monologue—asks:

> "Suppose… another scribe was dazzled by the coolness of the disinterest enough to realize how beauty burns over and around that rigid, frigid abstraction and so created a scorching rendition to tease and terrify us with its ever-proliferating suggestions for further readings?" (N 303)

Standing outside the space of the novel, we know that this rhetorical question directly indicates that other text against which this text stands in a complex mirror-relation—though Jue-Grutn, "inside" the text, cannot know this. By the same token, we observe that Jue-Grutn's monologue, in reviewing three samples of writing and itself being embedded in a problematic fourth, is yet another image of Venn's discussion of tale-telling—but with a difference: while Venn might be able to recognize the pattern her fourth retelling generates, Jue-Grutn, completely constituted by that fourth text, cannot recognize it as we do. But even his incomplete description of an originary and pervasive arche-writing inspires in Pryn a vision of a potential infinity of meanings, which recalls both the image of Norema's childhood vision of the simultaneous opacity of the world and the unboundedness of the "space of examples," as well as an image from a tale which the adult Norema had told Pryn at the opening of *Neveryóna*—and presents an unnervingly accurate image of the staggering density and complexity of the reflections and counter-reflections we have been observing at this particular point in the text (N 305–8).

But if *Neveryóna* leaves us dazzled by a vision of unlimited semiosis, both *Flight from Nevèrÿon* and *Return to Nevèrÿon* present a considerably darker vision, in which images become counterfeits and reflections become distortions. These tales are veritable fugues of misrecognitions, misunderstandings, and misremembrances. To pick only the most obvious examples (one could go on indefinitely): the young smuggler's obsessive gathering of information about Gorgik the Liberator in "The Tale of Fog and Granite" mirrors the Master's quixotic quest for information about Belham the inventor in "The Tale of Plagues and Carnivals"; the Master's misremembering of events on his quest mirrors Gorgik's misremembering, in "The Game of Time and Pain," of the mines from which he himself had originally been liberated; and the smuggler's misrecognition of Gorgik in "Fog and Granite" mirrors the barbarian Udrog's misrecognition of him in "Time and Pain."

This last example is worth pursuing a little further. We know that the smuggler's and Udrog's misrecognitions both arise from the same source, namely, a highway thief who has been impersonating Gorgik in order to dupe unwary travellers. Furthermore, the thief knows that he can pass himself off as Gorgik in his later encounter with Udrog, because, even though he'd lost an eye to Raven's double-bladed sword in his earlier encounter with the smuggler, he still fits one of the many conflicting descriptions of Gorgik (RN 25). But what the thief does not know is that these conflicting descriptions have been deliberately engineered by Gorgik's one-eyed lover Noyeed (an image of his earlier lover, Sarg) gone out into the land to impersonate him and thus create an "all-pervasive fog" of confusion around him (FN 16). And what very few people in all of Nevèrÿon know, except perhaps the very powerful and the very marginal, is that Gorgik had originally appropriated this strategy of obfuscation from the absentee Lord Aldamir of the southern province, whom we have already (not) encountered in "The Tale of Potters and Dragons." Clearly, the double- (or is it quadruple-?) edged sword of reflection and appropriation has reappeared in these last tales with a vengeance. Even Gorgik, master appropriator though he is, admits that he is confounded by the proliferation of reflections that the world—and his own self—present to him:

> "All I could come to… was that, years before… I had looked into a mirror, recognized that mirror for what it was, and seized the image within it for my use. Now, at a sudden turn of chance, in need of an image to seize, I'd glimpsed that what I'd thought were mirrors and images and an 'I' looking into and at them were really displaced, synthetic, formed of intersecting images in still other mirrors I'd never noticed before—mirrors whose angle, tactility, and location, because there were so many of them, because they were visible only through what was reflected of them in other mirrors, I couldn't hope to determine (much less locate a coherent pattern in which to place them), much less determine which, if any, were real and which were merely intersections in others." (RN 93)

But where does this leave us, the readers? Are we, too, confounded by these reflections—blinded by their brilliance as Norema is blinded, briefly, by a reflection of sunlight from an Ulvayn belly-mirror (TN 104)? In the end, are we only able to apprehend each new image put before us as "some endlessly shimmering sign, whose clear and concise meaning in the weave and play of meanings is merely terrifying rather than illuminative" (FN 261)? Gazing into this hall of mirrors, what image within can we seize for our own use?

Here we would do well to recall Spencer Brown's reminder, near the end of his argument, that "we are, and have been all along, deliberating the form of a single construction... notably the first distinction" (LF 68). We must remind ourselves that we have, all along, been deliberating the relation between two constructions, Delany's and Spencer Brown's. To discern the value of our crossing through Delany's texts, let us return, briefly, to *Laws of Form.*

IV.

> What is revealed will be concealed, but what is concealed will again be revealed.
>
> —G. Spencer Brown, *Laws of Form*

We recall that subsequent to its publication, *Laws of Form* became the subject of intense debate in the pages of the *International Journal of General Systems*, a periodical devoted to original research in the mathematical modelling of complex systems. Many of the contributors to the debate saw *Laws of Form* as an exciting and unprecedented contribution to the field of general systems, and used Spencer Brown's calculus to generate new models of networks and finite automata, and even to develop new axiomatic systems. Others saw *Laws of Form* as simply Boolean algebra written in a peculiar—and even misleading—notation. I submit that we can read this debate as an image of the debate that has grown up around Delany's work over the last few decades. I submit further that our reading can profit from precisely the exploration and critique of the content/image/reflection trope which Delany has undertaken, and which we have reviewed here.

Interestingly, both Spencer Brown's champions and his detractors often begin their arguments by translating his notation into more "familiar" algebraic forms; thus, the mark " ⏋ " becomes a "1," and the blank "   " becomes a "0," as in standard two-valued Boolean algebra. But if we accept this translation as valid, it becomes difficult to ignore the detractors, who offer convincing arguments that once it is reinscribed in classical notation, Spencer Brown's system is indeed isomorphic to Boolean algebra. But is this reinscription valid? Let us look to Paul Cull and William Frank's rather cantankerous critique of *Laws of Form*, which presents the most detailed discussion of the problem of translating Spencer Brown's typography. Although Cull and Frank actually change their minds in mid-argument about how to interpret Spencer Brown's calculus, both of their interpretations involve a general critique of Spencer Brown's use of the blank "   " in his equations. They argue that equation (2), " ⏋⏋ = ", uses the blank space on the right side of the equation as if it is a symbol, not a true void—in which case it becomes possible to interpret any empty space in a given equation as potentially containing many "blank symbols."[91] But if Spencer Brown's equations are not to be "infinitely ambiguous," the blank must be interpreted as simply an unclear way of indicating a single constant, in which case one must interpret the mark and the blank as constants in a two-valued logic. Cull and Frank thus conclude, along with several other mathematicians in the debate, that Spencer Brown's calculus is merely a "confusing" or "obscure" way of writing ordinary Boolean algebra.

At this point I simply cannot resist quoting Delany's response to a particularly vituperative review of one of his own more "confusing" and "obscure" works: "I wonder if it doesn't mean something when the most violent detractor hits the point precisely."[92] For while Cull and Frank are correct in considering the blank problematic, they miss the mark, as it were, in interpreting the blank as a constant, and consequently miss what is truly radical about Spencer Brown's project. Louis H. Kauffman, in a brief and elegant refutation of Cull and Frank's argument in the *Mathematical Review*, provides the key to understanding both the real status of the blank and the reason why Cull and Frank must interpret it the way they do. Using a model Spencer Brown himself spends much time exploring (LF 69–76), Kauffman interprets the expressions in the calculus as representing collections of embedded circles on a plane—in which case it becomes immediately apparent that one cannot have a "blank space" without a circle somewhere demarcating it: the relation between the mark and the blank is not truly a binary relation, but a container/contained relation. Blanks become "ambiguous" only if one reinscribes the mark and the blank into a more classical notation which obliterates their fundamental relational property. The point is that "a notion of 'many blanks' has arisen the moment we use a symbol… for the blank. It arises in the descriptive context."[93] This explains why Cull and Frank, later in their argument, must resort to using parentheses to convey the concept of

91. Paul Cull and William Frank, "Flaws of Form." *International Journal of General Systems 5* (1979): 202.

92. Delany is here responding, in *The Straits of Messina* (Seattle: Serconia Press, 1989, 38), to Harlan Ellison's review of *Dhalgren*.

93. Louis H. Kauffman, review of "Flaws of Form," *Mathematical Reviews* 812:00007 (May 1981): 1620.

embedded marks and blanks: one cannot literally embed a "0" inside a "1." Thus, Kauffman explains, the key to interpreting the calculus correctly lies in understanding that all expressions within it "stand for purely local situations that occur in larger collections" of expressions.

Do we find any equivalents to Kauffman's statement in *Laws of Form* itself? Yes, we do: immediately after his introduction of the concepts of content, image, and reflection, Spencer Brown mentions in passing that "an unwritten cross is common to every expression in the calculus of indications and so need not be written" (LF 43). Although Spencer Brown himself does not elaborate on this remark, we have just seen that it is absolutely crucial in preserving the coherence of his notation and more specifically, that it does indeed refute Cull and Frank's argument, since the disquieting "blank space" on the right side of equation (2) turns out to be implicitly "framed" by an unwritten mark:

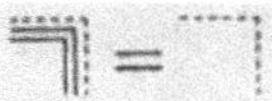

But this new understanding will have an absolutely shattering effect on our interpretation of the calculus as a whole. For if every expression in the calculus is understood to be framed by an unwritten mark, then there is no limit to the number of outer frames in which a given expression can be said to be embedded:

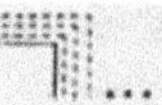

Which in turn means that when we reduce an expression down to its "unique value," we are really only reducing it down to the value indicated within the unwritten mark. If we decided to write that mark in, the value would reverse itself; if we added the next one, the value would reverse itself again, and so on.

Thus, to reduce any expression in Spencer Brown's calculus down to a single value is equivalent to suppressing knowledge of a frame.

Clearly this is an image of the interpretive dilemma Delany's work presents to us. For, as we have seen, to try to trace out any single privileged interpretation through the texts one must in effect ignore the elaborate destabilizing frames which Delany has set up around/within them. And it is precisely this sort of interpretive activity that has led some of Delany's critics to insist—rather as Spencer Brown's critics have insisted that his calculus is just a typographically obscure Boolean algebra—that Delany's texts are merely stylistically obscure fantasies.[94] But this sort of interpretive activity is just an image of thematic criticism in general, which tries to isolate as an object of analysis by interpretive methods which are restricted to what is allowable within one's given discourse—what is really a dialectical process of image and reflection. Thus it becomes clear why Spencer Brown's scholarly readers, operating within an institutionally sanctioned (and therefore conservative) discourse, must ignore the fundamental properties of his calculus and interpret it as a form of Boolean algebra, just as Delany's critics within the sf field must ignore the real readerly effects of his texts in order to interpret them according to a pre-existing template for the "well-formed" sf or fantasy story. Both Delany's and Spencer Brown's texts generate a situation which reveals a certain kind of interpretation to be equivalent to an act of concealment,

Along similar lines, we can expand on our earlier statement that finding a single value for expressions in Spencer Brown's calculus is equivalent to concealing the presence of a frame, and say that to interpret Spencer Brown's calculus as a two-valued logic is equivalent to concealing a relation that is not binary, but hierarchical. But this, of course, is an image of the concealment of hierarchy behind binarism that deconstructive criticism works to reveal. Spencer Brown's calculus can thus be read as a mathematical image of Derrida's logic of the trace, dropped into the binary stronghold of algebraic discourse—the effect of which has been the commencement of an ongoing dialogue between the conservative and progressive voices within, and the revelation of the discursive limits within which the dialogue operates. But Spencer Brown's text does not reside wholly outside the discourse, just as it does not reside wholly within it: as Delany's critique indicates, Spencer Brown's text is itself grounded in a conception of the metaphysics of mathematics which is not necessarily incompatible with the root-assumptions of the discourse it critiques—so any limit it reveals, it reveals at least partially from within. But this is just another image of deconstruction. In the Appendix to *Tales of Nevèrÿon*, Delany, ostensibly

---

94. See, for example, Darrell Schweitzer's review of *Neveryóna* in *Science Fiction Review*, Vol. 12, No. 3, August 1983: 46.

discussing Steiner's work (in the persona of the evocatively named conservative academic S.L. Kermit), addresses the problem of the status of Spencer Brown's:

> The question must finally be: Are Steiner's equations the expressions of a conservative collective speech, which would certainly seem to be the case with any probability work concerning myth and language; or, are they the expression of a radical individualistic authority—which seems, at any rate, to be the collective view of mathematical creativity, if not authorship/authority itself. (TN 260)

This self-deconstructing passage expresses the dialectic which Delany's analytical engine has set in motion, and, needless to say, of which it itself—neither wholly inside nor wholly outside its own discursive field—is constituted. And the readerly experience of this dialectical oscillation is not one of reassurance, of inevitability, of learning yet again what one already knows—but rather of ongoing recognition and revelation: that is, the experience of insight itself.

In *Laws of Form* we find a striking image of the kind of deconstruction/revelation that Delany's texts generate, as well as a model of the ungrounded ontology from which they generate it. Very early in his argument, Spencer Brown reminds us that just as expressions can be simplified, they also can be made more complex (LF 9–10)—which means that equations can be read from right to left as well as from left to right. Thus, by equation (1), any mark can generate an infinite number of "twins." And by equation (2), any blank (which we now know to be enclosed/defined by a mark) can be thought of as infinitely "productive," as concealing within itself an infinitely deep echelon of marks:

But if we connect this image with our earlier notion of the infinite number of unwritten frames which can be revealed to reside outside of any expression, then we see that any mark, and by extension any expression, can be understood to rest in a potentially infinite "corridor" of unwritten distinctions:

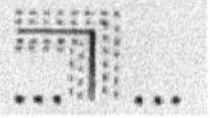

And this is quite literally an image of Delany's hall of mirrors. It is an image of what we are really doing when we call any distinction the first distinction, any content the primary content, any ontological ground the ontological ground: we are positioning ourselves within an unbounded field of possible revelations by performing a complex act of concealment. The act may be willed by us, or the act may be heavily determined by the discourse in which we are embedded (a dialectic with which we are now familiar); but in either case, we are suppressing revelation in the interests of intelligibility. But this process of reduction is just an image of language itself, which, as Delany says in his essay "Shadows," does not so much differentiate entities as indicate "any number of different things in the same way" (JHJ 117); thus it is also an image of any critical interpretation, any algebra, or any coin. The problem then becomes one of how to discern when this reduction shades over into oppression—for which a calculus grounded in the notion of ideal distinctions may not provide the optimum interpretive method. As Reverend Amy says in *Dhalgren*: "What we need is not a calculus of form but an analytics of attention, which renders form on the indifferent and undifferentiated plurima" (D 472).

Toward the end of his argument, Spencer Brown devises a complex method for generating infinitely extended expressions.[95] In these expressions he discerns a property which we have already seen to be potentially present in every expression in the calculus: namely, the property of indeterminate value. Such expressions, Spencer Brown argues, can be read as oscillating in time between two values, as alternately "transparent" and "opaque" to the space outside the expressions—an image of the dialectical process. Spencer Brown calls this property of oscillation a subversion (LF 62). But if every expression has this property, then every expression is a subverted expression—which Spencer Brown himself seems to realize, though he appears unwilling to pursue the idea. In his discussion of the phenomenology of distinction, following his discussion of subversion, Spencer Brown notes in passing

---

95. I would argue that Spencer Brown actually devises a much simpler method early in Chapter 6, with Consequence 4, interestingly named the "Occultation" or "Conceal/Reveal" function. All one has to do is write in the unwritten mark around the expression, and one gets a construction identical to, and expandable in the same way as, the step-generating sequence in Chapter 11.

that "in these experiments the sign '=' may stand for the words 'is confused with'" (LF 69). But this is just a restatement of the process of reduction-shading-into-oppression that we discerned above. And like his previous passing comment about the unwritten mark (are we now beginning to see why Spencer Brown can only make these comments in passing, why he must deprivilege them within the mathematical context which legitimates his argument?), this comment indicates a property which completely alters our view of the calculus as a whole: the property that not a single equating of one so-called distinction with another, be it the ideal first distinction, the mark, or the observer, is a perfect equating that every equation in the calculus of indications is a subverted equation.

In her essay "A Cyborg Manifesto," Donna Haraway mentions her indebtedness to Delany's writing, and to *Tales of Nevèrÿon* in particular, for being part of a group of texts which had provided much of the inspiration for her own conception of a radical political project founded in the celebration of the "confusion of boundaries" and the "leaky distinction"—in the transgressive crossing of borders between realms of knowledge and practice which discursive and coercive systems would endeavor to keep separate.[96] Clearly, Delany's deconstruction of *Laws of Form* makes such a crossing. The value of that crossing to us, standing in the space of the humanities, is the illumination of a whole realm of mathematical discourse (and more importantly, its limits) that might otherwise have remained concealed and opaque. The brilliance of this illumination and all of its reflections in other discourses, other texts—is a tribute to Delany's ingenious appropriation/contribution. But a critical essay such as mine can only present a much-reduced account of this illumination and what it suppresses in that account may ultimately be more important than what it privileges. For an incomparably richer experience of this illumination, then, the reader must turn away from my reflections and—here I echo the words of K. Leslie Steiner in her (authorial? or authoritarian?) "Preface" to the whole series—Return to Nevèrÿon.

---

96. Donna Haraway, "A Cyborg Manifesto," in *Simians, Cyborgs, and Women* (New York: Routledge, Chapman, and Hall, Inc., 1991), pp. 173–78, 150, 152.

The Making of *Hogg*

To explain why this essay/interview on *Hogg* closes out this collection of pieces on *Dhalgren*, I start by pointing out the overlap of the books' place-date subscriptions:

> *Hogg*: San Francisco, London, NYC, March '69—Oct '73.
> *Dhalgren*: San Francisco, Abaqii, Toronto, Clarion, Milford, New Orleans, Seattle, Vancouver, Middletown, East Lansing, New York, London, Jan '69—September '73.

Basically *Hogg* was written in some of the same places as *Dhalgren* and during the same months. The place-date subscriptions on all of my books tell when a first draft—or a draft of the book in which all of the structural decisions have been made—was completed.

I signed the first contract for *Dhalgren* when I was still in New York City, with George Ernstberger, then at Peter Meyer's Avon Books. I had explained to George that I wanted to write a series of up to five space operas, each of which would show how a future movement, much like the then-urban-counter-culture, would cause five different urban governments on five different worlds—an ordinary capitalist democracy, a fully collective government, an enlightened monarchy like England, another run by a combination of bribes and buy-offs like a South American dictatorship, and perhaps a fifth, which has some combination I had not yet figured out—to topple. The contract itself, I'm sure, was only for three books, but George was assuming that the series would be in the same genre as *Nova*, which he had already read and very much liked.

I had written a section of the first in what I thought might be part of the climax of the initial volume, in which one of the female characters wears a dress whose fabric changes color under a radio control (whether or not I had even shown that much to George, I don't remember): some will recognize it, even from this description, as the dress Lanya wears to the book party Calkins holds at his multi-gardened mansion in *Dhalgren*'s chapter VI; but between that sample and the published book, my whole view shifted, and instead it became a single near-future book set in a single city—Bellona—that represented all cities in the country at that time with everything other than racial and sexual politics swallowed up. Even capitalism does not mean the same thing in a city where money longer functions as anything except a symbol.

While I was rethinking *Dhalgren* in a single city, I wrote *Hogg* in longhand. The first draft filled five notebooks. It took place in the same city, except that it had a waterfront area called Crawhole, and the pier (halfway between Aransas Pass, Texas, where I'd worked in '62, and some vision of a wholly imagined dockside) was called Frontwater. Bellona is the same city minus that waterfront. Eventually, in my own mind, all such cities came to be known as Enoch.

When I came back to the East Coast, I forgot them in a San Francisco closet.

When I eventually returned to the city for more work on *Dhalgren*, by then Marilyn had left Natoma Street for England. Our friend Paul Caruso, who had inherited the flat, reminded me of the notebooks, and I was surprised to discover I had an entire novel. Both Marilyn and I spent a great deal of time traveling back and forth, getting back together, and separating again. By '72, I had made a film (*The Orchid*), with Barbara Wise producing, during which I was living at the Albert Hotel after a stretch in a tenement with Joe Manfredini on far West 10th Street. The film had just been completed when I got a call from Marilyn to join her in London and have a child, to which I eagerly said yes. On New Year's Eve, 1972, I left the Albert Hotel, where I had been staying, and flew to Heathrow, to be met by Marilyn and her business partner, John Simms, for a two-and-a-half-year stay at 21 Paddington Street.[97] Manuscripts of *Hogg* and *Dhalgren* went with me. Both were rewritten. *Dhalgren* was finished and sold, and *Hogg* came back to America, back to the Albert, and was not published until 1993. The difference is that structural revisions were going on in *Dhalgren* all the way through the time in

97. Just today via Google Maps, I learned that our four-story flat, with the Indian restaurant at street level, across from Paddington Park—once a graveyard—had been pulled down and replaced with a six-story building. It's another dwelling place, where I once lived and worked (with Tim Curry as an upstairs neighbor and an African import business just below), that, with the green grocers at the end of the block and the little restaurant where I regularly had lunch, no longer exists.

London. No structural changes were occurring in *Hogg* once the first draft was completed. Because they share a city, however, I am including this essay in this book on the malleable city, the changing city—sometimes with, sometimes without a waterfront—whose ruins can be explored in outer Mongolia and who even loaned its name to a city on Mars.

Hogg
a novel by
delany....

The Making of Hogg

[Harold Jaffe thanks Stephan-Paul Martin and Mel Freilicher for editorial assistance with the questions for the interview.]

The nameless narrator of Hogg *[Normal, Ill.: Black Ice, 1995] is a Huck-like eleven-year-old caught in society's most sinister seams. Unlike Huck, though, Delany's narrator passes no judgments on the violent actions he takes part in. Becoming the sexual slave of truck-driver Franklin Hargus (a.k.a. Hogg), he wants only to suck on his master's penis, toes, and fingers, drink his urine, and eat his feces.*

Hogg is no ordinary teamster, however. Various disgruntled men (and women) hire him to rape and brutalize their out-of-favor lovers and wives. Over large sections of the book, the narrator describes Hogg and his gang terrorizing women, sexually savaging them and their families. To relieve his perpetual erection, one gang member, teen-aged Denny, pushes a nail through his penis. Maddened by the pain, he goes on a mass-murder spree. About the same time, a local biker and another of Hogg's gang kidnap the narrator away and sell him (for ten dollars) to a brutal black fisherman on the Crawhole docks. As Denny is about to be taken by the police, Hogg rescues the killer, spirits the narrator away, and the two smuggle the teen-aged psychopath into a neighboring state, where, after receiving the flimsiest of promises to behave, Hogg turns him loose to commit who-knows-what further mayhem.

The novel ends in irony. For the first time Hogg admits he feels affection for his child companion, who has accompanied him on these horrific adventures. But now the narrator has decided to escape, seeking as new masters a pair of sadistic garbage men, Rufus and Red, who operate a scow out of Crawhole and whom the narrator met in passing when he was sold there. As the narrator plans his defection, Hogg asks him what's on his mind. The first he speaks in the book and the novel's last word, the narrator's answer is, "Nothin'."[98]

98. This synopsis is modified from one prepared by Harold Jaffe for the original publication of the interview in *Fiction International, #30*.

FI: You completed *Hogg* in 1973 and published it twenty-two years later. Can you detail some of the problems you had in finding a publisher?

SRD: In the paraliterary field—e.g., science fiction, comic books, pornography—the relationship between creation and publication is so very different from the relation that obtains in the literary precincts, it might help, in understanding the book's publication problems, if I spoke some about the circumstances under which *Hogg* was written.

In the late 1960s, a company called Essex House began putting out a highly literate line of pornography. Following the model of Maurice Girodias at Olympia Press, instead of exhorting the cynical, if not sub-literate, hacks who traditionally provided such textual fare to write for him, Essex editor Brian Kirby approached young poets and aspiring literary writers who were just not making a living, men and women for whom a seven-hundred-fifty or a thousand-dollar advance was a major bulwark against eviction or starvation. Formal parameters were relaxed. The books had to focus on sex—but that's all. What came out was extraordinary. Poet David Meltzer produced *Orf* (1968) and *The Agency Trilogy* (1968); Marco Vassi's works came out of this. To my mind, however, the most remarkable of these books was poet and critic Michael Perkins's *Evil Companions* (1968).

I met Michael just after he' d completed his extraordinary *roman noir* but before it was published. (See my "Preface" to the Rhinoceros edition reprint [1992] of *Evil Companions*.) The energy around these books and writers was immense, pervasive, and infectious. I was twenty-six years old —and it was hard not to be caught up in it.

Within that field of energy and excitement I wrote my first pornographic novel, *Equinox.*

Kindly, Perkins read my book in manuscript. One night in the first weeks of December '68 at Perkins's Avenue A apartment, we had a long, boozy critical session over it that lasted till dawn. As anyone who has read his criticism knows (*The Secret Record* [1992]; *The Good Parts* [1994]), Perkins is an astute analyst of texts.

The session had at least three results.

The first was a four-day hangover. Then, about ten days later, with a New Year's Eve flight, I moved to San Francisco.

The second and third were two new passages I inserted toward the beginning and end of *Equinox*, "The Scorpion's Log." Finally, that spring, I was ready to submit the manuscript to Kirby—only to learn that Essex House had gone out of business.

The manuscript went into the drawer.

The last Essex House volumes were, however, still making their way to my wife's Natoma Street flat in San Francisco where I was then living. The energy was still there.

"The Scorpion's Log" had been an attempt to patch up *Equinox* in light of Michael's criticism—criticism that boiled down to: You don't have to sacrifice a rich relationship between character and landscape just because you're writing about sex. As a novel, *Equinox* is largely a collection of set pieces. As such, "The Scorpion's Log" only added some new ones to those already there. At the same time, I was working on a large novel, *Dhalgren*. After having put together a fairly complex outline for it back in New York, I was having some difficulty getting beyond the opening chapter. In that way we writers have, I was looking for things to distract me: One of the things I did was to direct a little-theater production of Genet's *Les Bonnes*—in French. It played in our front hall for three weekends, moved to a church basement for a couple of months, and finally aired over KPFA-FM in Berkeley.

And, because I wanted to try my hand at writing a pornographic work more focused and with a greater psychological density, another thing I did (a fourth result of the session with Michael, back in New York) was to begin *Hogg*. On and off, between March and July '69, the novel's first, handwritten draft filled up two, three, then four notebooks. Next I took some time to co-edit with my then-wife, Marilyn Hacker, four issues of a quarterly called *Quark*. Finally I could turn my major energies to *Dhalgren* again; and this time it began to work.

The *Hogg* notebooks ended up in the back of a closet at Natoma Street.

And *Dhalgren* was taking up pretty much all my time.

In summer '71, after teaching at the Clarion SF Writers' Workshop, I came back to New York City and again got to work on *Dhalgren*. I'd already sent the manuscript of *Equinox* to my agent, Henry Morrison, who began marketing it around. In the Albert Hotel, where I was living, another project intervened—a film called *The Orchid*, produced by

Barbara Wise, which I wrote, directed, and edited on an old "chatterbox" editing machine that was moved into my tenth-floor hotel room. The eleven days of filming took place in February. The editing went on up through April and into May of '72.

Prints were ready at the end of June.

That summer's Clarion Workshop had three chapters, one in East Lansing, one in New Orleans, and one in Seattle: I taught at all three. After Seattle's Clarion, with a student I'd met in the class, Pat Muir (grandson of the naturalist John Muir, Pat was an electronics repairman and biker), I rode on the back of Pat's motorcycle up to some Oregon communes, then to Vancouver, where we stayed with Russell and Dora FitzGerald, saw George Stanley again, and met poet Robin Blaser. After the trip was done, I bussed down from Seattle to San Francisco, where my friend Paul Caruso was now staying at Natoma Street.

Between the San Francisco Greyhound Bus Terminal and the house, I stopped at the Empire Theater on Market Street, in the back balcony of which I managed to lose a notebook containing some forty-odd pages of *Dhalgren*, so that when I arrived at Paul's I was rather down. But now Paul asked me: "Do you want those old notebooks you left in the back of the closet?" I pulled them out, to realize I had the first draft of an entire novel that I'd all but forgotten. It kind of cheered me up.

I reconstructed the lost *Dhalgren* pages. Working on things carefully, sentence by sentence, with lots of notes (the way I'd been writing *Dhalgren*), makes such reconstruction easier. By no means is it fun. But it's only tedious—not impossible. A month or so on, the *Hogg* notebooks went with me to New York.

Later in '72, back at the Albert, I finished a draft of *Dhalgren*—just about the time Henry (my agent), told me he'd managed to place *Equinox* with Lancer Books, a small paperback company—three-and-a-half years after the book had been completed. They wanted to change the title to *Tides of Eros*. After dinner and a four-hour brainstorming session at the Albert, with the help of Warren Wexler, we compromised on *Tides of Lust*. Inspired by the sale of my first pornographic novel, on a portable electric type writer I borrowed from Henry's wife I typed up *Hogg* over the next six weeks.

"I think," Henry told me, a week later, when he'd finished it, "you're going to have a bit more trouble selling this one than you had with

Equinox." He didn't even want to try Lancer. (Financially they were pretty shaky; a week after they published *Equinox* in '73, they went out of business.) At my suggestion, we submitted it to Girodias at Olympia, which had opened up American offices.

The result was a pleasant lunch with Henry, me, and that urbane and charming old scoundrel. Girodias was interested but noncommittal. Sometime later, after he'd rejected the novel, he wrote me: "*Hogg* is the only novel in my career that I have declined to publish *solely* because of its sexual content. Should the book someday appear, please feel free to use this as a blurb, if you think it will help promote sales." Alas, when the book did appear, twenty-odd years later, Maurice was dead. Using that blurb would have confused more readers than not—though I'm still fond of it.

Days before Christmas '72, I flew to England to rejoin Marilyn. During the first half of '73, in our Paddington Street flat, *Dhalgren* went through another—and final—rewrite. Impelled by leftover energy, *Hogg* shot, once more, through the typewriter—and received its final subscription date, October '73, though my agent had been sending around earlier versions for the previous year and a half. In London, editing a string of British men's magazines, American poet Richard Deutch read it and became quite enthusiastic. He promised to publish some excerpts—but had a severe breakdown at about that time. A pleasant young woman I met through Richard, who worked out of her kitchen while her kids played around the table legs, typed the final manuscript. Besides typing, she wrote soft-core stories for British men's magazines. Supportive and enthusiastic about my novel, she was one of *Hogg*'s first fans.

I began to realize the problems to beset the finished book when the London copy shop, where I took *Hogg* to be Xeroxed, phoned me to say that they would not make copies of the text. The office manager had looked at it, read a page or two, and told them to return it to the customer.

At a self-service machine, I copied *Hogg*, feeding in a sheet at a time —and sent it to Henry. Still not sanguine about publication possibilities, he told me over the phone he' d start sending the new version around. I returned from England the day before Christmas Eve 1974 (I was now a father, with a daughter almost a year old), to start teaching at SUNY Buffalo in January '75. *Dhalgren* had just been published, and *Trouble on Triton* was in production. As Marilyn and I were coming through

Kennedy Airport, I saw a newsstand rack full of *Dhalgren*s, and—a few minutes later—a sailor in his blues sitting in a tubular chair, at one of the gates, reading a copy. Three days later, Bantam Books phoned me to say the book had already gone through three printings before its official publication date (January 1, 1975). It was scheduled for two more: I had a moderately successful novel on my hands.

A week or so later, Marilyn and I separated for good.

I don't really know *where* Henry sent *Hogg*. I'm not particularly interested in who rejects my work—only in who accepts it. That he tells me only of the latter has always been our arrangement. I know, however, he was sending it somewhere. A year or two on, I picked up a young, stocky Irish-American (complete with red hair, very thick glasses, and freckles) near the city's downtown waterfront, who took me back to his apartment in the industrial streets west of the Village. Our after-sex talk turned to books. At one point, getting up from the futon and putting on a paisley robe, he said: "Do you want to see the weirdest, most outrageous thing I've ever read? Just a second." He went to a drawer, pulled it open, took out a manuscript in a black spring binder, and brought it back to me. "Read five pages of that—*any* five pages. It doesn't really matter which ones—go on!"

I opened back the black cover and began to flip through what was obviously a Xerox of a Xerox of a Xerox—I could only guess at how many generations. There was no title page. It began simply at page one.

It was the manuscript of *Hogg*.

Somehow, to say, "Hey, you know, actually *I* wrote this…" seemed absurd.

So I read a few pages. Yes, it was my novel.

"That's… pretty amazing," I told him. "Where'd you get it?" He'd gotten it from a friend who'd gotten it from a friend who'd gotten it from a publishing company, where the manuscript, on arrival, had created a small furor in the office. Before returning it, someone had made a quick and unauthorized Xerox.

"I'd like to read the whole thing," I said. "Could I get one?"

"I guess so. Although it's pretty dim to copy once more…

Unfortunately we never ran into each other again. But I didn't really need one.

After the success of *Dhalgren* in '75 (and the smaller success of *Trouble on Triton* in '76), in '77 Bantam Books agreed to buy up all my earlier books, the rights to which had recently reverted to me. Lancer had gone out of business, so the rights to *Equinox* had also reverted. "You know," Henry told the folks at Bantam he was negotiating with, "Delany also has two 'erotic' novels, one of which has been published and one of which is still in manuscript. You guys are doing real well with things like Anaïs Nin's *Delta of Venus*. Do you want to buy the rights to those as well?"

Somebody said, "Sure. Why not?"

So *Hogg* was bought—in a large package with a lot of other books—and paid for—though no one at Bantam had actually read it. Henry felt that was the best he could do. One day at Bantam, however, I asked Lou Aronica if there was any chance of their publishing *Hogg*—not to mention reprinting *Equinox*.

Lou looked at me and laughed. "You know, I just got around to reading them last month. They're extraordinary books, Chip. Both of them. But will we *publish* them?" He chuckled. "Not a snowball's chance in hell!"

Of the twenty-odd years *Hogg* languished in Limbo, Bantam accounts for ten. The book was shown to a few other publishers during that time. Five? Fifteen? I didn't know, because I was working on other things, and (as I said) generally I'm not informed of rejections. Lou said as soon as there was some interest from someone else, certainly he wouldn't stand in the way of our buying back the rights. But as the '80s rolled on, with times becoming more and more conservative, there seemed less and less chance of the books appearing.

But those samizdat Xeroxes were (I guess) still generating rumors: In 1989, a group contemplating becoming a small publishing collective in Seattle, centered around Ron Drummond, Randy Byers, and the people at Serconia Press (who'd already done a nonfiction book of mine, *The Straits of Messina* [1989]) phoned me. They knew of the existence of *Hogg* from my bibliography by Peplow and Bravard.

All the people involved were pretty familiar with the range of my work—including *Equinox*. "The fact is, Chip," Drummond told me over the phone, "it would be hard to *conceive* of a book by you, even if it's about the strangest sex in the world, that we wouldn't want to do. Send *Hogg* to us, and I can all but guarantee you, sight unseen, we'll publish it."

"Don't do that, Ron," I told him. "If you're interested, certainly I'll show it to you. If you guys decide you want to publish it, I'll be delighted. But it's unrealistic to commit yourself to something like that without reading the manuscript first. Too many people have found it too great a problem. Make your mind up *after* you look at it."

But I agreed to send it.

A couple of weeks later, Drummond phoned again. "Well... eh, Chip. Yeah. You were right. We've all got lots of questions about the advisability of bringing it out."

"I'm not surprised," I said.

"What we want to do," Ron said, "is hold a meeting. We want to have a few more people read it. Then we want to have them all discuss it seriously." They decided to put together a discussion seminar of six people: four men and two women—all people who had read the book and who were familiar with my other work. They decided to record the discussion, and Ron told me they would send me a copy.

About that same time, in his Guest of Honor talk at Readercon, speaking of the problems he'd had with the publication of some of his own more experimental books, Barry Malzberg explained: "Some books are simply never going to be published by a committee."

After seventeen years, I didn't have much emotional investment in *Hogg*'s publication. But on the intellectual level, what I'd heard Malzberg say seemed pretty much to cover the situation.

Perhaps a couple of years later, at an SF convention here on the East Coast, Victor Gonzales just in from Seattle handed me a copy of the tape. On a Walkman in my hotel room, I played it that afternoon. One of the discussants, at the last minute, hadn't been able to make it—one of the women, I believe. Other than that, it was what they'd said it would be. A second woman, coming late, joined the discussion about halfway through.

The tape ran about an hour and a half. The meeting was held on July 2nd, 1989, with Randy Byers, Ron Drummond, Victor Gonzales, Carl Juarez, and Kate Schaefer. (Jerry Kaufman had, by this time, decided not to publish the book.)

No writer could have asked for a more astute and sensitive discussion of a manuscript. Listening to the dialogue, I felt that everyone on the panel had read the book carefully and intelligently. They'd all taken in its intentions, its various and several points. None of them had missed any subtleties or major moves in the text. All seemed to have found many sections moving. All agreed that the material was extraordinarily distasteful: It is.

The breakdown as to which people felt the book should be published and which people felt it would be dangerous to publish (not because of legal repercussions, but because of what it might do to unstable readers) was, however, interesting.

Schaefer felt that, as distasteful as it was, the book ought to be published. She even thought its publication imperative. Half the men felt that the danger to unstable minds was simply too great to risk.

Because the money for the venture was being put up by one of the straight men, however, finally it was decided to forego publication. With many apologies, they returned the manuscript. Randy Byers sent me a fine, thoughtful, and considered letter. I answered him with a letter of my own. At this point, Larry McCaffery became aware of the recent interest in the novel—and the controversy it was causing. I'm not sure whether he actually heard the discussion tape. (At one point, Ron said he was going to send it to him.) Larry asked to see *Hogg* and took it to Ron Sukenick and Curt White at Fiction Collective 2, who were just putting together a new line, Black Ice Books.

Did I want to see *Hogg* published? Yes.[99]

But I was now almost fifty and the author of more than twenty-five books—most of which had appeared in several editions. The truth is, in more cases than not, publication is painful enough to leach all but the most fleeting pleasure from the printing of a new book. To fixate on the realization of a forthcoming volume only intensifies the pain from the inevitable defects marring its actual publication.

From time to time, yes, I've found myself looking forward to the appearance of a new volume.

But I try not to.

Then working at *Reflex Magazine*, my friend Robert Morales volunteered to scan the manuscript onto disk. At that time, optical scanning and character recognition were not all that efficient. Proofreading the text and putting in corrections turned into a far more time-consuming job than I was ready for. Three months later, though, a pristine manuscript went to Seattle.

Fiction Collective 2/Black Ice are *Hogg*'s current publishers.

---

99. For an alternate version of what occurred, one should talk with Ron Drummond, whose memory of the details is notably different from mine.

Most of the problems the book encountered, even there, turned, again, on the committee nature of a collective publisher—and also on the fact that they are a small operation. Those problems ranged from some unauthorized last-minute "creative copy editing" that had to be undone, to a delay in the appearance of the book (anyone who looks at the hardcover copyright page will see the book is dated 1994, though it didn't appear until well into 1995), to the obligatory cover-confusion (it was supposed to be white dropout splat on an all-black cover, but a volunteer worker graduate student objected to it strenuously—or so I heard—and to appease her, they turned it into a black splat on a pale blue background, which now looks like a splat of blood, which was the last thing in the world I wanted it to evoke. Although there is a murder, I didn't want it to be advertised as a murder-mystery. It changes considerably the reading of that abstract splat—which is, yes, my significant other Dennis's seminal fluid), to a mix-up in the printing of the first paperback edition, so that the printing had to be pulped: Through dropped or doubled lines, more than ten percent of the pages didn't connect to the page following. It was unreadable.

Suffice it to say, however, that the current paperback printing now out in stores is a fine and largely accurate edition of *Hogg*.

The press and I are proud of it.

FI: Transgressive is a literary category that perhaps has been overused; still one could reasonably fit *Hogg* into that category. It is transgressive in terms of its extensively elaborated scatology; and it is more generally transgressive in that it is narrated from the point of view of the sexual recipient, or "victim," as some might choose to call your adolescent narrator. To what extent were you influenced by the writings of Genet and Bataille, two notable literary prototypes of so-called transgression? Did you have any other artistic models in mind?

SRD: That's a complicated question. First, there *are* victims in the book: the women that Hogg is paid to rape, abuse, and brutalize. But the narrator is *not* one of them. Perhaps that helps make the book as disturbing as people so often find it. We have an overarching sentimental model that says an underage child involved in sex *must* be a "victim"—or, if not (and this is the soiled, nasty underside of sentimentality), then some sort of monster of the *Bad Seed* variety. But *Hogg*'s narrator is neither, though he takes part willingly in rapes, assaults, and brutalization.

When I wrote *Hogg*, the only Bataille I had read was the old Ballantine paperback edition of *Literature and Evil*. Although Perkins was a great fan of Bataille's two pornographic novels, *Madame Edwarda* and *Story of the Eye*, and had recommended them to me highly, neither was then readily available in English. So, no, I *hadn't* read them. In 1961 I'd read *Our Lady of the Flowers* in the 1949 Editions Morihen translation (under the title *Gutter in the Sky*). And, as I said, I was directing Genet's *Les Bonnes* just before I started writing *Hogg*. As it happens, I first read *Miracle of the Rose* in the Frechtman translation *while* I was writing it. But though I enjoyed Genet's second novel immensely, if it was any sort of influence, it was a negative one: Genet's heightened rhetoric a-swirl all through the presentation of a succession of several objects of desire, with whom there is all-but-no bodily contact, is precisely what I *didn't want* to do in *Hogg*.

Guillaume Apollinaire's surreal pornographic masterpiece *The Debouched Hospodar* (Perkins published the first English translation in his magazine *Down Here*) was very much, and conscientiously so, a model for *Equinox*—though I wanted to achieve some of the same effects without recourse to the surreal. (I used drug-induced hallucinations instead.) But for *Hogg* there was no conscious pornographic model at all.

In an article on my several sex novels that first appeared in the *New York Review of Science Fiction* (reprinted in the James Sallis-edited volume *Ash of Stars* [1996]), writer Ray Davis makes a point I, at least, found interesting: *Hogg* is a novel—perhaps, says Davis, the only such novel—that really *is* filled with precisely what conservative forces in the country claim is rampant in *all* pornography: violence against women, torture, murder, racism, filth, the exploitation of children, and other acts too perverse to name. The only place it breaks with this (if we can call it such) classical and conservative description of pornography is that it is carefully written, not sloppily hacked out; and it examines those subjects not from the point of view of sociologists and psychologists with their ready-made categories of "victims" and "monsters," but examines them as seriously—and relentlessly—as the *people caught up in such acts* are capable of. That it finds touches of humanity here and there even among murderers and criminal psychopaths is, of course, troubling.

At the end of the book, the reader should ask: What punishment should Hogg receive for what he's done?

What punishment should Denny receive?

Is there some unwarranted cruelty in the narrator's decision to leave Hogg for what is a comparatively domesticated version of S&M with garbage scow workers Red and Rufus back on the docks?

And, of course, the final question must be: Personally, how are *you* engaged by these questions?

FI: Among the many atypical aspects of *Hogg* is the fact that it is not "naturalized"; that is, nowhere in the savage goings-on is any norm posited. Rather there is a collective radical deviation from so-called normalcy in which every major character participates. The novel's ending reinforces the significance of the destabilization of all norms, when the adolescent narrator rejects Hogg's plan to domesticate their situation. Would you comment on any of these themes?

SRD: Humbly I'd suggest that you're overlooking, among others, the "normal" couple, Harry Bunim, Mona Casey, and their infant son Chuck, living on the barge beside the scow belonging to Rufus and Red. But there are lots of relatively "normal" people in the novel: the hardware store owner and her daughter, for example; the bartender, Ray, at the Piewacket Bar; the harmonica-playing fisherman, Andy; and perhaps the most important, the director of the radio show. Generally, the "normal" people are the ones attacked and brutalized by Hogg—and, later, by Denny. One of the novel's tasks is temporally to normalize a moral frame outside the experience of most readers of the book: The frame that will triumph in the book *is* Red and Rufus's, which the narrator will finally—and sensibly—choose over Hogg's. One strategy the book employs to accomplish this normalization is the metonymic association of Red and Rufus with Harry and Mona.

The prevalence of and the focus on the deviant is high enough, however, that, for the first reading or two, readers are not likely to pay much attention to the strands of normalcy threading the brutality and sexual excess. Nevertheless, those strands are as carefully woven as the "abnormal" ones. If they weren't, the book wouldn't function.

Among the tasks the novel attempts is to mark out a discursive field in which, by the end, the reader can no longer even *say* the words "normal" and "abnormal" without putting them in quotation marks, ironizing them, or somehow or other placing them *sous rature.*

FI: The narrator rarely addresses his own emotional state, yet his description of the other characters and of the frequent S/M and scatological sexual acts in which he participates are exhaustively detailed, always precise, and often stylistically refined. This seeming discontinuity between an adolescent, unself-conscious narrator who is also a keen and even elegant observer/recorder seems central to the novel's impact. Can you discuss your narrator's character and function?

SRD: To begin with, the narrator is not an adolescent: He's *pre*-adolescent—he's only eleven. He is, however, pubescent. That's not the same thing. As a first-person narrator, however—like Huckleberry Finn, like Esperanza Cordero in Cisneros's *House on Mango Street*, like Holden Caulfield—my narrator tells his tale from some indeterminate future age. (Fourteen, seventeen, twenty, twenty-six… this last the age I was when, just before my twenty-seventh birthday, in San Francisco, I began drafting it.) This signals to the reader that he's survived the story's events and, like Ishmael, lived to tell them. Yes, he attempts to narrate Hogg's story as it struck him *at the time*—but, of course, there's a fibrillating quality to his sophistication, that registers (to you) as a discontinuity, or set of discontinuities.

Were the material more traditionally associated with children, you might be less aware of those "discontinuities" that of course exist between the character's various levels: the touches that signal the eleven-year-old to whom the events happened, the verbal turns that signal the older personality looking back on the events, and those places where, as it must to those looking for it, the "art of the novel" shows.

FI: In a certain way, Hogg's complexities seem complementary to the narrator's. A sexual torturer and murderer, he performs the most degrading, even bestial, acts with a fiercely relentless exhilaration. At the same time he is capable of astute self-reflection and of discoursing on so-called normalcy and the social construction of desire and identity in the manner of a poststructuralist and gender theorist. Did you have any literary or cultural precedents in mind for the characterizations of

Hogg and/or his mentor-protégé relationship with the adolescent narrator?

SRD: Sadism is classically known as "the perversion of philosophers." Presumably when you realize that you gain real and deeply desired pleasure by doing things that *truly* hurt other people, you face the sort of *aporia* that *must* start you thinking about the nature of the social world that defines good and evil and your own place—and the place of other beings—in it.

The same imperative is just not there, say, with masochism: "You derive pleasure from hurting yourself? Go on, then. Hurt yourself—as long as it doesn't bother me."

You call Hogg a murderer. But while he's probably killed a few people before the book begins, in the novel proper, though he threatens many and physically injures many more—injures them to the point they will need serious medical attention—the only *murder* he commits (some readers are surprised when they're reminded of this) is that of the morally loathsome Jimmy.

James Bond, Snake Pliskin, Dirty Harry—all are *far* more lethal than Hogg—in films any eleven-year-old is energetically welcomed by our society to view.

To call Hogg a poststructuralist or a gender theorist is a hyperbole that, I take it, you offer as a compliment. It's a hyperbole still. That he's all but illiterate doesn't mean, however, Hogg can't *think*. Yes, he's smart. (Were he not, he'd have been caught long ago.) Also he's the most active onstage character in the novel. (When Denny briefly becomes *more* active than Hogg, *he* moves *offstage* and his actions are only reported indirectly for the duration.) That goes a long way toward needling at the reader's sympathies. Hogg has a specific roster of things he wants to accomplish over the novel's course—and he puts a lot of energy into achieving them successfully, which is, in current narrative discourse, another way of evoking sympathy.

The reader is uncomfortable sympathizing with such a "monster." But when, at the end, the narrator realizes he can get the same sexual excitement from Red and Rufus, without actual murder sand rapes, and so chooses to return to the garbage scow and abandon Hogg (a sane, logical decision, which—at the *level* of logic—all of us have to concur with), many readers—if only for a moment—are going to find themselves caught up in the poignancy of Hogg's situation. That someone like Hogg could elicit our sympathy—that (even momentarily) we should find him poignant, human, and struggling for happiness (rather than monster or victim)—*is* going to trouble. Well, *Hogg* is a story written to trouble.

It's no more a feel-good novel than *Sentimental Education* or *Good Morning Midnight*. Davis sees in *Hogg* a combination of Mark Twain and Dashiell Hammett, with a goodly dollop of Sade. But I'd rather let readers —and/or critics—speculate on possible literary models, precedents, or origins than try to untangle them myself. To say that *Hogg* represents something new or unprecedented simply flies in the face of all we know of intertextuality, of the literary. Texts that are readable—and even texts that aren't—just *aren't* new in that transcendent way. I don't mind saying, though, that two dozen years ago when I was writing it, *Hogg* certainly *felt* new. But that's the illusion all writers need to put down words and finish their novels. (To appreciate a book richly, possibly readers need it too.) If it hadn't felt that way at the time, I wouldn't have been able to write it.

—New York City
August 10, 1996

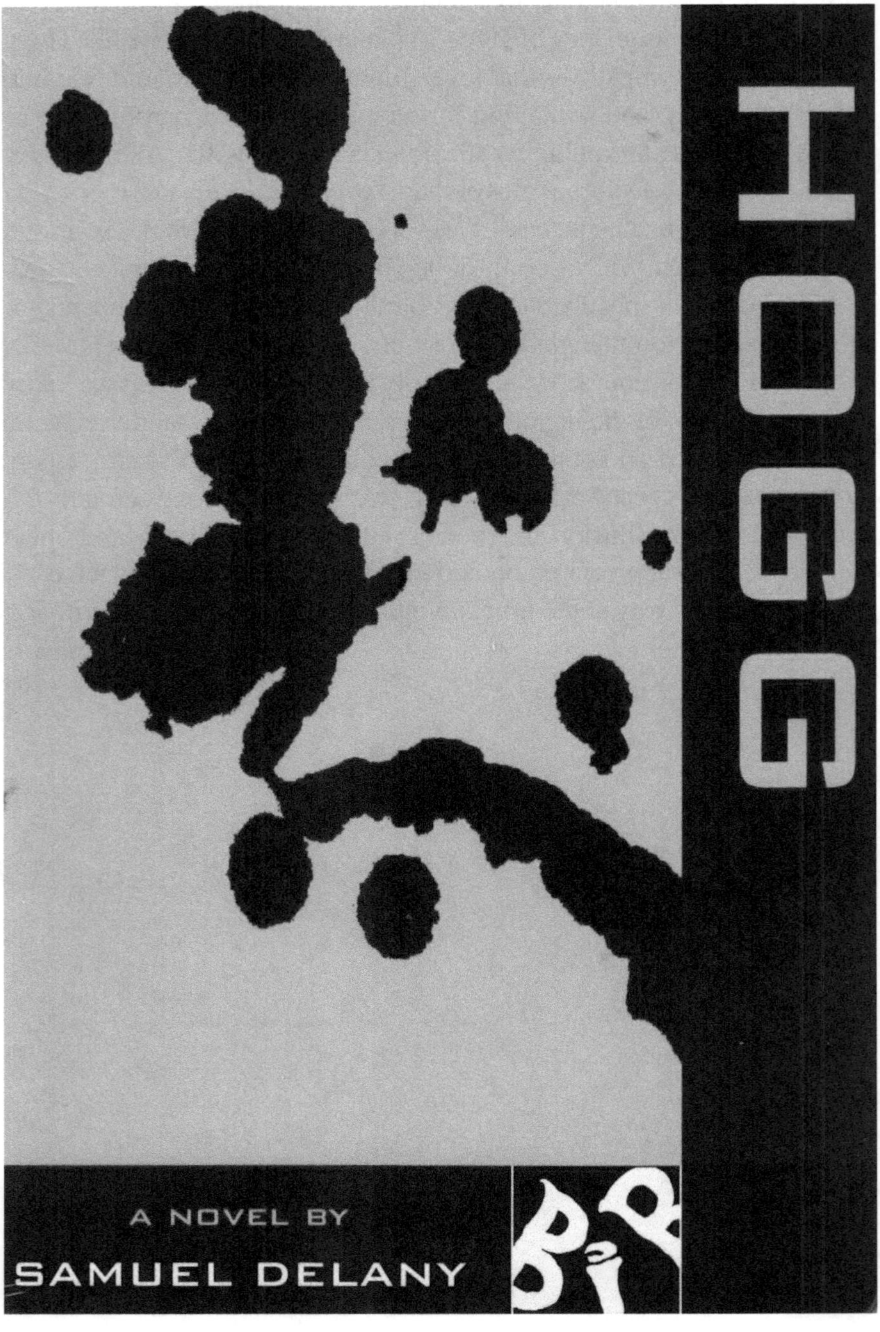

HOGG

A NOVEL BY

SAMUEL DELANY

Errata

The basic master correction list was compiled and annotated by Ron Drummond (as of 30 May 2002) in consultation with the author. (The third [as well as 4th and 5th] Vintage printing[s] contains 110 corrections —and at least one new error [791/(rubric) 16]—that the 1st and 2nd Vintage Books printings do not.) The list was updated over 2003 with corrections by Maurizio Natti and the Delany Listserve (Yahoo Groups), in the course of helping Natti with his Italian translation of *Dhalgren*. Subsequently it was supplemented with corrections by Kevin Donaker-Ring. The current version of this list was transferred to Kevin's website with the help of Zvi Gilbert and is approved and authorized by Samuel R. Delany.

Page 791, paragraph 16, left rubric:

"Lanya said you weren't writing too much in your place, either. She said she thought there were too many people around."

Note on "Mr" and "Mrs" in *Dhalgren* (December 16, 2003):

The last rewrite of *Dhalgren* was done in 1972 and '73 when I lived in London (in 21 Paddington Street), England. The hired typists (mostly Ginny Reddington, though there were at least two others for parts of the manuscript) naturally conformed to the British convention of using no period after honorific abbreviations. (For a more detailed history of the MS of *Dhalgren*, see "In the Once-Upon-A-Time City" in *1984: Selected Letters*, [pp. 336–41, Doc. 54].) "When the manuscript was sent to Bantam Books in New York, I just assumed that the copy editor would bring the MS in line with the American convention of using periods.

When the galleys were returned, however, it had not been done.

Inserting periods throughout the MS would have involved moving too much text around. Thus the original paperback had no periods after "Mr", "Mrs", "Dr", etc. When the MS was taken over by Wesleyan University Press, again I assumed (and even asked) that the American convention be observed. It wasn't. The same thing happened when Vintage Books produced their edition, using the original Wesleyan tapes—even though (indeed because) a number of other corrections were put in at that time: inserting the periods would have doubled their number.

For what it's worth, my own preference was and still is to have the book printed with periods.

—S.R.D.

A detailed list of corrections can be found at Kevin Donaker-Ring's website: http://oneringcircus.com/dh_errata.html

You can also access this website through the Samuel Delany website: www.samueldelany.com

Copyrights and Permissions

www.ingramcontent.com/pod-product-compliance
Lightning Source LLC
Chambersburg PA
CBHW071558030726
47593CB00001BA/226

9781515424192